LEAVING ORBIT

Also by Margaret Lazarus Dean

The Time It Takes to Fall

LEAVING ORBIT

Notes from the Last Days of American Spaceflight

Margaret Lazarus Dean

Graywolf Press

This publication is made possible, in part, by the voters of Minnesota through a Minnesota State Arts Board Operating Support grant, thanks to a legislative appropriation from the arts and cultural heritage fund, and through a grant from the Wells Fargo Foundation Minnesota. Significant support has also been provided by Target, the McKnight Foundation, Amazon.com, and other generous contributions from foundations, corporations, and individuals. To these organizations and individuals we offer our heartfelt thanks.

Published by Graywolf Press
250 Third Avenue North, Suite 600
Minneapolis, Minnesota 55401

All rights reserved.

www.graywolfpress.org

Published in the United States of America

ISBN 978-1-55597-709-2

2 4 6 8 9 7 5 3 1
First Graywolf Printing, 2015

Library of Congress Control Number: 2014960047

Cover design: Kimberly Glyder Design

Cover photo: Personnel in the Launch Control Center watch the launch of Apollo 11, July 16, 1969. Kennedy Space Center Media Gallery, NASA.

To Elliot, and the future

Lovell: Well, how about let's take off our gloves and helmets, huh?
Anders: Okay.
Lovell: I mean, let's get comfortable. This is going to be a long trip.
— Transcript of Apollo 8, first mission to lunar orbit, 1968

It is easy to see the beginnings of things, and harder to see the ends.
— Joan Didion, "Goodbye to All That," 1968

CONTENTS

Saturn V

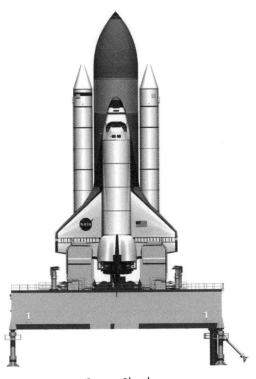

Space Shuttle

LEAVING ORBIT

PROLOGUE: Air and Space

The Smithsonian National Air and Space Museum in Washington, DC, has a grand entrance on Independence Avenue, a long row of smoked-glass doors set into an enormous white edifice. Most of the buildings nearby are marble or stone, neoclassical, meant to appear as old as the Capitol and the Washington Monument, which flank them. The Air and Space Museum, completed in 1976, is an exception: it is meant to look ultramodern, futuristic, which is to say it looks like a 1970s idea of the future.

I remember pulling open one of those doors as a child, the air-conditioning creating a suction that fought me for the door's weight. When I was seven, in 1979, I first visited the Air and Space Museum with my father and little brother, and for years of weekends after. This was what we did now that my parents had officially separated, now that our court-ordered visitation arrangements gave our weekends a sense of structure they had never had before. Divorce is supposed to be traumatic for children, and as time went on ours would become so, but not yet. For the time being, there was something festive about leaving our normal old lives and going on an outing with our father. Where we went each weekend was Air and Space.

We stepped over the threshold and into the chilled hush of the interior, one enormous room open many stories high to reveal old-timey relics of flight hanging by invisible wires from the ceiling. I knew the names of the artifacts long before I understood what they had done: The *Spirit of St. Louis.* The Wright Flyer. *Friendship 7.* As a child, I was vaguely aware that everything was out of chronological order, but I wasn't sure what the correct order was. The artifacts were simultaneously elegant and crude, all of them covered with an equalizing layer of dust. I liked to hear the sound of my father's voice, and I liked the way he explained to me things that most adults would assume were beyond my comprehension. My father was in law school, in the midst of switching careers, but being with him at Air and Space revealed how much he missed the math and engineering he studied most of his life, all the way through a PhD from MIT. He told me about orbits, gravity, escape velocity, the Coriolis effect. I tried to understand because I wanted him to think I was smart.

I was often bored in Air and Space, but I was often bored in general: boredom was a natural state for a dreamy little kid often left, benignly, to her own devices. At home and at school I read a lot, stared out windows blankly, and took in whatever music was floating through my fuzzy consciousness: Bach's Brandenburg concertos at my father's apartment, the Supremes and the Pointer Sisters in my mother's car, Top 40 radio at my school's extended day program where those of us with working parents went after class: "Rock with You." "Do That to Me One More Time." "Hit Me With Your Best Shot." "Another Brick in the Wall."

Even at its busiest, Air and Space was always hushed, the only sound the faraway murmurings of tourists who walked reverently past exhibits silent behind their glass. I looked at the exhibits. In the past, apparently, men ate food from toothpaste tubes while floating in space: here was one of the tubes, displayed in a case. In the past, men walked on the moon wearing space suits. Here was one of the suits, moon dust still ground into its seams. Here were the star charts the astronauts used to find their way in space—sometimes they had to do the math themselves, in pencil, and I could see their scrawled figures in the margins. Here was a moon rock, brought back to Earth in 1972, the year I was born. People lined up to touch the relic. At Air and Space, spaceflight seemed like an experience both transcendently pleasurable (the amniotic floating in zero G, the glowing blue world out the window like a jewel in its black velvet case) and also gruelingly uncomfortable (the cramped capsules and stiff space suits). No way to bathe and no privacy, the merciless nothingness just outside the spaceships' hastily constructed hulls.

In the lobby was an artifact that at first looked like nothing more than a large charcoal-gray circle, thirteen feet in diameter, on a low platform in the middle of the room, encased in glass. That circle was the base of a cone-shaped object, which turned out, when you walked around it, to be the crew capsule from Apollo 11. The museum's curators could have chosen to place the capsule on a pedestal, or to hang it from the ceiling, like so many of the others, but instead its position was unassuming, out on the floor where people could examine it closely. My father and brother and I did just that, and on the other side we encountered an open hatch revealing a beige interior with three beige dentist couches lying shoulder to shoulder facing a million beige switches.

My father spoke behind me. "Three astronauts went to the moon in here." I noted the reverence in his voice. "It took them eight days to get there and back."

"Mmm," I said noncommittally. This made no sense, this claim that three full-grown men had crammed themselves into this container the size of a Volkswagen Beetle's backseat, even for an hour. This story seemed like a misunderstanding best politely ignored.

"Neil Armstrong sat there," my father said, pointing at the couch at the far left. "Michael Collins sat here. And Buzz Aldrin sat here."

For the rest of my life, the syllables of those three names would call up for me this moment, those couches, that tiny cramped space, the way the capsule, then only ten years old, felt both futuristic and outdated at the same time. Already the moon landings were fading into history; already my father had in his apartment a computer much more powerful than the one carried on board this spacecraft. For a child in 1979, the moon landings seemed largely fictional, an event our parents remembered from their own youth and liked to tell us about, and therefore boring and instructive. Yet standing in Air and Space I found there was something pleasing about the contradictions contained in that capsule: the cozy utility of its interior combined with the risk of death just past the hull. There was something about all this I loved in a way I couldn't have described, still can't. The closest I can come is to say that this was the first time I understood that, despite their long and growing list of appalling limitations, grown-ups had at least done *this:* they had figured out how to fly to space. They had, on at least a few occasions, used their might and their metal machines to make a lovely dream come true.

As I grew up, we kept going back. On a visit in 1985, we watched *The Dream Is Alive,* a film shot by astronauts on three different space shuttle missions, in the museum's IMAX theater. The camera pans around the empty cockpit of the space shuttle *Discovery,* where along the far wall, two large bright blue bundles float horizontally. The camera approaches and finds sleeping people. One of them is a woman of surprising beauty, her dark curly hair floating about her. This is Judith Resnik. She sleeps, or pretends to sleep; her long lashes rest on her cheeks. Her tanned arms linger in the air before her, and the look of peace on her face is captivating. Judith Resnik sleeps in space.

I fell in love. My father, brother, and I came back to see this film over and over, and I practically memorized it frame for frame: the launch scenes, landing scenes, footage of Earth turning outside the windows of the space shuttle. Scenes of mundane domestic life lived inside the spaceship, smiling astronauts in shorts and sock feet. They work, eat, chat in their headsets with Houston, float companionably together. Judith Resnik sleeps in space.

Six months later, in January 1986, *Challenger* would explode in the sky with Judith Resnik on board. The metal machines were no longer invincible, it turned out; the adults were not actually in control of them or of anything else. The space shuttle program would never recover from *Challenger,* its goals scaled back and its future curtailed.

Seventeen years later, as I was writing my first novel, about children whose lives were changed by *Challenger,* space shuttle *Columbia* was destroyed during reentry, killing all seven astronauts and leaving debris across three states. The end of the program was written in its disasters: an accident board investigating the 2003 *Columbia* disaster recommended retiring the shuttle in 2010, a recommendation the government has adopted.

Together the five orbiters *Columbia, Challenger, Discovery, Atlantis,* and *Endeavour* have flown a total of 133 successful missions, an unequaled accomplishment of engineering, management, and political savvy. But it's the two disasters that people remember, that most shape the shuttle's story. The lovely dream of spaceflight I grew up with is marred by the images of *Challenger* and *Columbia* breaking apart in the sky, the lost astronauts smiling on hopefully in their portraits, oblivious. Some people took the disasters to mean the entire space program had been a lie, that the dream itself was tainted with our fallibility. But even as a child, I knew it was more complex than that. If we want to see people take risks, we have to be prepared to sometimes see them fail. The story of American spaceflight is a story with many endings, a story of how we have weighed our achievements against our failures. It may also be a story with many futures—new spacecraft will leave Earth one day, whether they belong to NASA or not, and some of the spacefarers traveling on those new spacecraft will be killed. We are at a moment of reconsidering what this means.

I kept going to Air and Space until, at thirteen, I would move away from Washington. But I would remember what I saw there, remember which artifacts were in which room, the way we remember our childhood homes. While I was doing research for my first novel, I would read that Gemini astronauts coming back into the airlock after the first space walks noticed a distinct smell coming in with them on their space suits, a smell of something cooked or burned, a smell both barren and homey. It was the smell of outer space itself. The astronauts found this smell hard to describe, but I could imagine it exactly: it smells like walking into the atrium of the Air and Space Museum with my father and my brother on a hot Saturday morning in the early 1980s. People often ask me how I became interested in space, and I usually share a more logical beginning—I tell about taking astronomy my first year in college, or about seeing *Challenger* explode on TV as an eighth-grader, or about witnessing my first shuttle launch in 2001. All these things are true, but the real truth is a little more confused and intimate, as it always is. The truth is the air-conditioned, musty smell of Air and Space, the crisp homey smell of the cosmos, a space-scarred Apollo capsule, the floating black curls of Judith Resnik, and my father's calm voice.

For Americans of my parents' generation, it takes no mental effort to conjure the feelings that came along with the heroic era of spaceflight from 1961 to 1972: the wonder and the awe, the risk and the ambiguity. But for those under forty-five or so, who are now in the majority, those feelings about spaceflight are clichés, the stories of our elders and the sound tracks of the movies, the lone trumpet signifying the daring and the grace.

Though I'm under forty-five, too young to have seen Neil and Buzz climb out of their lunar module, too young to have witnessed the prime of NASA, I love the idea of spaceflight. I love the audacity of the handsome young president challenging us to go to the moon not because it is easy but because it is hard; I love the young scientists and engineers who took his charge as their personal religion and made inestimable sacrifices to meet John Kennedy's challenge after his death. I love the fire and the rockets, the thundering wonder of building-sized objects hauling themselves off the launchpads and past the grip of gravity. The badass steeliness and crew cuts of the test-pilot sixties astronauts, the engineers in their short-sleeved dress shirts and dark ties, the technicians in their greasy uniforms. I love the old ladies wearing cat's-eye glasses and drinking tea while they stitch together the seams of the space suits that will be the only barrier between moonwalkers and the sucking black vacuum of space.

Above my desk is a photograph of the stainless steel plaque that rests on the Sea of Tranquility on the surface of the moon. Printed on it are these words:

HERE MEN FROM THE PLANET EARTH
FIRST SET FOOT UPON THE MOON
JULY 1969, A. D.
WE CAME IN PEACE FOR ALL MANKIND

Is this not stirring? Rarely is such grandiose language earned by such specific and deliberate action, and this action is the counterbalance to the legacy of the failures. Few Americans were aware of it at the time, but looking back we can see that the beginnings of the end of space-flight were already present at the triumphant moment of Apollo 11— the funding already reduced, the goals already compromised, three dead astronauts already martyred to the cause. In the future, fourteen more will die, and the shuttle project will never entirely recover from their deaths. But the plaque knows nothing of all that, and I love it for that reason, for the vigorous simplicity of its language. I love the language of spaceflight: the go and the no-go, the translunar injection burn, the nod and the twang. The names Neil Armstrong and Buzz Aldrin. The sonorousness of the very acronym NASA. These are the sounds of dreams. Can we who were not there be blamed for wondering whether it was all a dream?

The trees rose solid as a rampart, the last boundary of the Earth, and beyond stretched the spaceport for the space flight to the Moon: a silence of sand and water, a handful of islands thrown down by God on the seventh day when He couldn't think what else to do with them. . . . The tallest and biggest building seemed to touch the clouds.

—Oriana Fallaci, *If the Sun Dies*

The most important events in America seemed to take place in all the lonely spaces.

—Norman Mailer, *Of a Fire on the Moon*

Cape Canaveral was in Florida, but not any part of Florida you would write home about.   —Tom Wolfe, *The Right Stuff*

CHAPTER 1. The Beginnings of the Future: This Is Cape Canaveral

Family Day: September 25, 2010

Say the words out loud: Cape Canaveral. Say them in JFK's voice, in John Glenn's voice, in Walter Cronkite's voice. The very syllables connote rockets and bravery, the countdown to zero, heroes in helmets, banks of inscrutable computers. So it's strange that when you visit the Kennedy Space Center in Florida, when you make the drive from Orlando or from the beach towns south or north, you must first drive through miles of green flats, the low pulsing of insects all around you, alligators lurking in ditches, before you finally encounter the structures built by NASA in the sixties.

You wouldn't necessarily know that you were at the Kennedy Space Center, the swampy, improbable spaceport that inhabits 219 square miles of mostly untouched wilderness in central Florida. The only clue to what goes on here is a roadside sign with the NASA logo and changeable numbers reminding workers how many days remain until the next launch. Kennedy Parkway runs past a wild beach and, past that, the narrow strip of land from which American spaceships leave Earth. Most of this square mileage is a wildlife refuge, closed to any type of development for over fifty years because of the potentially explosive nature of what goes on here. In this way, the tour guides tell their busloads of tourists, technology and nature can help each other.

It's fall 2010. I'm sitting in the backseat of a rental car being driven by my father; in the passenger seat is his wife, Judy. We all found each other at baggage claim in the Orlando airport late last night, having flown in from two different cities, and shared a car out to the coast. There is a special urgency to this trip because the space shuttle program will end soon, and this is one of the last opportunities I or anyone else will have to see the Kennedy Space Center as a working spaceport. The era of American spaceflight that started in 1961 when Alan Shepard became the first American to travel in space is about to come to an end, and few people seem to notice or care. Two more space shuttle missions are scheduled: STS-133 and STS-134. (STS stands for Space Transportation System, the original name for the space shuttle program from the seventies). A third mission, STS-135, will be added if NASA can get approval from Congress. This would mean one final launch for each of the three remaining space shuttle orbiters: *Discovery, Endeavour,* and *Atlantis.*

The decision to end the shuttle program was made quietly, and as a result many people are still not aware it's ending. In the wake of the loss of *Columbia* in 2003, the investigation board tasked with uncovering the causes of the disaster pointed out the age of the fleet—the oldest surviving orbiter, *Discovery,* was then twenty years old. The investigation board's report includes, on page 227, an item titled R9.2-1, Recertification. It recommends that NASA, "prior to operating the Shuttle beyond 2010, develop and conduct a vehicle certification at the material, component, subsystem, and system levels." The destruction of *Columbia* had not been attributable to its age, but the board clearly feared the next disaster might be. The word sounds benign, but *recertification* would require the shuttles to be taken apart, examined, tested, and rebuilt from the ground up. This process would be prohibitively expensive, and everyone knew it; the inevitable consequence of this recommendation, barring some unforeseen change, was that NASA would have no choice but to retire the shuttle when this date arrived. In this paragraph the end of the shuttle is written.

By adopting the *Columbia* Accident Investigation Board's recommendations, the Bush administration in effect set a 2010 end date for the shuttle. That date will be extended a bit to allow for assembly of the final components of the International Space Station, but now in the fall of 2010, the last mission is in sight. Space fans and especially the spaceworkers around here have hoped the retirement decision would be reversed somehow, and still do, hoping against hope.

Wilderness, marshes, palm trees—then, all of a sudden, the Vehicle Assembly Building. From a distance, it looms. I'm directing my father from the backseat, using both the GPS function on my phone and a printout of e-mailed directions. I'm tempted to use the Vehicle Assembly Building as a landmark, but I know better because I've been here before: the vast size of the VAB makes it impossible to tell whether you are one mile or three miles away from it, and a turn that seems to be right before the VAB may in fact be three turns earlier. Marked with an American flag the size of a football field on one side and an equally huge blue NASA logo on the other, the VAB was the biggest building in the world by volume when it was completed in 1966, and it remains among the largest by volume to this day. No other single-story building comes close to equaling its size, if you are willing to accept that its 525-foot height constitutes a single story. The building is simply enormous in a way that people react to viscerally and emotionally, and its enormity is part of the reason the Kennedy Space Center was named one of the Engineering Wonders of the World. Visitors have not been allowed inside for over thirty years, and the tour buses that constantly crawl through the Kennedy Space Center all stop at the outer edge of the VAB's parking lot. Tourists pile out to take pictures of each other, leaning back in an effort to fit more of the building into the frame. My own picture of myself outside the VAB dates to 2001, and in it only a small part of the building is visible over my shoulder. But today, I have plans to meet a stranger who says he can take me inside.

I've been here at the Kennedy Space Center twice before, twice have ridden the tour buses past the launchpads and hangars and landing strip, twice have paid my admission at the Visitor Complex to look at the artifacts, watch the IMAX movies, and eat at the Lunch Pad. Both times I was here to do research for my first novel, which revolved around the *Challenger* disaster. On those trips I'd known that I could come back if I wanted to, take another tour, see another launch, and it's different now to approach the enormous facilities of the Space Center knowing how profoundly everything here is about to change. The relentless conquering of the future for which this place has always stood is now coming to a close.

I tell my father how far the turn will be from here. He grunts in agreement; he is following our progress using the GPS on his own phone. A terrible sense of direction is one of my father's legacies to me; another is a love of spaceflight. When I e-mailed to tell him about the invitation I'd received for a behind-the-scenes visit, my father first responded that he very much hoped to be able to join me, but that he would have to check on some things first, to see whether everything could be covered at work. He e-mailed me again a few minutes later to say that yes, he would go, regardless. This was a once-in-a-lifetime opportunity, and he was going to be there no matter what. I'm pleased that I will be able to get him access to this experience, a re-creation of the Saturdays we spent exploring the National Air and Space Museum when I was a child.

I've been instructed to wear long pants and closed-toed shoes for my safety. I've been told to bring a picture ID that confirms my US citizenship. I've been warned that my tour may be canceled at any time for any reason because the Kennedy Space Center is a working space facility. A few days before, I booked a last-minute flight, asked my husband, Chris, to care for our three-year-old son by himself, and arranged for a colleague to cover my classes. My father and his wife made similarly hasty plans.

Now that I'm here on the Space Coast, I'm feeling nervous about meeting my host, Omar Izquierdo, a spaceworker who has invited me here today as his guest. I feel I know Omar because we are Facebook friends and because we share a love for the space shuttle, but, my more pragmatic friends point out, I don't actually know him at all, don't know for sure that he even exists. I'm grateful my father and his wife are here with me, though I know I would have come even if they hadn't been able to make it. In my eagerness to visit restricted areas here and meet people who have worked to put spaceships into the sky, the risk that Omar is not what he claims to be is a risk I'm willing to take.

American spaceflight did not begin at the Kennedy Space Center; nor did it begin at Cape Canaveral Air Force Station across the Banana River from here. It began in the early twentieth century when three men working independently in three different countries all developed the same ideas more or less simultaneously about how rockets could be used for space travel. Konstantin Tsiolkovsky in Russia, Hermann Oberth in Germany, and Robert Goddard in the United States all came up with an eerily similar concept for using liquid fuel to power rockets for human spaceflight. I've seen this pointed out as an odd co-incidence, one of those moments when an idea inexplicably emerges in multiple places at once. But when I read through each of these three men's biographies I discovered why they all had the same idea: all three of them were obsessed with Jules Verne's 1865 novel *De la terre à la lune (From the Earth to the Moon)*. The novel details the strange adventures of three space explorers who travel to the moon together. What sets Verne's book apart from other speculative fiction of the time was his careful attention to the physics involved in space travel—his characters take pains to explain to each other exactly how and why each concept would work. All three real-life scientists—the Russian, the German, and the American—were following what they had learned from a French science fiction writer.

Spaceflight began in earnest on October 4, 1957, when the Soviet Union launched the first artificial satellite, Sputnik, into orbit. The degree to which Americans were shaken by Sputnik is all but incomprehensible to people born too late to remember the Cold War. We can only know it from books and films—my favorite is Homer Hickam's memoir *Rocket Boys,* in which he describes standing outside on cold October evenings to watch the tiny light of Sputnik go by. We can only imagine their panic when they heard on the radio that steady Soviet beeping. The thing was streaking by like a star over Americans' cities and towns. And what was to stop it from raining weapons down upon Americans from that vantage point? If Sputnik wasn't actually big enough to have weapons capabilities, maybe the next satellite would be.

It is fair to say that Sputnik completely changed the way Americans in positions of power thought about both weapons and spaceflight. Up until that fall of 1957, the idea of using the rockets developed for World War II to make science fiction fantasies come true was at best a tough sell. But once everyone heard that ominous beeping, the goal of getting an American satellite up there too suddenly became urgent.

A tiny government agency called the National Advisory Committee for Aeronautics had been in charge of overseeing the development of new airplane technology, including the plane that Chuck Yeager had flown to break the sound barrier in 1947, but their ambitious plans for sending pilots into space had always been dismissed as too expensive, too dangerous, and ultimately pointless. After Sputnik, President Eisenhower took a new interest in the activities of NACA and turned it into NASA, the National Aeronautics and Space Administration, with an infusion of funding. NASA was meant to beat the Soviets at their own game. The space race was on, and it seemed that the Soviets already might have won it.

Project Mercury began the same day NASA did, folding in a poorly funded Air Force project known as Man in Space Soonest. Everyone knew how far ahead the Soviets were, but it suddenly seemed there was no choice but to try to catch up. Not to do so would be to concede defeat. Entering the race would mean a justification for a huge upsurge in government spending, some for new projects, some for existing but underfunded ones. Public education was one of the first areas to feel the effects—high schools revamped their curricula to include more math and science, as well as Russian-language instruction.

At the end of World War II, the best of Germany's rocket designers had been recruited to the United States by a covert government group that later became the CIA. The project was called Operation Paperclip because the Germans' affiliation with the Nazi party and/ or the SS had to be covered up through fake documents, which were paperclipped to their files. The most important German rocket expert was Wernher von Braun, who had been responsible for the development of the V-2 rocket used to bomb Allied cities. Now an American citizen, von Braun had been working to develop rockets for the US Army since 1945 and had been finding the support and funding offered him and his staff at Fort Bliss to be insultingly inadequate. But all that changed in 1957 with Sputnik, and the rocket designers soon found themselves working for NASA and enjoying much better accommodations. Suddenly everyone was interested in what von Braun and his team could do and wanted them to have all the money they needed to do it.

As it turned out, the United States came close to being the first to put a human being in space, had it not been for a couple of setbacks and an abundance of caution. As it was, a Soviet cosmonaut, Yuri Gagarin, made the historic first flight into space on April 12, 1961, and Alan Shepard followed soon after, on May 5. Riding the wave of that enthusiasm, and needing a way to recover from the Bay of Pigs debacle in Cuba, President Kennedy made his move.

On May 25, 1961, Kennedy spoke to a joint session of Congress and made an ambitious pitch: "that this nation should commit itself to achieving the goal, before this decade is out, of landing a man on the moon and returning him safely to the earth." Not long before, Kennedy had had nothing but skeptical things to say about human spaceflight. The Soviets had changed the script for him. When I watch his speech to Congress now, I am struck first of all by his youth. He was forty-three years old, one of the youngest people in the room, and he appears younger than his years. I've always known that in this speech he urges lawmakers to strike out on a bold path, but I never knew until I watched the entire speech myself that he does so with such sincerity and humility. He emphasizes how difficult and expensive the project will be, that there is no guarantee of success. He admits that "I came to this conclusion with some reluctance," and then closes with this: "You must decide yourselves, as I have decided. And I am confident that whether you finally decide in the way I have decided or not, that your judgment, as my judgment, was reached in the best interest of our country."

What Congress decided was to embark on what would turn out to be the largest peacetime engineering project ever undertaken by the US government. They felt they had little choice, with the terrifying possibility of Soviet weapons in orbit and on the moon. The role of this fear in influencing space policy is not to be underestimated, and proponents of spaceflight would try to keep this fear alive as long as it had any plausibility. Kennedy's speech to Congress is a rousing piece of rhetoric and a key moment in spaceflight history, but it also shows us the first instance of a recurring spectacle: an impassioned spaceflight advocate begging a fickle Congress for money. The script would be rewritten again and again for the space shuttle and the International Space Station, and the results would never be as unequivocally favorable again.

Gus Grissom flew next, in July, repeating Shepard's suborbital flight, then John Glenn became the first American to orbit the planet, on February 20, 1962. Scott Carpenter and Wally Schirra followed, and Gordon Cooper made the last Mercury flight, becoming the first American to spend over a day in space and the last to travel in space alone. Already the Gemini project was under way, named for the two-man crews who would work through the problems necessary for getting to the moon: creating larger and more reliable rockets, mastering the biomedical challenges of enabling astronauts to survive in space for weeks at a time, developing methods for docking two vehicles together in space, and testing the space suits and other equipment necessary for space walks.

Of course, part of the plan for getting to the moon involved building a moon port. The facilities at Cape Canaveral Air Force Station were not going to be adequate—not for the size of the new rockets themselves; not for the numbers of people necessary to take part in assembly, maintenance, and launch control; not for the number of launches that would have to be prepared simultaneously. In 1962, NASA chose a site nearby on Merritt Island, the landmass just to the west of Cape Canaveral, and began acquiring the land and designing the facilities. Mission Control would be housed at a facility near Houston first called the Manned Spaceflight Center, later renamed for President Lyndon Johnson after his death in 1973. Kennedy visited Cape Canaveral on November 16, 1963, and was shown around by Wernher von Braun and other NASA luminaries. He looked over the new Saturn rocket and the new moon port with excitement. Kennedy then flew from Florida to Dallas, where he was shot to death six days later.

Historians have debated why Kennedy chose to put so much of his political currency into Apollo. After all, he had shown little indication of caring about spaceflight before Sputnik, and even after Gagarin's flight he seemed reluctant to make spaceflight a national priority. The most convincing discussion I've read is from historian John Logsdon, who argues that what caused Kennedy to make his decision was (1) "a conviction of American exceptionalism," (2) the geopolitical situation of the moment, and (3) JFK's individual values and style.

The day before he died, Kennedy gave a speech at the dedication of the nation's first aerospace medical health center, in San Antonio. He reiterated how important the moon project was, in spite of the risks:

> Frank O'Connor, the Irish writer, tells in one of his books how, as a boy, he and his friends would make their way across the countryside, and when they came to an orchard wall that seemed too high and too doubtful to try and too difficult to permit their voyage to continue, they took off their hats and tossed them over the wall—and then they had no choice but to follow them.
>
> This Nation has tossed its cap over the wall of space, and we have no choice but to follow it.

Back at home, I have hanging over my desk an image of the Kennedy Space Center as it looked in 1963, girders rising improbably out of the surrounding swamp. The wetland had been drained, then tons of sand packed into the earth to make it stable enough for the construction of the world's largest building. Workers who came out to pack the sand and drive the pilings found themselves covered with mosquitoes; many witnesses describe a white shirt turning black with blood-sucking insects within minutes. Histories of the Kennedy Space Center acknowledge without exaggeration that the obstacle posed by the mosquitoes was so serious that NASA quite literally could not have put a man on the moon by Kennedy's "before the decade is out" deadline without the invention of DDT. In this way, the challenges of spaceflight reveal themselves to be distinctly terrestrial.

When the Vehicle Assembly Building was finally completed, NASA invited *Life* magazine to do a spread about the new moon port. *Life* photographers were given full access to the grounds, where they shot images of the largest building in the world from every angle. After returning home and processing thousands of photos, the photographers admitted that they had failed. They had not found a way to capture, in a single frame, the outsize scale of the VAB. One photographer tried to convey how large it was by photographing a man standing next to the building, but at the distance necessary to get the entire building into the frame, the man had disappeared, smaller than the grain of the film. The size of the Vehicle Assembly Building was officially unphotographable.

After the last successful Gemini mission, in 1966, the next step was to test the new Apollo-Saturn, the largest rocket ever built. Three astronauts were training for the first Apollo mission to fly with a crew. On January 27, 1967, they were doing a rehearsal at Cape Canaveral when a fire broke out in the sealed crew capsule on the launchpad. Gus Grissom (the second American in space), Ed White (the first

American to ever do a space walk), and Roger Chaffee (who was training for his first spaceflight) all died in the fire.

Not long before, Italian journalist Oriana Fallaci had interviewed many of the astronauts and had asked them about the risk. John Glenn, whom Fallaci took a special liking to as "the most perfect fantastic Boy Scout in a nation of Boy Scouts," spoke eloquently about the risks:

> Up to today it has cost us little: only work and money. So many men went, so many came back. But it won't always be like this, I know, we know. Some of us will die, maybe a whole crew will die: but remember, it's worth it all the same. And because it's worth it, we will accept our losses and continue with those who remain. . . . Yes, we must go up there, we must. And one day those who are against it will look back and be pleased at what we've done.

The Apollo 1 fire made the risks of spaceflight seem real to Americans for the first time—up to that point, nothing had ever gone seriously wrong, and it had started to seem as though the exploration of space would be without human cost. NASA recovered quickly from the setback, but future disasters would take greater tolls. Some space fans suspect Americans had a greater tolerance for risk in the sixties than we do now, but it may be that this first disaster seemed like an anomaly. A second (Challenger) seems like a betrayal; a third (Columbia) seems like a pattern of failure.

The Vehicle Assembly Building was designed to house the simultaneous assembly of four moonbound rockets, and as such it stands as a monument to a long-past era in American history. There never did come a time when four Saturn V rockets were assembled at once. The history of American spaceflight is a history of doing less than had been planned, less than had been hoped for. Space fans angry about the end of the shuttle seem to think that their disappointment is something new, but in fact the dreams of space enthusiasts have been scaled back from the start. A lunar base, a permanent space station, a reusable spaceship with a booster section that could land like an airplane, a Mars expedition—all these were to have been undertaken by the eighties. Not only were the new projects tabled, but the last three Apollo missions were scrapped before the third crew of moonwalkers landed.

Family Day is a Kennedy Space Center tradition that began in the mid-1960s, when spaceworkers' families complained that they had no idea what went on behind the gates, what was keeping their spouses and parents so frantically busy for so many hours and so distracted even when they were at home. Certain Saturdays were established when workers could bring their families inside the gates and show them around. Family Days decreased in frequency after the debut of the space shuttle, with its more dangerous solid rockets. And after the terrorist attacks of 2001 led to heightened security at government facilities, Family Days stopped altogether. But now that the retirement of the shuttle is within sight, there is a last-chance feeling around the Kennedy Space Center, and a few final Family Days will be held before the end. Today is one of them.

My first contact with Omar Izquierdo was in 2007, when he sent me the first e-mail I received about my *Challenger* novel, the day after its official publication date.

> From: Omar Izquierdo <xxxxxxxxxx@gmail.com>
> Subject: **Comments about your Book, The Time It Takes to Fall**
> To: Margaret Lazarus Dean <xxxxxxxxxxx@gmail.com>
>
> I picked up your book last Monday night. I was first drawn to your book by the photo on the cover. I grew up on Merritt Island, and I was 6 years old when Challenger happened, and my dad worked (and still works) at the Kennedy Space Center. I also work out there now, and so when I saw the book, I instinctively decided to give it a closer look.

Mistakenly, I assumed at first that it was a true story about a girl who grew up on the Space Coast around that era, and since I also grew up under those circumstances, I immediately purchased the book, looking forward to see how similar this girl's childhood perspectives on that day and time would be to my own.

I was 25 pages into it, before I realized that the book was a work of fiction. I am a bonehead.

However, I decided to continue reading, and I finished the book 5 days later. Interestingly, I finished it at work while I was on break, sitting literally 10 feet away from the huge left wing of the Space Shuttle Atlantis, as it was being worked on in the VAB for the upcoming mission.

Anyway, I just wanted to say that I still did find your book enjoyable. Since I was 6 when Challenger occurred, and the character in your book was 13 (and a girl), I'm afraid I can't offer you relevant feedback and say that my experiences and hers during that era were completely similar. What we did have in common was an obsession with everything having to do with shuttle, and feelings of confusion when the Challenger accident occurred. Since my father (in 1986) worked with the shuttle main engines, his job was not affected by the accident as severely as Dolores' father was in the book.

Once again, thanks for the good read. It seems you did significant research, and your descriptions of the Space Center in particular are fairly accurate (with the exception of two things, 1.) It would be impossible for a child to sneak past security at KSC, and 2.) Nobody is allowed to bring non-employees into the Vehicle Assembly Building, ESPECIALLY while the Orbiter is hanging from the crane above the stack during Orbiter/ET Mate).

Thank you very much.
Omar Izquierdo

For a first-time author, hearing from a complete stranger the week my book came out, a stranger who walked into a bookstore of his own accord and chose my book from among all the other books, then actually read it, felt like a miracle. But when I got to the second paragraph about how Omar grew up near the Kennedy Space Center himself, and works there now, I felt a sinking dread. All the facts I must have gotten wrong suddenly seemed to glow like badly buried radioactive waste. This reader, this Omar Izquierdo, would expose my errors, would lead the charge against me. After all, I had taken his hometown, his childhood, and his life's work and made them into a backdrop for a story I, an outsider, had made up.

Soon after that initial exchange, I went on Facebook to create an identity for my book's main character (authors were encouraged to do this during the brief period after Facebook became ubiquitous and before Facebook's fan pages were introduced). When I went looking for Facebook groups my character might join, I came across one called "If You Oppose NASA in Any Way I Will Punch You in the Face." Perfect for Dolores. I clicked on it, and the first name I saw among the existing members was Omar Izquierdo. So I friended him.

A Facebook friendship evolves either more quickly or more slowly than a face-to-face one; mine with Omar evolved quickly. We are both on Facebook multiple times a day, both click Like often on each other's postings, especially ones that involve our shared interest in spaceflight. And his space-related posts are to die for: images of *Discovery* being prepared for launch, interiors of restricted spaces like the Vehicle Assembly Building and the Orbiter Processing Facility, or the often-dramatic weather at the Cape. But I've found you can also learn a lot about a person by what he finds funny, by his comments on everyday happenings, and I came to feel that I knew Omar well through his posts even if I'd never been in the same room with him.

Omar's father is a mechanical engineer who has worked at Kennedy his entire adult life. He was recruited right out of engineering school in Puerto Rico in 1979, when NASA was gearing up for the first shuttle launch, and was given a choice of whether to go to the Marshall Space Flight Center in Alabama or the Kennedy Space Center in Florida.

He chose Kennedy because he had heard that Alabama was more racist. He brought his young wife to Florida, bought a house, put down roots, and Omar and his sister were born here soon after.

Before leaving home, I'd looked back over all the e-mails and Facebook messages Omar and I have sent each other, and I'd reread that first e-mail in which one of the errors in my book he points out is a scene in which an employee brings an outsider inside the VAB. Neither of us could have imagined when he wrote those words that three years later he would be taking me inside the VAB himself.

Back in my hotel room I've left the stack of books I brought with me to Florida. Tom Wolfe's *The Right Stuff*, Lipartito and Butler's *History of the Kennedy Space Center*, William E. Burrows's *This New Ocean*, Diane Vaughan's *The Challenger Launch Decision*, Oriana Fallaci's *If the Sun Dies*, Michael Collins's *Carrying the Fire*, and Norman Mailer's *Of a Fire on the Moon*.

Each of these books offers different layers of the infinitely layered story—Wolfe's bombastic lionizing of the Mercury astronauts; Burrows's thorough tracing of the currents of history across three nations; Vaughan's tireless unpacking of the seemingly benign decisions that would doom two shuttles. When I was researching my *Challenger* novel, I'd thought at first that once I understood the outlines of the history of American spaceflight, I would be able to stop reading about it and get back to writing. But I found I loved reading multiple accounts of the same event—say, the first glimpse of the lunar surface on Apollo 8 in 1968, or the first space shuttle launch in 1981. When the point of view changes, details emerge and disappear, meanings shift, emotions transmute themselves. The very import of the event can change. My research was turning into something more like an obsession, and even once my *Challenger* novel was published, I kept reading, wanting to be able to grasp a historical era that in many ways seemed better than my own.

The books that mean the most to me are the firsthand accounts, the people who grapple with what they have seen and experienced, and by doing so take on the emotional meanings of spaceflight.

Michael Collins, who went to the moon with Neil Armstrong and Buzz Aldrin, is also a first-rate prose stylist with a natural feel for detail and a light touch with humor; his book sounds a lot like what you would expect if E. B. White had qualified as an astronaut and flown to the moon. Tom Wolfe undertook to grasp the courage of the astronauts and uncovered a brotherhood that is both unprecedented and ageless. Oriana Fallaci was an Italian journalist who traveled to Houston, Huntsville, and the Cape at the height of the excitement for Apollo but before the success of the first moon landing. She met astronauts, rocket engineers, and NASA managers engaged in the as-yet-uncertain project of beating the Russians to the moon, and she questioned the project constantly—will they get to the moon by the deadline, and if so what will that accomplish?—while also admiring the adventure and the adventurers. When she meets Neil Armstrong, for example, he is just another astronaut in a large group, described in terms of his resemblance to John Glenn, not as the first man on the moon. When she meets Deke Slayton, a chance remark reveals that he was one of the pilots responsible for a bombing raid on Fallaci's home city of Florence during World War II, a raid that injured her and destroyed her family home. If nothing else, this episode should remind us of how very recent the war had been, and the fact that Oriana and Deke became great friends anyway is an example of the way spaceflight brings people together. I envy Fallaci most in the scenes where she flirts her way through the astronaut corps, one by one, drinking martinis with them in the motel bars of the Space Coast, smoking like a chimney and eliciting from von Braun eloquent observations about the moon project. It can't be a coincidence that the sixties era of creative nonfiction overlaps so perfectly with the heroic era of American spaceflight, the big egotistical voices turning journalism inside out at the same time the innovators in Houston and Huntsville and the Cape were redefining what machines were capable of, what human beings were capable of.

Norman Mailer's book is about witnessing the launch of Apollo 11— *Life* magazine had commissioned him to go to the Cape to write about the launch in exchange for a sum of money rumored to be somewhere between extraordinary and obscene. I hadn't known, before I came across it, that Norman Mailer had written a book about Apollo 11—I knew him for having written the best-selling novel *The Naked and the Dead,* for cofounding the *Village Voice* and helping to spearhead New Journalism, for winning both the Pulitzer Prize and the National Book Award for *The Armies of the Night,* for running for mayor of New York and finishing fourth out of a field of five in the Democratic primary, and for stabbing his second wife, nearly to death, at a dinner party. But here, it seems, he had also written a book about spaceflight. The article in *Life,* and the book that subsequently expanded on it, are both ungainly wandering things with oceans of technical details and self-conscious linguistic tics. Norman Mailer could never quite get both arms around the subject, but he tries in a way that few have, and I witness in his very struggle one of the best expressions I've seen of what American spaceflight means: the boredom of waiting, the wondering whether one should be feeling something more, then, suddenly, feeling it—excitement, or patriotism, or pride in one's own species, the big-brained nonquitting species that would set itself such a ridiculous goal and then meet it so spectacularly.

When I read all these books, I'm encountering other minds struggling with the same questions while walking the same landscape. With Norman Mailer especially, the only one of the three to undertake to describe a launch, I feel as though he and I are tugging on opposite ends of the same thread, a thread forty years long. I am often struck with jealousy for the era he lived in. Sometimes it seems as though Norman Mailer's generation got to see the beginnings of things and mine has gotten the ends.

Juan Ponce de León stumbled across Cape Canaveral in 1513 while he was searching a new land for gold, slaves, and the Fountain of Youth. He'd left his home in San Juan Bautista (now called Puerto Rico) aboard the ship *Santiago* and headed north, toward a landmass that had been sighted clearly enough to be included on maps, but upon which no European had yet made a landing. The chronicler Antonio de Herrera writes in 1610:

> And thinking that this land was an island, they called it La Florida, because it presented a beautiful vista of many blossoming trees and was low and flat; and also because they discovered it during the time of Easter [Pascua Florida]. Juan Ponce wanted the name to conform to [agree with] these two aspects [reasons]. They went ashore to gather information and to take possession.

Books still use the word *discovery* to refer to this voyage, but that term doesn't quite seem to apply when some of the natives Juan Ponce encountered on the shores of the new land had actually traveled to San Juan Bautista; some even greeted him in his own language. The landmass we now call Florida was not understood, at first, to be a peninsula, and in fact Juan Ponce died believing that what he had "discovered" was a largish island.

We don't know where exactly on Florida's east coast Juan Ponce de León first landed, but we do know that shortly afterward, in April 1513, his travels down the coast brought him to Cape Canaveral. There he found only scrubland and unwelcoming natives. By all accounts, Juan Ponce and his men declared Cape Canaveral uninhabitable and piled back into their boats to see what else this new land had to offer. After they abandoned the Cape to the wind and the mosquitoes, no Europeans returned for nearly three hundred years, by which time the native people who had inhabited the Cape had either been wiped out by disease and violence with other tribes or had migrated elsewhere. A few European families raised citrus groves—the Indian River region is especially well suited to growing high-quality oranges—but aside from them, the area remained almost entirely uninhabited. That is, until after World War II, when the Air Force was scouting sites for testing rockets. A rocket range has some odd geographical requirements: it needs to be as close to the equator as possible (so Earth's rotation can help propel lifting bodies), it requires a great deal of undeveloped space in case of mishap on the ground, and ideally it should border on a great deal of water, in case errant rockets fail or have to be shot down. Cape Canaveral met all of these requirements.

According to an uncredited Air Force publication about the history of the Cape charmingly titled *From Sand to Moondust,* Ponce de León sailed the coast of Florida "meeting at every landing hostile Indians whose appearance gave no indication of wealth and who did not offer to lead him to hidden treasure or magic fountains." It's true that Juan Ponce would never find either, but his fantasies of youth and wealth have somehow embedded themselves into the underlying fantasy of Florida itself. At any rate, *Florida* is the oldest surviving European place name in the United States. Today, the landscape around the Kennedy Space Center is in most ways oddly unchanged from the day Ponce de León abandoned it in frustration. This incidental preservation is one of the many strange gifts of spaceflight.

My father drives calmly down Kennedy Parkway, the Vehicle Assembly Building filling the windshield. I'm glad he's driving; I'm anxious about being late to meet Omar and might have been prone to speeding. I try to anticipate what our first face-to-face conversation will be like. As I'm considering what we might say to each other, we pass an SUV being driven slowly, just below the speed limit, and when I glance out the backseat window over at the driver, a young Hispanic man chatting with his passenger, I think, *Oh, that's my friend Omar.* I've only seen small blurry pictures of Omar on his Facebook page and would not have thought I would recognize him. But a few minutes later, when we find the parking lot with the Redstone rocket Omar has told me to look for, the SUV is there too. The driver steps out and asks, cautiously, "Margaret?"

Omar is neatly dressed in an athletic shirt and khaki shorts. He is about my height with a round, kind face and a buzz cut like a Mercury astronaut's. It's not until that moment, as I'm introducing myself and my family, that I consider that Omar took a risk by meeting me too, that he might not have known what to expect from a female English professor with a spaceflight obsession—that he might have been as anxious about our meeting as I was, and he went out of his way to invite me here anyway.

"I hope you didn't have too much trouble finding it," Omar says politely after shaking everyone's hands, though he's given me both detailed directions and an iPhone map image with a pin dropped at the exact spot. "I realized later that 'Redstone rocket' might not be the most helpful landmark for everyone."

"I know my rockets," I assure him.

"Ah. I figured you might," Omar says. A second later he adds, "You don't really look like your picture. But I knew you anyway."

Here under the Redstone rocket, I reach out and hug him, though I am not generally a touchy person. I'm so pleased to discover that this is my friend Omar: he is exactly who he seemed to be, exactly who I thought he was all along. My father snaps a picture of the two of us together under the Redstone, the first of many he will take today.

Omar has brought three other friends for Family Day, all of them locals who grew up with space shuttles rattling their windows. We all climb into Omar's SUV and approach the checkpoint at the south gate to the Kennedy Space Center. Omar shows his work badge to the armed guard, who allows us through. Now on NASA grounds, we pass the DAYS TO LAUNCH sign. *Discovery*'s last flight is scheduled for November 1, 2010, thirty-six days from now. *Discovery* is already stacked on the launchpad—if all goes as planned, we'll get to see it up close later today.

As we drive toward the VAB, Omar tells me more about his job. He is one of the thousands of people who work at the Cape doing various things that need to be done in order to get spaceships off the ground—in his case, making sure that only authorized people get access to *Discovery* at the various points along its work flow and making sure that any object that enters the crew cabin comes out again. His official title is orbiter integrity clerk. Delightfully, part of his job involves watching for birds to make sure they don't damage the vehicle on the launchpad (this responsibility was added in the nineties after woodpeckers damaged an external tank to such an extent that it had to be rolled back to the VAB for repairs). Omar loves what he does—I know this already from the cumulative impression of his Facebook postings—and he takes pride in what his employer does, more than anyone else I know. In another context, a person with his job description might be called a security guard, but I would not call Omar that. Partly because in his job the stakes are so high—a single errant screw could endanger the mission, the spacecraft, and the astronauts. But also because Omar's pride in his work here, like that of every single person I have ever met at the Cape, makes the job title itself almost irrelevant. Omar works on the space shuttle. Specifically, he works on *Discovery,* and though he is modest and unassuming by nature, I have heard him refer to *Discovery* in conversation as *his,* as in, with reference to a specific mission, "that was *my* bird."

Now *Discovery* has only one mission left to go. This upcoming flight was supposed to be the final mission for the shuttle, but then NASA announced one more would follow, on *Endeavour.* Now rumor has it they might add one more, which, if it happens, will be on *Atlantis.* I ask Omar as we drive up Kennedy Parkway whether this adding-on will continue, whether NASA can tack on one more mission, then one more mission, indefinitely.

"I don't think so," Omar says. "The site in Louisiana that makes the external tanks delivered the last one, and now they're shutting the facility down. If NASA wanted to contract for more, they'd have to start it up again."

"Oh," I say, disappointed. "I'd hoped they might be able to keep extending it."

"I mean, that's just what I've heard," Omar clarifies. "I don't know that for sure." As I get to know Omar, I will continue to be impressed by his insistence on differentiating what he knows to be true from claims based on unofficial sources, rumor, or his own extremely educated guesses. He is an epistemological purist, an orbiter integrity clerk of truth.

"It seems like a waste to retire the shuttles when they still have life in them," I say experimentally. I have never known Omar to make a negative comment about NASA, and I'm wondering whether he'll open up a bit more in person.

Omar nods, but doesn't elaborate. He knows he will almost certainly be laid off after *Discovery*'s retirement in a few months. Yet for now, he's always at work. For now, the Kennedy Space Center is bustling, as it has been for forty-eight years, with the effort to prepare spaceships for multiple missions simultaneously.

There will be two or at most three more launches, and then all this will be over. I think about my favorite books about spaceflight, those writers who faced the task of rendering an exciting, brand-new, seemingly limitless future. They struggled to define what these achievements were going to mean, where all this innovation was going to lead us. And where exactly *has* it led? Even with the knowledge I've spent the last ten years gaining, I realize I still don't know. If Mailer and Wolfe and Fallaci were here, what would they say? The more I think about it, the more clearly I can imagine them—Mailer cussing and snarling at everything, Wolfe sweating through his trademark white suit, Fallaci bristling at all the no-smoking signs. All of them disgusted that the future they worked so hard to understand and to put on the page has been canceled.

What would it mean to go to the last launch and write about it the way Mailer wrote about the launch of Apollo 11? To spend time with the people involved and write about them the way Fallaci did? The last launch of the space shuttle would unfold with all the glory and boredom and strangeness of Apollo 11, would provide an ending to the story. I think about how time-consuming and expensive it would be to try to do this—after all, fewer than half of shuttle missions launch on the first attempt; some have taken as many as seven attempts (separated by days or weeks or months) to get off the ground. A person could travel to Florida five or six separate times and never manage to catch a launch at all. Some space fans have suffered similar bad luck.

In humid weather, clouds sometimes gather within the unprecedented single-story height of the Vehicle Assembly Building. Technicians feel raindrops, then look up from their work assembling the spacecraft to find that it's raining lightly, the far-off ceiling windows obscured by indoor rain clouds.

Omar has never seen this himself, he tells me when I ask, but he has heard that it happens. He pulls into the enormous parking lot, and we pass the point where the tour buses always stop, where I've stood twice to try to get the VAB into my camera's frame. It gives me a thrill to ride right past that point and keep going, all the way up to the gate surrounding the building. We pile out and approach the VAB. I soon give up trying to tip my head back to take it in, as doing so impedes my ability to walk in a straight line. The entrance is like that of any large industrial building—heavy rolling door, polished concrete floor, safety signs posted on either side. BICYCLES PROHIBITED IN VAB. HAVE A SAFE DAY. But then I step into the interior, which is not like any other space in the world. I hold my breath while I follow Omar across the threshold and look up.

The sweeping vertical expanses made possible by flying buttresses in the twelfth century were meant to draw the eye up, and thus the spirit—the architecture was meant to stir the emotions and connect visitors with God. I look up. Other visitors, other NASA families, stream in on either side of me while I stand and gape. The space comes into focus in all its unphotographable enormousness. I have studied many images of the VAB, but I have never before quite grasped the way it all fits together, the way the four high bays mark four corners divided by the transfer aisle through the center of the building. Like all cathedrals, the Vehicle Assembly Building is laid out like a cross.

I can recite all the tour guides' facts about the VAB: Each of its four doors opens wide enough to take in the United Nations building and tall enough to take in most skyscrapers. Its volume is three-and-a-half times that of the Empire State Building. Its roof is big enough to contain more than six football fields.

But I couldn't ever have pictured quite how big it really is. Looking up, I see floor after floor of girders with their orderly rows of little white work lights twinkling. I peer into one of the four high bays in which the rockets are stacked. The ceiling windows whirl at a dizzying height that seems higher than the zenith of the sky itself. The human beings at the other end of the building disappear, too small to make out, even though we are all in the same room. In his book about Apollo 11, Norman Mailer wrote that the Vehicle Assembly Building may be the ugliest building in the world from the outside, but that from the inside it was a candidate for the most beautiful. I can finally see what he means.

This is where spaceships are assembled, every rocket to the moon, every space shuttle. I feel the enormity of the work that has been done here, the days and weeks and years of work, birthdays missed, children grown up, the endless and delicate work of assembling machines for going to space. I feel tears form in my eyes. I have been to Notre Dame and the Supreme Court and the Grand Canyon and Fallingwater and other sites imbued with a special grandeur, an urgent frisson of importance and here-ness, but none of them has made me cry. I look around at the other Family Day visitors chatting, wandering, pointing things out to each other in normal tones. None of them are weeping. I dry my eyes, hoping none of my companions have seen. Most people are milling through, in one door and out the other. I try not to judge them too harshly. To be fair, just to walk from one end of the building to the other does take a significant amount of time.

I feel Omar materialize at my shoulder.

"What do you think?" he asks. I'm surprised by the hopeful tone in his voice, the expression on his face when I turn to meet his eyes. He is actually concerned that I might not be having a good time.

"It's stunning," I tell him. "I'm stunned." He laughs before moving toward the mobile launch platform in one of the high bays. He tells me how the space shuttle launch vehicle is stacked vertically on the MLP before the crawler transporter lifts the whole business to move it slowly out to the launchpad. If Omar noticed I had tears in my eyes, he does an admirable job of not letting on. My father wanders over, and Omar explains more about how the platform works. My father snaps a picture of it.

The first segment of the first Saturn V reached the Vehicle Assembly Building in August 1966, and for the first time workers used the VAB's full height to stack the vehicle's stages one atop the other. I have a photo of the crew capsule being lowered onto the Saturn second stage, the Vehicle Assembly Building's cranes being put to use for the first time. Workers, ridiculously tiny, stand upon the enormous cylinder of the second-stage rocket, heedless of the massive spacecraft dangling above their heads. I would love to have seen the VAB then, when it was new and first being put to its intended, and still fantastical, use. It took a full year to stack that first Apollo/Saturn. When the assembled vehicle was finally complete, the access doors opened almost the full height of the building, and Apollo 4 rolled majestically out, its bright black-and-white paint job visible for miles, as the spaceworkers who had built it sat on picnic blankets with their families and applauded.

Only since the collapse of the Soviet Union have we learned that the Soviets were in fact developing a moon rocket, known as the N1, in the sixties. All four launch attempts of the N1 ended in explosions. Saturn was the largest rocket in the world, the most complex and powerful ever to fly, and remains so to this day. The fact that it was developed for a peaceful purpose is an exception to every pattern of history, and this is one of the legacies of Apollo.

We pile back into Omar's SUV and ride around to the other sites that are open to visitors. We visit the Orbiter Processing Facility, where the space shuttles are prepared horizontally before being rolled over to the VAB for stacking. We visit the launchpad where *Discovery* is poised nose up and ready to go. We see the Landing Facility and the mate/demate device, a ten-story contraption for lifting an orbiter onto and off of the 747 that ferries it back from California when it has to land there. We visit the Launch Control building, where on one wall of the seventies-style lobby are hung the mission patches of every human spaceflight that has ever been launched from here, 149 to date. Beneath each mission patch is a small plaque showing the launch and landing dates. Two of them—*Challenger*'s STS-51L and *Columbia*'s STS-107—are missing landing dates, because both of these missions ended in disasters that destroyed the orbiters and killed their crews. The blank spaces on the wall where those landing dates should have been are discolored from the touch of people's hands. This would be unremarkable if this place were a tourist attraction, or regularly open to the public. But with the rare exception of Family Days, this building is open only to people who work here. In other words, it's launch controllers, managers, and engineers who have been touching these empty spaces with their hands, on their way to and from doing their jobs.

After getting back on the road, we pass the Press Site, an agglomeration of buildings and decks centered around a large open field facing a body of water known as the Turn Basin, and beyond that, the launchpads. At the edge of the grassy field stands the huge countdown clock, the one you've seen in photos and news footage of launches, alongside an enormous flagpole flying an American flag. The buildings that belong to various news outlets have logos painted on them. I can make out only the ones closest to the road: CBS (whose Walter Cronkite narrated the iconic news coverage of the moon landings) and *Florida Today*. I crane my neck to see as much of the Press Site as I can, feeling a surprising jealousy of the people I see moving in and out of buildings there. They get access to people and places I can't, even as Omar's guest.

Near the Orbiter Processing Facility, Omar points out a gantry being constructed for Constellation, the program meant to follow the shuttle's retirement. President George W. Bush had announced Constellation in 2004 with great fanfare—it is designed to be more modular and flexible than the shuttle program, allowing different boosters and different crew or cargo configurations for missions of varying lengths. The plan is to get astronauts and payloads into low Earth orbit again within ten years and, eventually, on to the moon, asteroids, and Mars.

But even at the time of the announcement, few people believed a second wave of moon landings could actually take place on anything resembling the schedule Bush described, a schedule that required future Congresses to increase NASA's budget precipitously.

Like many ambitious projects, it's set up such that a future president and Congress will be forced to either foot the bulk of the cost or else kill the program, a time-honored way for politicians to claim credit for a bold move without having to pick up the tab. To no one's surprise, President Obama announced in February 2010 that he planned to cancel Constellation and by doing so earned the ire of many NASA employees and spaceflight enthusiasts. That summer Congress voted to approve Obama's NASA Authorization Act, a plan to increase NASA's finding by $6 billion over five years, a continued commitment to support development of commercial capabilities in low Earth orbit, and a more streamlined long-range space vehicle, which would come to be called the Space Launch System. Constellation contracts would remain in place until Congress voted to overturn the previous mandate, leaving workers at the Cape to continue work that was almost sure to be undone sometime in the future. Obama's bill also allowed for one more launch to be added, STS 135, on *Atlantis,* though this mission had yet to be funded and so was not certain to fly.

We drive to the Visitor Complex, an independently funded tourist attraction adjacent to the space center, and browse through the gift shop. There, while my father and Judy pick out space-themed gifts for my son, Omar and I stand shoulder to shoulder for a long time in the book department. He shows me the ones he likes (he's read most of the books here), and I tell him about the ones I've read. He shows me the big-ticket items in the glass cases that he covets: detailed metal models of all five orbiters, signed glossy photographs of Apollo astronauts, space-flown medallions in jewel boxes.

"I'm surprised you know so much about Apollo, not just shuttle," I say. Over the course of my day here I've learned to say "shuttle," not "the shuttle," when I'm referring to the entire program rather than a single vehicle.

"Oh, I'm interested in all of it," Omar says. "Ever since I was a little kid. Maybe it's because I grew up here and because my dad works here."

"For some people, growing up with something like this makes it *less* interesting," I say.

"That's true," Omar says thoughtfully. "I guess I'm lucky. The things I think are really cool are the things I get to see every day."

Omar lets us use his employee discount to buy the things we've picked out. My father buys an astronaut suit and astronaut teddy bear for my son. I buy NASA T-shirts for my husband and son, a coffee mug for myself, books and key chains for friends. Omar gives me a mission patch from the most recent flight that he got from his father. Patches are sold in the gift shop as well, but this is one of the patches the NASA insiders give to their friends and families.

Standing in the gift shop in front of a wall displaying all the mission patches from every spaceflight, I think about all I've seen today, all that will still occur here over the next year. The idea forms in my mind again that I could witness and write about these last launches. Or rather, it might be more accurate to say it's at this moment the idea solidifies into intent. Because it's been brewing all day, the idea I keep pushing to the back of my mind, this feeling that I should come back for these launches and write about them. I felt it in the VAB, and I felt it in the Orbiter Processing Facility, where it seemed I could almost reach up to touch the landing gear of *Endeavour*. I felt it at the Landing Facility with its three miles of runway dotted with alligators who are under the impression that the warm concrete has been laid out for their sunbathing comfort. That night at dinner with Omar and my family, he tells us about the excitement of launch days when he was little, about being awakened by the sonic booms of orbiters punching through the atmosphere in the middle of the night. He tells us about the terrible day his father came home from work after having spent the day in Launch Control searching his data screens for some sign of what had happened to *Challenger*.

All the books I've read about American spaceflight are about a trajectory still on the upswing. Even the books written post–*Columbia* envision a shuttle program righting itself, restoring our faith, and carrying us over until the next vehicle is ready to launch. No one has yet tried to grapple with the end that is now in sight. Only when something ends can we understand what it has meant.

In the parking lot, my father and Judy shake hands with Omar and thank him for everything he's done today. While they get into the rental car and set the GPS for the airport, Omar tells me I should come back for the *Discovery* launch.

"I'd love to," I say. "But it'll probably be during a busy time in my semester."

"Sure," Omar says nodding. "I understand it's hard to get away. But remember—it's the last one."

I hug him before getting into the backseat of the car with my family. Omar stands in the parking lot waving as we pull away, until he is a tiny dot in the rearview mirror.

I've read that the twentieth century might be remembered only for the atomic bomb, the industrialized slaughter of human beings, and the first steps away from our home planet. If this is true, the end of American spaceflight is going to be one of the more significant moments of my lifetime, significant beyond the three missions left and the sixteen astronauts still preparing to go into space. By the end of Family Day, when we are all saying our good-byes, I have come to feel that the end of the space shuttle is going to be the ending of a story, the story of one of the truly great things my country has accomplished, and that I want to be the one to tell it.

The night I get home from Cape Canaveral, I e-mail Omar to thank him again for inviting me, then go to the NASA website and find the shuttle launch manifest. One more mission for *Discovery* in the fall and one for *Endeavour* the following spring. A last mission for *Atlantis,* if it's added, will be in the summer. After that there will be no more.

In another window on my computer is a Flickr photo set belonging to a woman I don't know. The photo set shows the woman visiting the Kennedy Space Center on some sort of special escorted trip. The way her captions are written tells me she doesn't know nearly as much about shuttle as I do—she uses slightly the wrong terms for everything.

Worse, her writing lacks the enthusiasm I feel properly befits her experience. Not only does she not report crying upon entering the Vehicle Assembly Building, she doesn't even seem to understand it as a special privilege. As the photos continue to scroll by, I get more upset, because here she is donning a full-body cover-up and climbing into the crew cabin of an orbiter, an enormous privilege. The astronauts themselves don't take this lightly. In the pictures, the woman looks pleased and amused but not mind-blown. It was NASA's message about the space shuttle from the beginning that it would be cheaper, safer, more routine, than Apollo, more like commercial air travel. Maybe that message sank in too far with some people, and maybe this is part of what has doomed the shuttle. I stare at the woman's pictures for a while longer, then close the browser window.

"I know my rockets," I'd assured Omar, but did I? There are always people who know more, have seen more. I've seen one launch, which is more than most people can say. But Omar has kept company with the orbiters themselves. He has seen dozens of launches and has spent workdays, workweeks, work years inside the buildings I've waited a lifetime to enter. I've been inside the VAB now, but this horrible woman has been inside the crew cabin. There will always be someone who has seen more.

I print out the launch manifest and make some notes in the margins. After we get our son to bed, I show the printout to my husband, and though he clearly dreads the chaos this project will cause in our household, he agrees that this story needs to be written. Chris is a writer too, and a freelance editor; each of my absences will seriously cut into his time to work. He will care for our three-year-old son while I go to Florida multiple times and on a maddeningly ever-changing schedule. I will have to drive twelve hours each way to save money and to give me flexibility in those cases when the launch scrubs until the following day. When launches are delayed for longer periods of time, I will leave Florida empty-handed and start over. I will have to impose on my colleagues to cover classes for me when the launch schedule conflicts with my academic calendar. In order to start this project, I will have to set aside the novel I'm already halfway through, a novel

I'm expected to publish soon in order to qualify for tenure and keep my job, which is the sole source of benefits for my family. And I will have to impose more on Omar, the only local and NASA insider I know. All this might well turn out to be for nothing. But I've decided to try.

Over the following months, people will ask me what I expect to find by going to the last launches, and I will have to admit that I have no idea. I'll find it when I see it, I tell them—or else, I won't, and all this will have been a waste. I know I want to write about those places where the technical and the emotional intersect—like the smell of space, or the schoolchildren watching *Challenger* explode with a teacher aboard, or an adult woman hiding her tears in the cathedralic heights of the Vehicle Assembly Building, or a bored child in a movie theater watching a beautiful astronaut float in her sleep. I want to see the beauty and the strangeness in the last days of American space-flight, in the last moments of something that used to be cited as what makes America great. I want to see the end of the story whose beginning was told by some of the writers I admire most. I want to know, most of all, what it means that we went to space for fifty years and that we won't be going anymore.

The astronauts walked with the easy saunter of athletes. . . .
Once they sat down, however, the mood shifted. Now
they were there to answer questions about a phenomenon
which even ten years ago would have been considered material unfit for serious discussion. Grown men, perfectly
normal-looking, were now going to talk about their trip to
the moon. It made everyone uncomfortable.

—Norman Mailer, *Of a Fire on the Moon*

CHAPTER 2. What It Felt Like to Walk on the Moon

Southern Festival of Books: Nashville, Tennessee, October 10, 2009

Maybe you've seen it. Many people have—at least 800,000 have
clicked on various YouTube iterations of the same moment. It looks
like nothing at first. The video is fuzzy, amateur, handheld. We hear
the muffled verité sound of wind against the microphone, of the excited breath of the camera operator. People are standing around, their
postures reflecting boredom, their faces and movements obscured by
the shaky camera work and low resolution.

On YouTube, of course, this poor video quality, combined with
a high hit count, contains an inverse promise: *something is about to
happen.*

We can make out a white-haired man in a blue blazer, partially obscured by a sign. He seems to be talking to another man, in a black
jacket, whose back is to the camera. Out of any context, the white-
haired man would be unrecognizable because of the bad video quality, but if you know to look for him—and you do, because of the
title on the YouTube page—the man is recognizable as astronaut Buzz
Aldrin, lunar module pilot of Apollo 11, one of the first two men to
walk on the moon.

The muffled audio obscures the voice of the black-jacketed man, who is speaking now. Passion or nervousness makes his voice waver.

"You're the one who said you walked on the moon when you didn't," the man says. He is holding an object out to Buzz. A subsequent Google search reveals that it's a Bible—he is trying to make Buzz swear upon it.

Overlapping him, Buzz Aldrin's voice says, clearly and unwaveringly, "Get away from me."

"—calling the kettle black. You're a coward and a liar and a thief—"

At that moment Buzz's arm comes up and cracks the black-jacketed man in the jaw. Even with the poor video, we can see that it's an impressive punch, well-aimed and powerful. We can't see the punched man's face, but we see his head recoil backward. The camera recoils too, as if in sympathy. Something has changed in the scene, you can sense it. One public figure's image has been complicated, another person now has a story to tell, a video to put on YouTube.

"Did you get that on camera?" the man in the black jacket asks breathlessly, a note of joy in his voice. The black-jacketed man is Bart Sibrel, moon hoax conspiracist. He believes that all of the trips to the moon were faked, were in fact physically impossible, and that the Apollo astronauts have agreed to uphold the lie because they benefit personally and financially. (He has also stated at other times that the astronauts are not consciously lying but were subjected to mind control by the government to convince them that they did in fact go to the moon. Today, clearly, he is working from the former theory.) He has made it his life's work to expose the conspiracy.

"Did you get that on camera?" This line of dialogue, spoken so clearly and happily, subsequently helps to acquit Buzz Aldrin, seventy-two years old at the time of the incident, of assault charges.

Everyone agrees that NASA's finest hour was the journey of Apollo 11, which left Earth with Buzz Aldrin, Neil Armstrong, and Michael Collins aboard on July 16, 1969. During the three days it took them to get to the moon, the astronauts grew beards, took measurements of the stars out their windows using sextants to make sure they were still on course, chatted with Houston, listened to music on tape, shot films of each other doing somersaults and making ham sandwiches in microgravity, got mildly on one another's nerves, and refrained from considering the enormity of their undertaking. Each of them has said in the years since that they actively kept themselves from thinking about the long chain of risky events it would take to get them back home. This particular avoidance was an ability they had honed as test pilots of experimental aircraft. It seems desirable for astronauts to be able to resist grand and potentially panic-inducing trains of thought, yet all three of them have expressed regret that this same character trait kept them from being able to adequately convey to us spectators what it was like to experience the things they experienced.

It's difficult for those of us born in a later era to imagine the historical phenomenon of Apollo, a moment when Americans came together over an enormous science project funded entirely by the federal government. We must take our elders at their word when they talk about what this was like, as we've never seen such a thing ourselves. Some years, during the run-up to Apollo, Congress voted to allocate NASA a larger budget than NASA had requested. The effects of this kind of public support were unprecedented outside of war, and may never be seen again. As important as this financial support was for the early days of Apollo, it also created a tragically inaccurate impression within NASA that its projects would continue to be funded at this rate. In the midsixties, everyone thought the construction of the Kennedy Space Center was taking place at the start of an exciting new era. No one could have known that in fact 1966 was to represent the zenith of that unanimity. The public's imagination for fulfilling President Kennedy's challenge would prove more shortsighted than anyone at NASA had hoped.

Space historians divide the fifty-year period of American spaceflight into two eras: the "heroic era," which includes the Mercury project to put the first Americans into space, the Gemini project to expand NASA's abilities and test techniques for getting to the moon, and the Apollo project, which achieved the moon landings. The second era of American spaceflight is known as the "shuttle era," and its being named for a vehicle rather than a lofty attribute says a lot about the difference between the two, about the loss of grandiosity in the goals we set ourselves, about the ways in which NASA had been forced to repackage spaceflight as an economical and utilitarian project. The heroic era spanned only eleven years (1961–72) compared to the shuttle's thirty, with a much longer list of firsts, and this fact contains an important lesson about the history of American spaceflight as well. We did a lot in a very short span of time, and then we did a lot less for a lot longer. Soon, of course, we'll be doing nothing at all. Faced with the fact that we are losing American spaceflight altogether, suddenly the workhorse shuttle seems as beautiful and daring as the Saturn V did in the sixties.

This is the paradox of growing up in the shuttle era: the vehicle is more complex and advanced, its reusability makes it much more cost-effective, and its versatility makes possible missions the Saturn V never could have accomplished, such as repairs to the Hubble Space Telescope and construction of the International Space Station. Yet the sense of danger, the sense of achieving the impossible, was what made the heroic era feel heroic. If we could somehow get that back, many people feel, we could restore NASA to what it once was. The sense of collective adventure from the heroic era has never left us. At the same time, it's the shuttle's disasters that brought about its end. We want the danger, but without any actual risk.

Here is one way to conceptualize NASA's heroic era: in 1961, Kennedy gave his "moon speech" to Congress, charging them to put an American on the moon "before the decade is out." In the eight years that unspooled between Kennedy's speech and Neil Armstrong's historic first bootprint, NASA, a newborn government agency, established sites and campuses in Texas, Florida, Alabama, California, Ohio, Maryland, Mississippi, Virginia, and the District of Columbia; awarded multi-million-dollar contracts and hired four hundred thousand workers; built a fully functioning moon port in a formerly uninhabited swamp; designed and constructed a moonfaring rocket, spacecraft, lunar lander, and space suits; sent astronauts repeatedly into orbit, where they ventured out of their spacecraft on umbilical tethers and practiced rendezvous techniques; sent astronauts to orbit the moon, where they mapped out the best landing sites; all culminating in the final, triumphant moment when they sent Neil Armstrong and Buzz Aldrin to step out of their lunar module and bounce about on the moon, perfectly safe within their space suits.

All of this, start to finish, was accomplished in those eight years. I have read many detailed accounts of how this happened from scientific, engineering, and political standpoints. What it *means* that all this happened—what it means that it couldn't happen again—is yet to be written.

The astronauts did well not to linger too much on the meaning of their undertaking, because the number of steps it would take to complete the mission was daunting. As command module pilot Michael Collins put it, "The press always asked what part of the upcoming flight would be the most dangerous, and I always answered, that part which we had overlooked in our preparations." In his memoir of the journey, Collins lists the eleven points in Apollo 11's flight plan that "merited special attention": (1) leave Earth's surface under the power of the world's largest rocket and attain Earth orbit; (2) burn the engines to set course for the moon and spend three days traveling a quarter million miles; (3) separate the lunar module and remate it with the command module; (4) achieve lunar orbit; (5) separate the lunar module (carrying Neil Armstrong and Buzz Aldrin) from the command module (now carrying only Michael Collins, who, while he was on the far side of the moon, set a record for being the farthest a human has been from any other); (6) land the lunar module safely on the moon; (7) put on space suits, open the hatch, and climb down the ladder to step onto an alien planetary body, gather moon rocks, plant a flag, conduct a few experiments, talk to the president, pose for pictures, climb back into the lunar module; (8) burn the engine to leave the moon's surface; (9) rendezvous with the command module in lunar orbit (which is to say, line up the two spacecraft and remate them, easier said than done when the two spacecraft are traveling at different speeds in different orbits); (10) ditch the lunar module and burn the engines again to set course for Earth; (11) survive the heat of reentry and hope the chutes deploy properly, allowing the capsule to splash down into the Pacific, from which the astronauts will be fished out by a helicopter rescue crew from a nearby aircraft carrier.

Different people give different estimates of the odds involved, but Michael Collins privately gave the whole chain only about a fifty-fifty chance of success. A failure at any one point would mean failure of the mission, and most would also mean the deaths of at least two, maybe all three, crew members. (Wernher von Braun told Oriana Fallaci that "fifty percent of the risk is that before they set off they'll die in a car crash here on Earth: they drive like madmen. The other fifty percent is that they'll die going to the Moon.") Many of these steps had never been attempted before, and some of them could not be properly tested on Earth. By far the riskiest step in the sequence was (8): burn the lunar module's ascent engine to leave the moon's surface. This step simply had to work, or Neil and Buzz would be left to die there. But designing an engine to ignite in a vacuum in one-sixth Earth's gravity was at best a series of educated guesses.

The lunar module, on its own going by the call name *Eagle,* undocked from the command module, now called *Columbia,* leaving Michael Collins behind, on July 20, 1969. *Eagle*'s descent toward the surface of the moon was not without incident: multiple computer alarms went off and the data screens went blank during the riskiest part of descent, with only sixty seconds of fuel left; neither Neil nor Buzz had ever seen these particular alarm codes in their training simulations. A twenty-six-year-old computer engineer in Mission Control in Houston had a fraction of a second to choose whether to call out "no-go" or "go"—whether to abort the mission and send *Eagle* back up to redock with the command module, losing the chance to land on the moon, or whether to continue.

"Go," the engineer said into his microphone.

"Go," repeated Mission Control to Neil and Buzz, "we are *go.*" In fact, none of them had any way of knowing whether the computer error might prevent *Eagle* from lifting off properly when it was time to rendezvous with *Columbia,* and the possibility weighed on them all for the next two days. The Apollo computer was one of the many components that simply had to work or the astronauts would die; its total memory was smaller than the file size of a song I just downloaded on my phone.

Neil Armstrong climbed out the hatch and set his boot onto the surface of the Sea of Tranquility at 10:56 p.m. Eastern Daylight Time on July 20, 1969. Some people suspect that NASA hired a team of copywriters, or poets, to come up with the historic first words to utter along with his first step, but in fact no one told him what to say or even asked what he would say, if all accounts are accurate. "That's one small step for a man . . . one giant leap for mankind." We've grown so used to this sentence, we don't even really hear it anymore. In fact, I grew up with a mishearing of it ("one small step for man") that renders the words senseless. It turns out that a quirk of Armstrong's regional accent led to the confusion—among Ohioans, "for a man" can come out "fra man," and the indefinite article was lost. But even with the misunderstanding, the line still rings in schoolchildren's ears.

Buzz Aldrin once told me that he envies writers their ability to put things into words. Yet one of his first utterances after stepping out of the lunar module, in an attempt to describe the landscape to Mission Control, was the phrase "magnificent desolation." This is surprisingly poetic for an astronaut, and it has stayed with me ever since I noticed it in a NASA transcript years ago. Every minute of the astronauts' time on the moon was planned, and they wore printed copies of their schedules on their wrists to keep them on track. But I have to imagine that, once in a while, Neil and Buzz looked up at the far-off mountains at the edge of the Sea of Tranquility and thought to themselves, *I am on the moon. This is all happening, right now, on the surface of the moon.* Buzz Aldrin said many years later, "Every step on the moon was a virginal experience. Exploring this place that had never before been seen by human eyes, upon which no foot had stepped, or hand touched—was awe-inspiring."

Neil, Buzz, and Mike traveled farther than anyone ever had and were gone only eight days. The images they brought back are among the most beautiful ever produced—all the more so, perhaps, because none of it was particularly intended to be beautiful. The jettisoned interstage adapter of the Saturn V tumbling, on fire, in a slow-motion ballet toward the gorgeous blue of faraway Earth. Buzz Aldrin smirking in a shaft of pure sunlight streaking through the command module window. Neil Armstrong overbundled in his space suit like a child dressed for cold, standing on the ladder and cautiously dangling one boot above the dusty surface of the Sea of Tranquility. The three astronauts confined to an Airstream trailer for quarantine after their return, smiling out at the president through a picture window. The perfect blue earth, thumb-sized, hanging in a deep black sky.

If someone asked to me to sum up what is great about my country, I would probably tell them about Apollo 11, about the four hundred thousand people who worked to make the impossible come true within eight years, about how it changed me to see the space-scarred *Columbia* capsule in a museum as a child, about how we came in peace for all mankind. Yet I feel the built-in pointlessness at the heart of Apollo as much as I fiercely admire it—it's the same pointlessness shared by any artistic gesture. I feel it most at that moment when Neil and Buzz have stepped off the ladder, taken their bearings, picked up a few moon rocks, photographed the scene, and looked around them. A weird thought hovers over their helmets in the bright sunlit vacuum. *What now?* It's a peculiar feeling, after the unspeakable effort and expense. None of the answers are entirely satisfying.

I'm watching the YouTube clip of the Punch because I've just confirmed that I'm going to meet Buzz Aldrin. I'm going to spend most of a day with him, actually. We will both be at the Southern Festival of Books, held each October in Nashville. Buzz is in the middle of a huge book tour behind his autobiography, whose release has been timed to coincide with the fortieth anniversary of Apollo 11. I had committed to being at the festival long before, to talk about my *Challenger* novel, and the organizers had quickly figured out that I would be the only other writer at the festival with much knowledge about spaceflight. After I agreed to give Buzz's introduction (which, I was told many times and in no uncertain terms, could absolutely not go over two minutes), I began to panic. What does one say about Buzz Aldrin in under two minutes? I looked back through everything I'd learned about his accomplishments—my books about Apollo, my copies of Buzz's previous autobiography and his forays into science fiction, Michael Collins's memoir and Neil Armstrong's biography, the many documentaries and interviews in which Buzz has participated. I could write a book about him if I were asked; it was harder to sum up everything about him in one hundred twenty seconds.

I imagined standing up in front of a packed auditorium and telling the crowd, "You guys, you know the greatest achievement of humankind? Okay, this guy? Right here? He did that." Point dramatically at Buzz, take my seat. Well under two minutes.

Buzz Aldrin was among the third group of astronauts, chosen in 1963. Those early astronauts, crew-cut Caucasian men, family men, military men, all seemed immune to the emotion of what they were doing. They never waggled their heads at the wonder of it all. There are no reports of them tearing up upon entering the Vehicle Assembly Building. They quickly changed the subject when they were asked about the possibility of their deaths, and politely filibustered questions about God and the heavens. This was what was expected of them, of course—this calm in the face of danger. This is what Tom Wolfe found remarkable about them. Their ability to step onto unstable rockets, to take perilous risks seemingly without fear, their ability to carry out the greatest achievements of their species without raising their heart rates or losing their swagger. This was exactly why they had been chosen as test pilots and then as astronauts. Yet—and here was the contradiction—people wanted to see emotion from them.

I knew that before being selected as an astronaut Buzz Aldrin earned a PhD in astronautics at MIT, where he designed orbital rendezvous techniques for spaceships docking in orbit (still a highly theoretical prospect in 1963). According to all reports, this was a project that required a freakish level of intelligence, a mind-spinning application of

physics, intersecting multiple orbits that young Buzz, in that time before computers, calculated by hand with a slide rule. (His fellow Apollo
astronauts also recall that he was unique among them in his ability
to calculate orbital rendezvous in his head.) The techniques he created were critical to early spaceflight, and some of them continue to
be used today.

Out of curiosity I decided to get hold of Buzz's 1963 PhD dissertation through my father, whose status as an MIT alumnus allowed
him to download a copy from the MIT library site. The dissertation
is titled "Line-of-Sight Guidance Techniques for Manned Orbital
Rendezvous." Hand-typed, the equations make me imagine Buzz (or
maybe it was his wife, Joan) painstakingly rolling the platen up or
down half a click to create superscript and subscript numbers, dozens of them per page. The abstract introduces the project as a study of
"the inertial rotation of the line of sight throughout three dimensional
Keplerian rendezvous trajectories." A whole page reads like this—
words I don't know, or words I thought I knew that are clearly being
used in an extremely specific way.

But on the sixth page I find a dedication:

> In the hopes that this work may in some way contribute to their
> exploration of space, this is dedicated to the crew members of this
> country's present and future manned space programs. If only I could
> join them in their exciting endeavors!

I feel a surge of happiness. Here is my reward: Buzz Aldrin has,
unwittingly, dedicated his dissertation to himself.

When I'd first learned about the orbital rendezvous piece of Buzz's
story, the math genius piece, I was surprised by it. I'd known that
Buzz Aldrin was handsome and brave, unnervingly competent, but
not that he was the sort of person capable of doing complex math
in his head. Those people are necessary to spaceflight, but we think
of them as the guys in short-sleeve dress shirts and dark ties, slide
rules in their pockets, the *nerds*—not the astronauts, possessors of the

Right Stuff who actually get to fly the missions and bag lots of babes along the way. The Apollo astronauts were avatars for our own dreams of spaceflight, in the same way that movie stars are our avatars for romance and relevance, and it's perhaps not entirely flattering to us as a culture that we require of astronauts that they be athletic and daring, but not especially book-smart. The truth is that the astronauts were and are book-smart, all of them, and by most accounts Buzz Aldrin was the book-smartest of them all. Alan Bean, a fellow Apollo astronaut, once said: "One thing I know about Buzz: he's one of these guys that's a lot smarter than most of us. You didn't want to sit near him at a party because he would start talking about rendezvous."

It's hard to say precisely when the first moon hoax theory emerged, and harder still to say when it picked up steam. Maybe there were always people who doubted, even in the moment, even as the images were playing in black and white in their living rooms. Maybe some people's trust in government had already eroded that much—maybe in certain circles it was starting to be a more fashionable stance to question everything.

What we do know is that by the thirty-year anniversary of Apollo 11, in 1999, about 6 percent of Americans told Gallup they believed the moon landings were staged and another 5 percent said they had no opinion, leaving only 89 percent who firmly believed we went to the moon. Things were worse by 2004, when a survey of people eighteen to twenty-five years old revealed that 27 percent of them "expressed some doubt that NASA went to the Moon," with 10 percent of them indicating that it was "highly unlikely" that a moon landing had ever taken place.

No one from NASA Public Affairs has ever undertaken to answer the hoax charges in a systematic way. The only rebuttal to appear anywhere on the nasa.gov domain is from the Science and Technology Directorate at NASA's Marshall Space Flight Center and dates from 2001, shortly after Fox aired a special called *Conspiracy Theory: Did*

We Land on the Moon? You can see why there wasn't a larger, more of-ficial response from within NASA—to do so would be to engage in, and thereby dignify, an argument that should not be mistaken for an actual controversy.

I have met moon hoax True Believers in my daily life, and while many of them are precisely the sorts of libertarians and *X-Files* fans you would expect to relish such a juicy conspiracy, I've often been surprised by stealth conspiracists, the non-paranoid-appearing, buttoned-up types whom you wouldn't expect to question much of anything. They smirk at me condescendingly, shake their heads a couple of times, and explain to me why we couldn't have done it. *Couldn't have.* If they seem open to discussion, I have a couple of key pieces of counterevidence I like to offer.

One I like to repeat is from Michael Collins: over four hundred thousand people worked on Apollo at its height, he points out, and not one of them has come forward to spill the secret in the interven-ing decades. "I don't know two Americans who have a fantastic secret without one of them blurting it out to the press," he points out in a documentary interview. "Can you imagine thousands of people able to keep this secret?" The idea that so many people, many of whom would have to be in a position to know of the deception, kept such an incendiary secret for decades strains even the most generous under-standing of human nature.

My other favorite counterargument draws on evidence that is more empirical. All six missions to land on the moon brought back pounds of moon rocks. These rocks have been made available to scientists, who have studied them using technologies that had not yet been invented during Apollo. Either NASA figured out a way to create fake moon rocks convincing to the molecular level, or the hundreds of scientists from all over the world who have been allowed to study the rocks over the years are in on the conspiracy. Neither seems likely. It seems much more likely that if NASA wanted to fool people with a fake moon land-ing, their first order of business would be to come up with a plausible reason why the spacecraft couldn't carry back any rocks.

But none of my counterevidence will make much difference, I

know. There is a pleasure in doubting. I've felt it too, about other things: a satisfaction at being smarter than those who have been duped, a satisfaction at being ungullible. I once met another Apollo astronaut, Jack Schmitt, a geologist and the first scientist to travel in space. I told him that his name is in my novel—my main character was born in 1972, the same day Schmitt and his crewmate Gene Cernan fired their lunar module's ascent stage and lifted off the surface of the moon for the last time. I asked him what he says to moon hoax conspiracists.

"Well," he said, slowly, "I describe to them my personal experience of walking on the moon. And if they choose to believe I am a liar, there is nothing I can do to help that."

"Good answer," I said.

It's the condescension in the conspiracist's smirk that drives me insane. The smirk makes me a credulous dupe, one of the clamoring naive who believes the bedtime story. The conspiracists want to erase from the official record the achievement that some call the greatest achievement of the United States, the greatest achievement of the twentieth century, the greatest achievement in the history of humankind. The rage this elicits in me (a tiny flame, entirely controllable in social situations, yet *rage* is the word for it nonetheless) is hard to describe. It is a *patriotic* rage, on behalf of forces much larger than myself, people much greater than myself. The doubters are calling people I admire liars, men who risked their lives for their country before they risked their lives for the exploration of space. Buzz Aldrin a liar, Neil Armstrong a liar, Michael Collins a liar. And the worst kind of liars—those who would manipulate our highest values for their own personal gain. It makes more sense to the doubters that NASA is an organization of frauds and opportunists than that a government agency achieved something beautiful and important, and this angers me on behalf of both the past and the future.

I've talked to people, friends and strangers, about what it means that the shuttle era is ending, and I'm both heartened by the sadness people seem to feel over its loss and frustrated by the general ignorance about spaceflight and its costs. People tell me that the shuttle program is being sacrificed so the money can be diverted to wars in Iraq and Afghanistan, that the shuttles had to be retired because they have flown more missions than they were designed for, that we are stepping aside as leaders in space in order to create a "more egalitarian" position in the world as part of our president's general move toward socialism. None of these claims have any truth to them.

"Why *are* we stopping then?" people ask me. I'm always a little more flummoxed by this question than I should be, given how much time I've spent reading and thinking about it. *It's complicated,* I say. The loss of *Columbia* was the beginning of the end—that much is true no matter whom you ask. After that disaster, politicians in Washington would have had to spend a lot of political capital to save the shuttle, and a recession would be an especially treacherous time to do that. All this sounds weaker than what I really want to say, though, which is partly that the public's own apathy is to blame. It's closest to the truth to say that the fundamental problem is that most people had not really noticed that we were still flying in the first place.

I watch the video of the Punch that night after my family is asleep, over and over, trying to get some feeling for the man. But we are not ourselves at our most extreme—not in a moment of rage at being called a coward, not in the moment of the utmost courage, guiding an untested spacecraft down, down, down toward the surface of a desolate alien world while the alarms blare and the fuel runs low. I know only that I don't yet know Buzz Aldrin at all.

Waiting on a street in downtown Nashville for Buzz Aldrin's limo to arrive from the airport, I decide not to ask him about the Punch, or about Bart Sibrel, or about hoax conspiracy theory in general. That's what everyone else asks him about, people who don't know much about spaceflight. They ask him about the Punch, they ask him whether Buzz Lightyear was really named for him (he was), they ask him what it felt like to walk on the moon. Buzz Aldrin has been surrounded by space groupies since he was selected as an astronaut forty-six years ago; he has been followed and accosted and approached and stared at and flirted with by people who know only that he is an astronaut, which is to say that they know he is famous, or that he is a hero, without really understanding the details of his fame or his heroism. I want Buzz to know that I am not one of those people.

In my hotel room the night before, I'd looked over everything I had learned about him: Buzz Aldrin graduated from West Point and served as a fighter pilot in the Korean War. He became a war hero when he shot down two MiGs and was decorated with the Distinguished Flying Cross. He then earned a doctorate in astronautics from MIT by the age of thirty-three.

Buzz has also been getting quite a bit of attention lately. Around the fortieth anniversary of the moon landings, he did interviews with *USA Today,* the *New York Times Magazine,* the *Today Show,* CNN, NPR, C-SPAN, Fox News, the *Guardian, Interview,* and *GQ.* He rapped with Snoop Dogg; appeared in ads for Omega watches, Louis Vuitton luggage, and Krug champagne; and started tweeting actively. He did a cameo on *30 Rock,* served as an announcer for a professional wrestling match, and held up his end of a cha-cha on *Dancing with the Stars.* For a few weeks before I met Buzz Aldrin, I couldn't poke around online or turn on my TV without seeing him. The three-man crew of Apollo 11 has displayed the full range of approaches to life as an aging moonwalker: near-total recluse in the person of Neil Armstrong until his death in 2012; active autographer and occasional interview subject Mike Collins; and at the other extreme Buzz Aldrin, who, at least for a while there, was constantly in the public eye.

The idea of introducing Buzz Aldrin to a huge crowd later today terrifies me, but I've agreed to it specifically because I want to have the chance to talk with him one-on-one about the impending retirement of the space shuttle. I've tried to anticipate what he might think about the end of shuttle, the fact that the fifty-year era of human spaceflight he participated in so admirably is ending, and my best guess is that he will say it's a failure of imagination. Everyone who lived through Apollo, it seems, bears a memory of a time when nothing was going to be impossible, when those first steps would be the beginning of a new era in which we would accomplish more and more in space. If it felt this way to people who watched Buzz walk on the moon, I can't imagine what it must have felt like to Buzz himself.

Sitting at the undersized desk in my Nashville hotel room, I wrote a two-page introduction outlining Buzz Aldrin's accomplishments. I decided to end with the inscription on the stainless steel plaque that he and Neil left behind on the surface of the moon. I stood up to practice reading the introduction out loud to make sure it was under two minutes, and when I reached the end, I tried to deliver the inscription boldly: "Here men from the planet Earth first set foot on the moon. . . . We came in peace for all mankind." But, embarrassingly, I got choked up. Some people are the same way with the preamble to the Declaration of Independence or the last verse of "The Star-Spangled Banner"; for me, this is the poem that most stirs my patriotic sentimentality. It's still hard to believe that these words rest on the surface of the moon two hundred and fifty thousand miles away, have rested there since before I was born; it's even harder to believe that the plaque so modestly refrains from bragging. I've always thought this was part of the answer to my question about what the era of American spaceflight has meant.

So I wait on Seventh Avenue in downtown Nashville, where I am to meet Buzz. It's a disconcerting sensation, waiting on a sidewalk with my coat over my arm, dress and lipstick on, like waiting to be picked up for a date. Book festival patrons on their way to events meet my eye, seem to wonder why I'm standing here. *I'm waiting for Buzz Aldrin,* I want to tell them. But I would sound like a lunatic.

When the limo finally pulls up, Buzz Aldrin pops out of it as if on springs.

"I'm Buzz Aldrin," he says as I approach him. But I'd know him anywhere. He is nearly eighty years old, but he is still cartoonishly handsome in a Dudley Do-Right way, with the deep chin cleft and sparkling eyes of a forties movie star. To my delight, he wears the same blue blazer he wore in the YouTube punch video; the color brings out the startling blue of his eyes. Buzz Aldrin is animated, twinkling, even, while we shake hands. He has absolutely no trace of the frailty or hesitation one might expect from a man his age. I introduce myself, and he repeats my name back to me, which thrills me.

I realize I am holding on to Buzz's hand too long. I can't help it. I am exquisitely aware, in that moment, of the fact that his hand *has been on the moon*. This hand—this eighty-year-old white man's hand—has traveled farther than anything I will ever again have the chance to touch. This hand, I think in that split second, may still have residual moon molecules on it. I think to myself: *I am touching a moon hand*. These thoughts are goofy and vaguely childlike, like so many we have about spaceflight, but I know the day is coming, not too long in the future, when there will no longer be any living human beings who have walked on the moon, no more moon molecules lingering in the creases of aging men's hands. All this makes a handshake hard to pull off elegantly.

Buzz turns to help his wife, Lois, out of the car. Lois is tiny and elegant, dressed in a sequined NASA shirt. They both carry Louis Vuitton overnight bags, part of his compensation for appearing in the ads connecting the brand with the fortieth anniversary of the moon landings. They have just arrived from a long flight but appear perfectly pressed and alert.

Once we reach the authors' green room, Buzz and I put on our name tags, look in our author goodie bags (each containing, among other things, a Moon Pie and an airplane-sized bottle of Jack Daniel's), and settle in to wait for our event. We have nearly two hours until his talk is scheduled to begin. Lois has brought a magazine and leaves Buzz and me to chat. This is my chance.

I don't really know how to bring up my question, though. I am suddenly conscious of how annoying it must be for Buzz Aldrin to have these big questions sprung at him without warning, knowing that his answers may appear in print. He would probably rather relax and make small talk like anyone else. I hate to be the one to do this to him, to force him into interview mode.

While I dither internally, Buzz asks politely about my book. I hand him a copy (having finished my own book event earlier in the day), then watch as he scans the jacket. Even though my book has been out for a while, has withstood reviews and polite corrections from people like Omar, this still makes me extremely nervous.

"Did you read *Encounter with Tiber*?" Buzz asks.

I murmur vaguely. *Encounter with Tiber* is a 1996 science fiction novel Buzz cowrote with John Barnes. I own the book—it's a mass-market paperback with a debossed alien solar system on its cover. I've read the chapter that describes a fictional space shuttle disaster with great attention. But the novel spans centuries—millennia, actually—and begins with a seventy-five-character dramatis personae, longer than those of most Russian novels. Despite glowing reviews from the likes of Alan Shepard, Michael Collins, and Arthur C. Clarke, I've never gotten around to finishing it.

Buzz asks a few polite questions—what kind of research I did, whether I, too, had been a thirteen-year-old when the space shuttle *Challenger* exploded. I tell him I was.

"A terrible thing," Buzz says. "We always thought the shuttle project was so much safer. Going to the moon was supposed to be the big risk, and the space shuttle was supposed to be this move toward safety and reliability."

This was part of the problem, of course—people thought the shuttle was as safe as an airliner, and were bored by that safety; they felt that much more betrayed when it turned out not even to be reliable. Buzz is right that it was a big risk going to the moon—I'd read the night before that President Nixon's speechwriter, William Safire, had drafted a speech for the president to give in the event the lunar module of Apollo 11 was unable to lift off the moon's surface. The speech is eloquent and moving, a haunting voice from an alternate universe in which the worst has happened. It begins with the line: "Fate has ordained that the men who went to the moon to explore in peace will stay on the moon to rest in peace."

"It was a terrible thing that one of the crew was a teacher," Buzz adds.

I consider telling Buzz about my theory that the inclusion of a schoolteacher on the flight, and the ill-fated attempts to publicize that particular flight to schoolchildren, altered irrevocably my generation's feelings not only about spaceflight but also about our country, about the way the world works. American spacecraft had been taking astronauts safely to space and back since long before we were born, and so we understood human spaceflight as a normal state of events, a preexisting condition, a birthright. For those who were already adults, *Challenger* was a terrible accident, but for children it was something more like a betrayal of our deepest trust. It permanently damaged our faith that the world made sense and that the adults were properly in charge of it.

But I'm not confident this line of thinking will interest or engage Buzz. At a certain level, I'm afraid of seeming guilty of a particular type of unappetizing generational self-pity ("Boo-hoo, we watched a rocket explode on TV") when everyone knows that, especially compared to his, my generation was strangely immune from tragedy. That an accident resulting in the deaths of seven people was, for us, the worst thing that had ever happened was evidence of how very sheltered we had been.

"I always thought John Denver should have gotten to go on that flight," Buzz says, interrupting my thoughts.

"John . . . Denver?" I repeat, wondering whether he really means the singer.

"Yeah, you know, 'Rocky Mountain High'? He was a great advocate of spaceflight, and when NASA first talked about sending a civilian, they considered sending a creative person, a performer. John Denver could have written a song in space that would inspire generations to come."

I find myself unsure what to say to this. "I wonder if NASA feared that sending John Denver to space would have seemed more like a publicity stunt," I offer.

Buzz furrows his brow at this. He seems to have no idea what I'm talking about.

"The whole *point* was publicity," he says. "A schoolteacher might be a wonderful person, and teachers perform an important role in society, but a popular songwriter like John Denver reaches a lot more people. It's just the numbers." Satisfied, Buzz goes back to perusing my book. It's true that Buzz's own approach to publicity seems to bear out this philosophy.

When it's time, we gather up our things and prepare to depart the safety of the green room. There is a growing crowd of space enthusiasts gathering outside, and it's time to face them.

Buzz offers me his arm as we make our way toward the door, and I wish someone would take a picture of us so I can prove to my friends later that this is happening. On our way to the auditorium, we pass through a courtyard, where a table is set up for Buzz's book signing after his talk; already a line of people, at least a hundred, snakes back and forth in front of the table. Some of those in the line are holding large stacks of books. It is an awkward moment, though one I suppose Buzz is accustomed to—passing within arm's reach of the autograph seekers who would choose to stand out here for the duration of his talk, to hold their places in line rather than go inside to hear what he has to say. It's uncomfortable to see the autograph seekers light up when they recognize Buzz, then look away sheepishly.

Luckily, there are still far more people who want to hear Buzz talk than those who hope to turn a profit from selling his signature. The auditorium seats sixteen hundred and is packed to capacity when we arrive. We loop our way around to the front, where seats have been reserved for Buzz, Lois, Buzz's ghostwriter Ken Abraham, and me. I turn in my seat to take in the crowd, all of them watching us intently, and only then does my panic really set in. These people are hungry for Buzz Aldrin. You can see it in their eyes, especially the men of a certain age—the way they lean forward in their seats, fiddling nervously with their hands, searching Buzz's face with awe. Squint a bit, and you can see them as little boys hunching in front of their TVs in the summer of 1969, their faces bathed in the silver light of the Sea of Tranquility.

I take the stage shakily and get through my introduction. I start with F. Scott Fitzgerald's line about American lives not having second acts, a claim Buzz Aldrin's life has clearly refuted. I run down a condensed list of Buzz's accomplishments, quote from the plaque on the moon, refrain from weeping patriotically. Applause. Two minutes exactly.

Buzz Aldrin takes my place at the podium and faces an audience now applauding wildly. He greets the crowd.

They don't stop clapping. In fact, they jump to their feet and clap harder.

Buzz Aldrin stands calmly at the podium. He is in no hurry. He watches me walk away, down the length of the long stage.

Then he turns to the audience and says, "Now, that's a special lady."

This is a polite gesture from Buzz, nothing more, but it's a moment I expect to see play back before my eyes during any near-death experience. I feel the attention of the crowd flick to me, but they know better than to fall for the distraction. They return their attention to Buzz. The applause grows to a thunderous peak; no one is even thinking about sitting down. Buzz nods graciously, gestures for the crowd to quiet. Sort of a papal gesture.

I've never seen anything like this: it's as if Elvis came back from the dead, or if the Beatles got back together. It's palpable, this outpouring of love, of gratitude, just for his being here today, for having done what he did, so long ago.

Buzz Aldrin speaks for an hour with no notes. His verbal style is round-about, tangential, loopy, anecdotes starting out and never quite reaching their points; clauses starting out and never quite reaching their verbs. He is charming and handsome and he has walked on the moon, and we hang on his every word. He tells stories about getting to the moon and back, about the world tour he, Neil, and Mike took upon their return, about the travel reimbursement form he received from NASA that detailed his work-related travel: Houston to Cape Canaveral; Cape Canaveral to Moon; Moon to Cape Canaveral; Cape Canaveral to Houston. His total reimbursement for the trip was thirty-three dollars. He tells us about his idea for the Aldrin Cycler, a series of spacecraft put into permanent orbits around Earth and Mars that would allow humans to travel to Mars by hopping from one to the next. (This proposal might sound silly coming from most public figures, but Buzz's expertise in orbital mechanics demands that we take the idea seriously). He ends by telling us about his idea he calls ShareSpace—a way of paying for human spaceflight through a lottery. Buy a ticket, get a chance in a random drawing to be selected to go to space. If you don't get chosen, you have the satisfaction of knowing that your money went to help further the project. It's actually a pretty great idea.

After Buzz's talk, followed by more thunderous applause, we make our way out to the table in the courtyard for the book signing. The line of people waiting now traces a winding path though the courtyard and out of sight, several hundred people at least. Buzz is unfazed. We take our seats at the table. Buzz greets the first person in line, signs the first book. The first person in line is, of course, a hard-core autograph collector—a white man in his forties, glasses and sweatshirt, with a workmanlike air and a complete lack of fawning. Though Buzz is polite, the exchange between them is one between people who have agreed to live with a certain amount of animosity. The autograph collector may in fact be a fan of spaceflight, may at one point have worshipped Buzz Aldrin and dreamed of being like him. Buzz, for his part, has probably met this autograph collector before, and at any rate has come to spot the type from a hundred paces. In addition to free events like this one, Buzz also participates in autograph trade shows, where attendees pay fees, often quite steep, for autographs. Buzz charges $500 for a simple autograph, more for signing an artifact, and even more as a "completion fee," meaning a single photograph or artifact has been signed by all three Apollo 11 astronauts or both Gemini 12 astronauts. These items have exponentially higher value in the autograph market.

The autograph seekers: there are droves of them, wherever astronauts are to be found. A combination of fandom, profiteering, and cottage industry, the trade in autographs has created an offshoot to the public appearances of astronauts, especially moonwalkers. A person standing in line with a stack of four hardcover copies of Buzz's book has invested about sixty dollars; once all the books are signed, the same stack will be worth hundreds or thousands of dollars. These people follow Buzz and the other moonwalkers everywhere they go, and their presence is both a reminder of the depth of fascination people have for astronauts and of the limitless drive to profit from that same fascination.

Buzz encounters autograph collectors like this one at the trade shows, and in that context their relationship is more clearly defined—this man pays Buzz money, and in exchange Buzz signs whatever the man wants. But the man's presence here today is a gray area—by showing up at a free book festival where Buzz is supporting his new book, the man is taking advantage of this appearance in a way that cheats the system, and both he and Buzz know it. The next in line is also an autograph collector, and the next. Buzz refuses to sign more than one book for the second man, though he'd done it for the previous one without complaint. The third autograph collector in line hands Buzz a book missing its title page. This is a trick some autograph collectors pull to get two autographs for the price of one book—he'd had Buzz sign the title page once, then knifed that page out to get the same book signed again. Buzz opens the book to find the title page gone, then slams it shut again and slides it back to the man with a scowl. The autograph collector accepts it and goes on his way without a word.

Soon we start seeing real space fans, die-hard fans, who want to talk to Buzz about his time on the moon. After an hour, the line has barely moved; things are progressing slowly because every single person not only wants to have a book signed, each also wants the chance to *meet* Buzz, to speak with him, to get a picture with him. They all want to touch the moon hand. A lot of people in the line are of the right age for the space obsession born in childhood, but not all of them—plenty of autograph seekers are old enough to have already been adults when Buzz walked on the moon or young enough to have missed it.

Among those of the right age range, everybody wants to tell Buzz Aldrin where they were and what they were doing while he was walking on the moon. These stories are almost uniformly uninteresting, as stories about watching TV tend to be. Buzz Aldrin nods and smiles politely. He is so patient with these stories it's easy to forget that he has been listening to them for forty years.

Some people bring objects they want Buzz to sign: a moon-shaped nightlight, the yellowed and brittle front page of a small-town newspaper with Buzz Aldrin's face, along with those of Neil Armstrong and Michael Collins, under the enormous headline MAN WALKS ON MOON. A T-shirt with the NASA logo on it. A book about the planets published in the fifties. Buzz is not entirely consistent in his policy on signing these things—many times he simply takes the object and scribbles on it without comment, but other times he refuses— he's here to sign his new book today, he explains to those people. One thing he is consistent about is Buzz Lightyear action figures. He signs them all happily. He even carries a special indelible pen that writes well on the white plastic of Buzz Lightyear's thigh. The connection that ignites between Buzz Aldrin and the children who love Buzz Lightyear is truly adorable to behold.

Most people accept Buzz's refusals politely and move on quickly. The professionals know that arguing or complaining will make no difference and could potentially get them blacklisted from future events; those who wanted his signature for themselves usually seem embarrassed and stammer out an apology.

But one woman argues with Buzz. She is middle-aged, with dyed red hair and a slightly harried look. She carries a huge autograph book under her arm. She doesn't have a copy of Buzz's autobiography, and holds the autograph book out to him instead. For a moment he seems to waver, but he sizes her up and signs the autograph book wordlessly. The woman watches him do it, lips pursed. She does not try to tell him where she was and what she was doing while he walked on the moon.

"I want to get the autographs of all the men who have walked on the moon in this book," she says. "Do you know what is the best way to do that? Can I just mail it to people and ask them to mail it back?"

"Oh, I wouldn't do that," Buzz answers sensibly. "We all get a lot of mail and a lot of requests for autographs, and things can get lost. If you really want to get as many as you can, you could go to trade shows."

"What's that?" she asks suspiciously.

"They're held at convention centers and such. They charge admission, and all of the astronauts set their own fees for autographs and memorabilia and what have you."

"You mean you charge *money?*" the woman asks, recoiling. I'm a single *parent*. I can't afford to pay hundreds of dollars to go to these places and get these signatures."

Buzz shrugs. "We all get a lot of requests for autographs," he explains. "Some of us are reaching a point where we would think about saying no to everyone, and this is a way where we can do it where it's a little more fair."

"I don't see how it's *fair,*" the woman answers as she takes her autograph book back from Buzz. I don't know who else has signed it, but it's now worth at least $500.

"I'm sorry to disappoint you," Buzz says evenly. He may be sincere or completely sarcastic. He may be trying to get rid of her. This puts her over the edge, and she raises a single finger to lecture Buzz and me.

"I'm an American *citizen,*" she says firmly. "I helped pay for the moon landings. I helped pay for *your trip* to the moon. Now I want the autographs of the astronauts I paid to send, and you're telling me I can't get them unless I pay them money?"

"Neil Armstrong won't do it at all," I put in. "He doesn't make public appearances anymore." She gives me a look of hatred before turning her attention to Buzz again.

Buzz apologizes noncommittally, and she wanders away. It's an interesting question, actually. Surely we who help pay for spaceflight have a right to the knowledge and images that come out of those missions. But how much access to these actual human beings have our taxes bought us? For how many years, how many decades afterward do they owe us their autographs and their answers to the question, yet again, how it felt to walk on the moon?

Over the course of the afternoon, as the line slowly wanders its way through the courtyard, I hear Buzz Aldrin asked dozens of times what it felt like to walk on the moon. He does not have a pat prepared answer—he tries to answer sincerely each time he is asked, and the answer takes on different nuances each time.

We were really just focused on staying alive, he says to some people.

We had a lot of work to do so we didn't really have time to reflect, he says to others.

The feeling of one-sixth gravity was a lot of fun but also challenging to get used to, so we really had to concentrate on doing our jobs and not falling on our faces.

When we got back, we sort of felt we'd missed out on the whole thing.

When Buzz Aldrin expresses frustration at not being able to describe his impressions of space as well as a writer might, his statement is, on one level, merely a polite thing to say when he is excusing himself from answering a tough question for the millionth time. But taken literally, it means something quite startling. It means that Buzz Aldrin envies Tom Wolfe and Norman Mailer and Oriana Fallaci, that—even more ludicrous—he envies me. Yet the thing we space writers have in common is the extent to which we admire and envy Buzz his experience of walking on the moon. We envy him so much that at times it's hard for us to see Buzz at all, to see his accomplishment as something *he* did, a risk *he* took gambling against his own death, rather than simply as something we will never get to do.

Leading up to our day together, I'd tried to imagine what Buzz Aldrin would say about the retirement of the space shuttle. I anticipated that someone who has risked his life to walk on the surface of the moon probably thinks that the space shuttle, which can only reach low Earth orbit, has been a frustrating waste of energy and maybe a step in the wrong direction. But I would not have predicted that a conservative eighty-year-old Korean War veteran would support government funding for a massive science project as a general principle, or even less that he would support President Obama's decision to cancel the Constellation project the following year, calling this "Obama's JFK moment."

It's hard to reach conclusions about my day with Buzz Aldrin. One unavoidable fact: he is a pro at all this. Meeting hundreds of people who are in awe of him, people who ask the same questions over and over. The day I spent with him was an honor but also an exhausting ordeal—speaking to a packed auditorium, meeting hundreds of people, including several weepy and/or emotionally disturbed space enthusiasts. For Buzz and Lois, the event in Nashville was bracketed by two flights and followed by *another* event that same evening in another city. By the end of our day together, I was in need of a strong drink and a lie-down with a cold washcloth over my eyes, but Buzz was still going strong. He has had days like this nearly every day since he came back from the moon forty years ago. One can forgive astronauts like Neil Armstrong who found they simply could not take it and tried to disappear from the public eye. For his part, Buzz Aldrin is completely accustomed to being Buzz Aldrin and the fawning energy that generates itself around him, the way people want to have their pictures taken with him, the way they hold on to his hand a little too long.

When Buzz and I are saying our good-byes, I decide to blurt out my big question. "I have to ask you," I stammer, "what do you think of the end of the space shuttle?"

Buzz shrugs.

"It's too bad," he says thoughtfully. "It's all still perfectly good hardware, and we've got the facilities and the people who know how to keep it flying. We should have something newer by now, but we should be building on what we already have, not starting over."

Buzz kisses my cheek before bundling Lois back into the limo with a daredevil's wave.

In the end, Buzz Aldrin can't tell me what to think. It's hard for anyone to say, on this particular October day in Nashville, Tennessee, when seven hundred miles south of us *Atlantis* is stacked on the launchpad for the 129th space shuttle flight, what it means for American spaceflight to be winding itself down. Only when an era ends do you get to figure out what it has meant. Buzz Aldrin is a human being who personally planted an American flag on the surface of the moon. He doesn't care if the shuttle is retired now or a few years from now. He knows, better than most of us, that the space shuttle is late-seventies technology. He had hoped to see an American go to Mars and has dedicated much of his post-Apollo life toward that goal. But he knows as well as I do that after the last shuttle launches, NASA won't send up another crewed spaceship of its own until after he is gone from this earth.

The world will hardly admit of an excuse for a man leaving a Coast unexplored he has once discover'd, if dangers are his excuse he is than charged with *Timorousness* and want of Perseverance and at once pronounced the unfitest man in the world to be employ'd as a discoverer; if on the other hand he boldly incounters all the dangers and obstacles he meets and is unfortunate enough not to succeed he is than changed with *Temerity* and want of conduct. The former of these aspersins cannot with Justice be laid to my charge and if I am fortunate enough to surmount all the dangers we may meet the latter will never be brought in question.

—Journals of Captain James Cook, 1770

CHAPTER 3. Good-bye, *Discovery*

STS-133: February 24, 2011

I have in my phone a picture of the space shuttle *Discovery* stacked on the launchpad for its last flight. I snapped the picture out the window of Omar's car as we drove by at a crawl on Family Day. There is no visual evidence of the circumstances under which the picture was taken—I was careful to keep the edges of the car window out of the frame—but I still feel that sense of motion when I look at it.

A few weeks after Family Day, my son was looking through my phone and, in that uncanny way small children have of intuiting technology, he found the photo of *Discovery* and reset it as the phone's wallpaper, replacing a picture of himself. He showed me, pleased with his work.

"Face shuttle," he lisped.

"That's right," I agreed. It occurred to me to wonder, not for the first time, whether he understands the difference between the shuttle and imaginary space vehicles like the *Millennium Falcon*. Because there are models and images of space shuttles all over his house, and he has only flown on planes a couple of times, space travel seems to him much more common than air travel. He has a charming habit of asking out-of-town visitors whether they traveled here on the space shuttle.

I got distracted before I had the chance to change the picture back; the next time I went to use my phone, I was surprised and pleased to see *Discovery* gleaming there. As the memory of that day quickly receded behind the pressures of the semester, it was nice to be reminded that I had been there, that I was going back for the last launch. In the picture, the Rotating Servicing Structure has been pulled back, presumably so the Family Day visitors could see the whole spaceship. *Discovery*'s white back is to us in the picture, its wings' full spread visible. Behind it, the orange external tank peeks up over its shoulder. On either side of the tank, the white solid rockets stand like sentinels. One of the rockets is partially obscured by the arm extending from the gantry to *Discovery*'s hatch, the walkway the astronauts will cross to reach the crew cabin a few hours before launch. I can make out the path of tan gravel used by the crawler transporter and the complicated metal gantries that surround the shuttle stack. A lightning rod balances upon the highest point of the launch tower. Central Florida is prone to lightning, and many spacecraft have attracted strikes during their time waiting on the pad or, more frighteningly, during launch.

In the foreground of the picture squats a low guard building, a few cars and trucks belonging to the employees working the pad that day. A flagpole flies both the American flag and the shuttle flag that will later be hung in the Vehicle Assembly Building as a souvenir of this launch. The elaborate fencing and gates, blocked off with cones that day. Behind it all, the weird Cape Canaveral sky, the clouds pressing down on the launchpad in a way that's almost menacing.

The image remained as my phone's wallpaper. It's there still as I write this, as *Discovery* is gathering its first layer of cobwebs at the Air and Space Museum. In the long delays leading up to the launch, every time I looked at my phone, I was reminded that *Discovery* still stood poised on that launchpad, just as in this picture, still stacked and ready to go.

First it was a problem in the orbital maneuvering system, the thrusters that allow the space shuttle to maneuver itself while in orbit. An OMS pod was leaking helium and nitrogen. Launch date was moved one day to November 2, 2010.

Then a slip to allow more time to refuel the helium tank. Launch date No Earlier Than November 3, 2010.

Then another scrub, after fueling had already begun, due to problems with a controller on the center main engine. Launch date NET November 4, 2010.

Then a scrub due to predictions of bad weather later in the day. Launch date NET November 5, 2010.

Then a scrub due to a hydrogen leak discovered during tanking. In addition to the leak, inspectors found a crack in the foam insulation on the external tank. This crack especially captured the attention of engineers and managers because it had been a chunk of foam falling from the external tank that had doomed *Columbia*. Fixing the shuttle while it is assembled and stacked vertically on the launchpad is difficult and time-consuming. Launch date NET November 30, 2010.

Then another slip to allow more time for repairs to the external tank. Launch date NET December 3, 2010.

Then another slip to allow more time to determine the likelihood of additional cracks in the external tank during launch. NET December 17, 2010.

Then another slip to make more time to validate repairs to the external tank. NET February 3, 2011.

Then another slip because engineers needed even more time to assess the cracks that were still forming, inexplicably, on the tank. The same day that slip was announced, US Representative Gabrielle Giffords was shot, along with eighteen other people, at a public appearance in Tucson, Arizona. The incident caused a national uproar and a renewed debate over gun control, but for space fans the shooting had an additional meaning. Giffords is married to astronaut Mark Kelly, who was slated to command the next mission after *Discovery's*—*Endeavour's* last—less than three months away. Would he leave his wife in critical or uncertain condition to go to space? Or would he back out of the last mission he could ever hope to fly, leaving the end of the shuttle program in chaos, as a new commander would barely have time to train? Launch date NET February 24, 2011.

A week after Gabrielle Giffords was shot, an astronaut on the *Discovery* mission, Tim Kopra, fell off his bicycle and broke his hip. With the target launch date now less than six weeks away, it wasn't clear whether the launch would have to be postponed. Let us take a moment to pity Tim Kopra: he trained for this mission for over a year, suited up for multiple scrubbed launch attempts, and then once it seemed all the problems for his launch had been solved, he injured himself in a leisure activity and lost his chance to fly on the shuttle ever again. Media and space fans waited anxiously to learn whether Mark Kelly would be replaced as well.

In late January, another mission was added to the manifest. A contingency mission, to be launched only if the crew of *Endeavour* was in need of rescue, became an official mission, STS-135, on *Atlantis,* with a target launch date of June 28, 2011. This was something of an audacious move on the part of NASA, since STS-135 still hadn't been funded. A few weeks later, NASA managers announced that STS-135 would fly regardless of the funding situation in Congress. Omar and I communicated about these developments via e-mail; I told him I appreciated NASA's boldness in planning for an unfunded launch and suggested they should take this approach more often.

So now we knew for certain what the last space shuttle launches would be: first *Discovery,* if the kinks could finally be worked out; then *Endeavour* in the spring, and *Atlantis* would be the very last, in the summer. In photographs, the crew of *Atlantis* all looked slightly bewildered that they were being pressed into service as the Last Crew, representatives and spokespeople for the entire shuttle program.

I texted Omar:

How likely do you think it is the problem w Discovery is really fixed?

Hard to say, Omar texted back. I'll let you know if I hear anything.

After thanking him, I went to turn off my phone, but stopped to look at the image of *Discovery* gleaming there on the glass screen. *Discovery* looked enormous and permanent, like it wasn't going anywhere. I found it hard to believe that Omar and I were discussing plans for this thing to leave the ground. The history of spaceflight teaches us that the more serious the cause of a shuttle delay, the less accurate the first guesses as to how long it might take to fix it. Omar and I both knew the No Later Than date of February 24 was a guess.

Yet as weeks went by, February 24 stayed on the manifest. I could, if I got lucky, witness in person the last launches of each of the three orbiters. Of course, it was also possible I could travel to Florida many times only to witness many scrubs and never see a launch at all.

I-75 starts at the Canadian border in Sault Ste. Marie, Michigan, and traces a path south through the lengths of Michigan, Ohio, Kentucky, Tennessee, Georgia, and Florida, all the way to Miami. From my house in Knoxville, Tennessee, it's only fifteen miles to get to I-75; then after a full day of driving and an exit near Orlando, it's only a couple of hours to cut across the middle of Florida to the eastern shore.

It's boring to describe one's interstate route, or any driving directions. But I've never given as much thought to any interstate as I have given to I-75 in recent weeks. I will drive this route alone, down and back, for each launch attempt I go to. The space shuttle's likelihood of getting off the ground in any one attempt, though it's gotten better over the years, is still not a very good gamble. With the shuttle's millions of delicate and critical moving parts and Florida's volatile climate, the possibility of delays remains high. I know I will spend a great deal of time on I-75 over the coming months.

When I first thought to write about the end of shuttle, I had neglected to consider that three of the things I have avoided most in my life are driving long distances alone, talking to people I don't know, and getting up early in the morning. I have ruled out entire careers because they interfere with these aversions. So I-75 looms large in my imagination in the weeks, then days, before the last launch of *Discovery*. Twelve hours is a long drive. But I've decided to go.

For a while there, the target dates had been falling during my university's winter break, which would have worked nicely in terms of my teaching schedule, but the additional slips have placed the February attempt squarely in the middle of my semester. A fellow professor is covering one class for me today, and one of my graduate students is covering the other. My husband, Chris, has had to plan his week around being a single father. With each slip, he has listened patiently when I gave him the new No Earlier Than date, then answered with a nod and a "Just keep me updated." Once I leave for Florida, I can't say for sure when I'll be back. If the February 24 attempt slips till Friday, I'll stay till Friday; if it slips to Saturday, I'll stay till then.

So I pack some warm-weather clothes and a few supplies into the back of my car, then hit the road after dropping my son off at pre-school. The sun is shining as I pull onto the freeway and join traffic. I'm not used to interstate driving, and I feel like I'm going too fast even before I get up to the speed of the other cars on the road. My little car feels too light, insubstantial, its engine whining at the frequency of a mosquito. I think of the tires that have to grip the road, of the brake lines that have to transmit the signals from my nervous foot to the brake, of the pistons and fuel lines, steering fluid and god knows what else—I have no idea how cars work. All of it Criticality 1, in the language of NASA. All the worn pieces, nicked and abraded and fatigued, that are checked and fixed before each shuttle launch.

One can only stay panicked so long, though, especially in as boring a situation as long-distance driving. And, I discover, I-75 is a generous and forgiving road. It offers few major interchanges, no surprise exit-only lanes, very little construction work, and light traffic. I find myself settling into the task of driving enough to start letting my mind wander. I have loaded some long audiobooks onto my phone, and I will listen to them at some point, but for now it's pleasant to just drive. Georgia goes on and on at some length, with the appalling traffic of Atlanta right in the middle of it, and I don't mind that much either. I-75 is studded with many gas stations and Waffle Houses and even Starbucks and Paneras in the more suburban stretches. Roadside vendors sell peanuts and peaches. A billboard in Georgia reads WHERE'S THE BIRTH CERTIFICATE?—a succinct expression of a faddish right-wing skepticism about the president's birthplace. I stop for dinner at Cracker Barrel somewhere past Moultrie and watch the stars come out near Valdosta. Through to north Florida and on into central Florida, where I cut over to Orlando.

In a song that keeps coming on the pop stations, a woman sings plaintively, "Baby, you're a firework." Yesterday I was reading a book about the early developments of rocket science, and it had included the observation that, from an engineering standpoint, there are no real differences between rockets, fireworks, and bombs. Norman Mailer's description of the launch of Apollo 11 compares the light of launch to "the most beautiful of fireworks." The "firework" song is not about rockets or bombs but, I suppose, about letting one's inner light shine, a cliché of teen anthems. Still, I sing along.

On the morning of February 24, 2011, I wake up in a motel near the Orlando airport, pack up what I'll need for the day, and drive an hour to the coast. I would have liked to stay closer to Cape Canaveral, but I waited to make my travel plans until the last minute, and this is all that was available. Each launch creates a huge surge in tourism, even more so now that these launches are to be the last. My hotel room, I discovered when I arrived late the night before, is saturated with a swampy mildew smell that we don't have in climates farther north. As on my last visit, I'm struck with the strangeness of the terrain here. Palm trees, giant bugs, a long, low horizon, and huge sky a hot blue. At points in my hour's journey, I'm unsure which landmass I'm on, whether the mainland or Merritt Island or Cape Canaveral—or even if I'm on one at all, given that some of the causeways were constructed by bulldozers. The geography itself eludes me—I have only a rough outline in my mind. Going west to east: there's the coast of the mainland, with the town of Titusville to the north and Cocoa to the south; then there's the Indian River (which is actually an estuary); then Merritt Island (which is actually, I think, a peninsula) with the Space Center on the north half and the town of Merritt Island on the south; then the Banana River (which is actually a lagoon); then the headland we call Cape Canaveral (though we also call this whole area Cape Canaveral) and the Cape Canaveral Air Force Station that sits at the point of that cape, and the barrier island that extends southward, which includes the (confusingly named) town of Cape Canaveral, and south of that Cocoa Beach (not to be confused with the town of Cocoa, of course, back on the mainland); then the Atlantic Ocean.

Each of these places has a different look and feel to it, a different history and a different idea of itself. At certain moments I think to ask Omar what it's like to have grown up on such an uncertain landscape, but I can never quite think how to phrase the question.

I reach the 528 causeway where it spans the Banana River. Hundreds of people drive across this causeway, this unbeautiful strip of land, every day to get from Merritt Island to Cocoa Beach and back, but today is one of the few days of the year when this scrubby margin of sand and grass becomes precious territory. The RV people have been camped here for days, staking their claims, and when I pull up, I find clumps of cars already parked, families setting up as if for a day at the beach. It's even busier than I had anticipated, almost completely packed, though the launch is still nearly nine hours away.

I find one of the last spots with an unobstructed view on the north side of the causeway. I've packed a cooler with food and cold drinks, books to read, student work to grade, a transistor radio, sunscreen, bug repellent, and emergency supplies in case I'm stuck in traffic for an extended period of time after the launch. By the time I set up my lawn chair and settle in, the astronauts are suiting up and the tanking of cryogenic gases has begun—I watch all this streaming live on the NASA app on my phone. All around me, couples and families are setting up their lawn chairs, talking and playing, eating sandwiches, smearing sunscreen on each other, listening to their radios, throwing Frisbees, going for walks. Most of all, people are looking out, either with binoculars or with the naked eye, toward where *Discovery* stands on pad 39A. And all of them are listening to the NASA announcer on their radios and watching the NASA app on their phones, shielding their screens with one hand against the glare of the white Florida sun.

Discovery stands upright on the horizon, fourteen miles north of us across the Banana River. It looks about the size of a paper clip. Fourteen miles sounds far, but this spot is one of the very best vantage points for viewing a launch—that is, for people who don't have access to NASA grounds. And the only people who have access are employees (including Omar and his father) and credentialed media. NASA gives credentials only to journalists who can prove they are representing an established media outlet or who can show a contract with an established publisher. When I was working on my novel, it struck me as tragic that this policy excluded me altogether in a catch-22—I couldn't get a contract with a publisher until I had written my book, and I felt I couldn't write my book properly without first getting access to the Kennedy Space Center. (Though I did have to admit, especially after the terrorist attacks of 2001, that a policy allowing someone like me unfettered access to a secure government installation would be in effect a policy without security at all, since any lunatic could claim to be "working on a novel.") So I paid for a ticket to ride the tourist bus, and I drove to a causeway in the middle of the night to watch the launch of STS-102, *Discovery,* a beautiful night launch in unseasonably cold weather that lit up the sky for miles around. I had to write the parts of my novel that took place on the grounds of the Kennedy Space Center using films, pictures, guesswork, and sheer fabrication—all the more reason to be terrified by that first e-mail from Omar, an eyewitness to my omissions and errors.

At any rate, my lack of press credentials today is a mixed fate. Although part of me wants access to the NASA viewing site from which Norman Mailer watched the launch of Apollo 11, I also want to see what it's like to watch a launch with other regular space fans, with people who have taken time off work to travel out here to see this event because they care about it, not because this is their job.

First-time visitors tend to imagine sitting at the base of the stack and feeling the heat of ignition on their faces, but this a misunderstanding caused by the footage we've all seen in movies. Those sequences are shot using remote cameras; any living thing that close to the launch-pad would be killed instantly. Even the emergency rescue teams wait out the launch from bunkers three miles away. An explosion on the launchpad, always a risk with tons of rocket fuel coursing through many miles of fuel lines, would destroy everything in sight.

I check my phone: T minus eight hours and counting. Because I've been to a launch before, I know that spaceflight is all about waiting. Five hours, eight hours, twelve hours. First-timers are often confused, then annoyed, then stupefied by this waiting. You can spot them the minute they pile out of their cars too quickly, with too much bounce, their adrenaline high as they scan the horizon for the launch gantry and point and shout, "There it is!"

Relax. There it will remain, until no earlier than 4:48 p.m., or maybe until tomorrow, or maybe until May. Space fans need to learn to pace themselves. Best not to use up all of your enthusiasm too soon. If there's a scrub you'll feel disgusted and vaguely humiliated; you will mistakenly view the scrub as a failure of NASA's, and this will mark you as an outsider more than anything else. Insiders know that scrubs are part of spaceflight.

While I wait, I read from *Of a Fire on the Moon*. Norman Mailer gripes about being packed into buses with the other journalists, all of them sweating through their shirts and ties, smoking and cursing the brutal Florida heat. I have the luxury of driving my own air-conditioned car; instead of a shirt and tie I wear a sundress, a beach hat, and enormous sunglasses that I hope make me look like Joan Didion.

When Norman Mailer gets off the bus at the Press Site, he recounts his impressions (in the third person) of feeling slightly disconnected from the events happening so near yet so far away. He says that people had built up for him how unforgettable the launch experience would be, that he had been promised that the ground would shake. But he couldn't match his lived experience with this expectation. "He had no sense at all of three psyches full of awareness on the edge of the horizon. Just that gray stick out there." I see it too: only with binoculars does that gray stick come into focus as black-and-white *Discovery* against its orange external tank, flanked by white solid rocket boosters. The astronauts' "psyches full of awareness" (six, in this case) are as hard to imagine today as they were in 1969. The idea of that gray stick lifting itself into the sky is still as hard to imagine as it was then, the fact of people on it just as wondrous.

Discovery first flew in 1984, the third orbiter to join the fleet. It was named for one of the ships commanded by Captain James Cook. Space shuttle *Discovery* is the most-flown orbiter; today will be its thirty-ninth and final launch. By the end of this mission, it will have flown a total of 365 days in space, making it the most well traveled spacecraft in history. *Discovery* was the first orbiter to carry a Russian cosmonaut and the first to visit the Russian space station *Mir*. On that flight, in 1995, Eileen Collins became the first woman to pilot an American spacecraft. *Discovery* flew twelve of the thirty-eight missions to assemble the International Space Station, and it was responsible for deploying the Hubble Space Telescope in 1990. This was perhaps the most far reaching accomplishment of the shuttle program, as Hubble has been called the most important telescope in history and one of the most significant scientific instruments ever invented. It has allowed astronomers to determine the age of the universe, postulate how galaxies form, and confirm the existence of dark energy, among many other discoveries. Astronomers and astrophysicists, when they are asked about the significance of Hubble, will simply say that it has rewritten the astronomy books. In the retirement process, *Discovery* will be the "vehicle of record," being kept as intact as possible for future study.

Discovery was the return-to-flight orbiter after the loss of *Challenger* and then again after the loss of *Columbia*. To me, this gives it a certain feeling of bravery and hope. *Don't worry, Discovery* seemed to tell us by gamely rolling her snow-white self out to the launchpad. *Don't worry, we can still dream of space. We can still leave the earth.* And then she did.

Around me, cars and trucks cruise up and down the causeway, looking for places to wedge themselves in. T minus five hours and counting. We all watch our phones and wait. It's been my observation that each launch offers a different experience of waiting, different shades of waiting, flavors of waiting, moods of waiting. Buddhists might appreciate the way each launch wait brings about in spectators a different quality of boredom, then acceptance, then calm, then something like a childlike openness, an ability to take in the sight we are about to see with minds wiped clear of desire, warped of time.

All along the causeway, those of us who got here earlier take walks and greet our fellow space fans. I'm reminded of Jules Verne's description of the people who showed up in Florida to see the first space launch in his 1865 novel. He imagined a tent city of space enthusiasts from all over the world, speaking different languages and "mingled together in terms of absolute equality." He describes a sense of anticipation that includes a hint of something like fear—"a dull, noiseless agitation, such as precedes great catastrophes." Verne got a few things wrong in his invention of what spaceflight would be like, but this is one of the many details he got right.

I've experienced the specific enthusiasm of space people before, at my other visits to the Kennedy Space Center and especially at the launch I saw in 2001; I saw more of them at Buzz Aldrin's book event in Nashville. Among the people I met on those occasions were some serious space fanatics, people for whom space is the main thing in their lives—the interest they read about, talk about, spend eBay money on, and chat with other people over the Internet about. Some of these people work in vaguely aerospace-related fields, but for more of them this has nothing to do with their jobs. They just love space, and for these people the Kennedy Space Center is something of a mecca. I am not really one of the space people, as much as my friends might mistake me for one of them. I've read a hundred books about spaceflight and traveled here to see a launch in person, but I did so as research for a book I was writing. I can't imagine putting this much energy into it just for its own sake.

When the space people come in contact with each other, which they do in great numbers on launch days like today, they have a sort of code for interacting. They list the previous launches they have seen, share thoughts on controversial subjects within the community (Did Gus Grissom really screw up and blow the hatch early on the *Liberty Bell 7* in 1961, or did it go off by itself as he claimed? Will any of the private aerospace companies be able to get astronauts into space safely, and if so which one[s]? Who was the most badass moonwalker? And so on). They exchange reviews of recent space books, trade the names of aging astronauts whose hands they have shaken. They wear T-shirts and caps and buttons and pins and patches and memorabilia from other launches. I'd almost forgotten about these people, how obsessed and knowledgeable and friendly they are. At a time when it seems all but self-evident that shuttle is ending because the general public no longer cares about spaceflight, these people controvert that broad claim with every molecule of their being. They care enough for all of us, and they are heartbroken by our leaders' shortsightedness.

The car nearest mine has license plates from Ohio. A friendly couple in their early fifties, just starting to gray, who drove two days to see their first launch before it was too late. The husband wears wraparound sunglasses and a T-shirt that says LIFE, LIBERTY, AND THE PURSUIT OF THOSE WHO THREATEN IT on the back. The wife is carefully made up and coiffed, but she wears baggy capris and sensible shoes, a popular look for women at shuttle launches. After locating the launchpad through his binoculars with my help, the husband tells me that we are all going to be forced to live under sharia law before too long, a conclusion based on "the way things are going in

England." (When pressed, he reveals that his main piece of evidence for England's inevitable transition to Islamic theocracy is the fact that Mohammed is the most popular name for newborn boys in London.)

"Do you know why Obama killed the shuttle program?" he asks me, as his wife joins us to offer everyone Combos. "The answer may surprise you."

"Um, I don't think Obama really killed the shuttle program," I reply vaguely, helping myself to some Combos. "That decision was made after the *Columbia* disaster, in 2003." I restrain myself from adding the obvious: *under Bush.*

"But Obama could have *revived* it." The man points his finger at me in a *gotcha* gesture. He leans toward me in his excitement; I can see myself reflected in his sunglasses. Next to him, his wife fiddles with her iPhone, trying to get NASA TV to come in.

"Obama's under orders by the Bilderberg Group." The man pauses, waiting to see whether I know what the Bilderberg Group is. I do, from reading Jon Ronson's *Them:* it's a group of global leaders and captains of industry that holds mysterious meetings, a cabal popular with conspiracy theorists. "He's under orders to destroy as many sources of national pride as possible. I mean, think about it. If the American people aren't proud of their country anymore, the One World Order can take over and we won't rise up in defense of our country."

"Don't you think it's more likely that he needs to make a show of austerity during a recession? Extending the space shuttle would look too spendy while people are losing their homes."

"Austerity," the man repeats. He looks at *Discovery* off on the horizon. "That's a good point, actually."

"I'm going to go get a Coke from my cooler," I announce. "Would you like anything to drink?"

"No, thanks. You might actually be right, though, about that austerity thing. I hadn't thought about it that way."

Crouched by my cooler, I scribble down everything the man said. I imagine getting similar interviews with other people, assembling a catalog of the kooks who show up for shuttle launches. Then it occurs to me that I am the only person within sight to have arrived by myself, to have driven twelve hours alone. I may be the only professor here missing classes today, the only mother to have left her child for three days, all to see a space shuttle launch. I feel a moment of shame for wanting to mock the Ohio man. But I write down everything he said anyway.

Later in the morning, the woman from Ohio with the Combos approaches me. Her hair has flattened a bit in the humidity, and some of her makeup has sweated off. She wants to know whether there is any officially sanctioned place for women to pee.

"I've been wondering about that too," I admit. All morning we have watched men and boys stroll down an embankment and disappear briefly into some tropical foliage, but it's not clear what our options are.

"Let's shield each other," she suggests. A third woman joins us, and the three of us set up a makeshift stall using two beach towels in some secluded bushes. The third woman, who is from West Palm Beach, has a bad knee, and so she needs to hold on to my shoulder to keep her balance while she squats. I brace myself against her weight, hold up my end of the beach towel, and look up at some helicopters passing against the clear blue sky. They will monitor the weather up until the moment of launch. Today six Americans are going to space.

Forty-two years ago, Norman Mailer woke up in a motel in Cocoa Beach, Florida, after two hours of sleep and drove to the Kennedy Space Center. He felt cranky, out of sorts, and hot. Too many other Very Important Persons had turned out for the launch, and Norman Mailer disliked them both individually and as a group. But in the moments right before liftoff, he had an insight: *He knew now why he was so irritated with everything and why he could not feel a thing. It was simple masculine envy. He too wanted to go up in the bird.*

I know what he means. The masculine envy of which he speaks is not masculine at all. It's integral to the experience of watching people soaring into the heavens while we, with pen and paper, are stuck on the ground. I feel it too, and that envy is at the heart of a kinship between Norman Mailer and me that transcends forty-two years, a change in space vehicle, and even gender—a difference not insignificant to Norman Mailer, who once remarked to Orson Welles in a television interview that all women should be kept in cages. But I understand him, I feel him, just the same. I've read accounts of the launch of Apollo 11 by each of the three men on board, by the flight director and dozens of other people closely tied to the mission, and I've clung to every word; yet it's Norman Mailer's wrestling with his own detachment, his own desire to feel something for that gray stick, that stays with me, that makes me feel I've been let in on what it was like to be there.

While I wait for the launch of *Discovery,* I text back and forth with Omar about whether the launch will go off on time, about weather predictions, about where we should have dinner afterward. He is watching the launch across the street from the Vehicle Assembly Building in a van equipped with badge boards and walkie-talkies, the equipment he will need in the event the launch is scrubbed and he has to go back to work resecuring the launchpad.

I haven't been to Florida since Family Day five months ago, but I still see Omar at least once a day on Facebook, and we play a lot of online Scrabble. He is a surprisingly serious opponent and beats me more often than not. I've started to think of him in the same category as my siblings—people I feel respect and affection for and don't see as often as I'd like. In the intervening time, I've gathered more of an idea of his life: he works a lot and enjoys it, both because he takes pride in doing the work well and because there are spaceships and astronauts at his workplace, which he never stops being excited by. There are things he learns that he's not supposed to tell anyone, and he is absolutely scrupulous about following those rules. He'll mention to me once in a while that he took a picture of something, but that he can't post it until he's given permission, which will probably not be until after the shuttles are retired. So he doesn't post it, and won't even tell his friends exactly what it is. When he is not working, he spends time with friends and family—there are pithy quotes here and there from his grandmother. He also helps out a lot with horses that belong to his girlfriend, horses whose snapshots populate his Facebook feed. A picture starts to come together of a man whose overwhelming attribute is reliability rather than ambition. (Or rather, a man whose single ambition—to be near space shuttles as much as possible—has been satisfied.) Either way, he is a person who does what he says he will do, and he does things for others rather than for himself.

After *Discovery*'s last flight, Omar might get another year or so working here—there will be a great deal of work to be done removing *Discovery*'s engines, cleaning it up and readying it for its new life as a flightless museum display. After that, he will have to find another purpose, like thousands of other people at the Cape.

Several "holds" are built into the countdown, pauses to provide a cushion in case the launch crews encounter any complications and need to catch up. One is at T minus twenty minutes, another at T minus nine. Traditionally, the T minus nine minute hold is when people start getting serious about their viewing spots. Floridians who don't care to go out of their way to see a launch will often at least stop what they are doing and step outside, find a roof, or pull over in their cars when they hear the announcement for the T-9 hold, then look in the direction of the launchpads.

At T-9, I take the lens cap off my camera and clamber up onto the roof of my car. The metal is hot and bumps about under me disconcertingly, but I persevere. Now the causeway is packed—in the last hour, people have started trying to cram their cars and trucks at odd angles into any tiny gap between the vehicles of those of us who arrived earlier, and some tension results. A sedan manages to slide past the Ohio couple and park on the other side of them, partially blocking their view. The Ohio man steams about it to his wife, hands on his hips. When the driver of the sedan emerges and turns out to be brown-skinned, Arab or South Asian, I fear what ugly confrontation might ensue. But the driver is an elaborately polite older man with very little English, making it hard for the Ohio man to start any kind of real argument. Soon the two are sharing binoculars, the Ohio man pointing out the stack on the horizon. I eavesdrop for a while, but when I don't hear the words *sharia* or *Mohammed* after a few minutes, I lose interest.

It continues to startle me, the range of political ideologies that are compatible with enthusiasm for spaceflight. Tax-and-spend liberals of the Great Society stripe, obviously—but also spending-slashing Tea Partiers, hippie peaceniks, fierce libertarians, military loyalists, and apathetics of every shade. So very many of us seem to feel that a love of human spaceflight is reconcilable with our beliefs, and we can all explain why. This belief doesn't always translate to actual funding; the launch we witness today was made possible by budget squabbles that happened last year, ten years ago, forty years ago. This man from Ohio sees the space shuttle as a natural offshoot of military aviation and an expression of American exceptionalism; I see it as a grand act of civic performance art. We are both right. This man and I are far apart on pretty much everything else (he tells me later that women are genetically disabled in terms of our spatial relations, especially at night, a disability responsible for as many traffic accidents as alcohol; when I ask him politely why, if this is so, women have successfully landed the space shuttle—the most difficult feat any pilot or astronaut can face—including twice at night, he answers, "affirmative action"), but we have spaceflight in common, and so today we share binoculars, information, and snacks. We look off agreeably into the sky together, and our companionship today, the companionship of many unexpected groupings and pairings like this one, is one of those things the space program has given us that is hard to put a value on.

The night before the launch of Apollo 11, Norman Mailer visited sites where tourists had gathered to watch the launch—maybe this very spot, he doesn't specify. He describes the people he saw there:

> And men and women, tired from work and travel, sat in their cars and sat outside their cars on aluminum pipe and plastic-webbing folding chairs, and fanned themselves, and looked across the miles at the shrine. Out a car window projected the sole of a dirty foot. The big toe pointed straight up to Heaven in parallel to Saturn V.

The scene here today is oddly like the scene here forty years ago. Not much has changed. People still drive for days to get here, still camp out, still sit on lawn chairs. People still look across the miles at the shrine.

In Mailer's book, he spins a fantasy of an archetypal working-class couple, a ridiculously offensive composite born of Mailer's imagination and class prejudice—the man all faded high-school glory and physical work and beer belly, the woman all aging sass and sexuality. I can only imagine that if Norman Mailer had watched the actual launch from here among everyday Americans, rather than from the NASA Press Site surrounded by credentialed journalists, he and the man from Ohio would have bloodied each other's noses by mid-afternoon. Or they may have gotten drunk together at a postlaunch celebration in a local bar. Or maybe both. There are ways in which I won't follow in Mailer's footsteps.

T minus five minutes. T minus two minutes. I start to feel a buzzy anticipation in my fingertips, a bit like stage fright. Time moves differently at this point, and I've read that it does for the astronauts as well. Each second seems to take forever, yet there is also something merciless about the way the seconds keep spilling forward. The time it takes to speak a sentence or check a camera setting feels like it should have taken thirty seconds, but when we check our watches again, only two seconds have gone by.

T minus thirty seconds. The announcer starts chanting the countdown at *fifteen*, and we pick up the count and chant along with him. *Ten. Nine. Eight. Seven. Six.* These words, spoken with such reverence and emphasis, are part of the poetry of spaceflight. But when we get close to zero, the countdown stops.

A general groan goes up. The announcer explains that there is an electrical problem.

There is only a ten-minute window each day during which the rotation of Earth brings Cape Canaveral within rendezvous range with the space station; if *Discovery* can't get off the ground within this launch window, we'll have to wait until tomorrow for the next attempt. I will have to tell Chris I'll be away for one more day; I'll have to find someone to cover another day of classes. We lean toward our phones and turn up our car radios and squint through our binoculars at the horizon while those ten minutes slowly tick away.

When the time is nearly up, we see a light on the horizon. Only two seconds before the end of the window, the main engines ignite, creating an orange glow. Then the solid rocket boosters. The stack lifts itself, silently at first. The sound takes longer to travel the fourteen miles than does the light, so the first bright moments of launch always have a silent-film majesty.

And now the sound comes toward us: bassy, crackly, like a fireworks display that never lets up. The sound goes right through you, and if you have become too emotionally involved in the space program, this sound will make you cry. It's the sound of American exploration, the sound of missiles put to better use than killing or threatening to kill, a sound that means we came in peace for all mankind. The man from Ohio is trying to watch through binoculars and shoot video of the launch with his phone at the same time; his wife is exclaiming "*Oh* my God! *Oh* my God!" over and over. We cry and tip our heads back to trace the bright light up.

At T plus two minutes, the solid rocket boosters drop off. Like others who have watched the *Challenger* footage too many times, I'm never fully satisfied that a space shuttle has launched successfully until I see with my own eyes those boosters drop off safely and arc away. From this distance, *Discovery* now looks mostly like a flare of flame followed by a streak of white arcing up into the sky, a streak that seems to curve inward with the bowl of the heavens until it's almost directly overhead, where it slowly disappears into a single point like any star.

Good-bye, *Discovery*.

I dry my eyes and gather up my things. I wonder whether Omar is crying. I feel I don't know him quite well enough to ask. A few seconds later, I get a text from him.

2 words. Buzzer beater.

A few people pull out onto the causeway and drive off while *Discovery* is still visible in the sky, the sort of people who leave baseball games during the eighth inning. But most of us stand and watch the whole thing, which takes ten minutes, long enough to take our eyes off it and talk to other people and check Twitter while we are still tracking its progress up, up, up to the top of the sky. The couple from Ohio seems to be in no hurry to leave. They are watching NASA TV on her phone and taking pictures of each other with the steam trail, taking pictures of their car against the backdrop of palm trees and faraway gantries, of the crowd up and down the causeway. But then they consult each other quickly, hop into their car, and drive away. The woman barely has time to call good-bye to me as they pull out onto the road. Up ahead, we can see, traffic is already getting backed up at the first interchange, and I suppose they are smart to leave now. I feel oddly lonely once they are gone. But now that I'm alone I am free to take notes on everything they said. I scrawl some notes in my unprofessional-looking children's black-and-white composition notebook. They're not even notes, exactly, but triggers, strange details that I hope will be the spark that contains the whole moment, as our every cell contains the whole of our DNA.

Thinking about the Ohio couple now, it pleases me to think that I am in some of their pictures, a part of the online album they will share on Flickr or Facebook. Even though we never exchanged names, I'm glad they will remember me, my beach hat and lawn chair and car with Tennessee plates.

Omar and I have agreed to meet at a Mexican restaurant as soon as traffic slows enough to let us through. The streets of Merritt Island are busy but not clogged—as Omar had predicted, most people have headed east or west. Waiting at a red light, I notice that the car in front of me is covered with space stickers. Patches from multiple missions, bumper stickers advertising the visitor centers at multiple NASA sites, as well as the two versions of the NASA logo: the blue circle with the stars and chevron dating to NASA's founding in 1959, and the simple stripped-down letters from the seventies. A few days ago I was reading about the two versions of the logo. The NASA website describes the components of the old version: "the sphere represents a planet, the stars represent space, the red chevron is a wing representing aeronautics (the latest design in hypersonic wings at the time the logo was developed), and then there is an orbiting spacecraft going around the wing."

This logo was hard to reproduce after the invention of the photocopier, and by the seventies some felt it had started to feel dated. In the pause between Apollo and shuttle, NASA hoped a redesigned logo would refresh the agency's image as forward-thinking and futuristic, and the new logo reflected this ideal: just the four letters NASA, so simplified and stylized that even the cross strokes on the As were removed as if to make the acronym more aerodynamic. You can see in the new logo an aesthetic argument that a stripped-down space program, a lean-and-mean reusable shuttle, was a thing to be proud of rather than a compromise to apologize for. If the old logo was made for lofty and expensive goals, the new logo was made for deploying satellites for paying customers and conducting experiments in low Earth orbit. The agency in the seventies and eighties didn't need to compete with the agency of the sixties on its own terms; the new agency would pay its own way or come close to it, and that would be its own achievement. The new design was given the unflattering nickname "the worm." (The old logo, to differentiate it, was called "the meatball.") Arguments about the logo became encoded arguments about NASA's narrative. What did it mean for NASA to be a collaborator with commercial interests rather than just a standard-bearer for our dreams? It should shock no one that this new worm logo, as appealing as it may have been to members of Congress, was bewildering and uninspiring to the public. In the midnineties the meatball came back and has been the dominant logo ever since. The reassertion of the meatball may mean that our affection for the spirit of the heroic era is still as strong as ever; it also may mean that the agency's best days are behind it.

It's been long enough that I'm a bit nervous again about seeing Omar—I even wonder as I'm approaching the restaurant whether we will have trouble recognizing each other. I have come to feel I know him well, but we only spent one day together, five months ago. Everything else we know about each other is through life lived online.

But of course I do know him the moment I see him, in a booth near the door, and he knows me too. We greet each other easily, without any of the awkwardness I feared. It seems we will be the sort of friends who can pick up where we left off. The restaurant is packed, the waitresses turning sideways and lifting their trays over their heads. All the patrons are sweat-stained, sunburned, wind-rumpled, and smiling, like us.

"So what did you think?"

"Awesome," I reply. I have trouble thinking what more to say about the launch. Sometimes the most complex experiences are best summed up in a single word.

"It was a nice one," Omar agrees. "How did it compare to the one you saw before?"

"That was a night launch, so—really different," I say. "But I guess I assumed that for the most part day launches are all the same, and night launches are all the same."

Omar shakes his head. "The funny thing is, they're all different. They all have a really distinct look to them. I guess it has to do with weather—how much cloud cover there is, humidity, wind, especially. Each one puts on a different show."

It occurs to me that there are a lot of people who have seen a single launch, but relatively few can compare multiple shuttle launches. There are people out here—not many, but they exist—who have seen every shuttle launch. I read about one man who has seen every single launch of anything, including probes and satellites. His father worked for Cape Canaveral Air Force Station even before NASA was formed and took him to see the first secret launches when he was a toddler. There is always someone who has seen more.

Omar and I talk more about how the day went. He shows concern over whether I had trouble finding the location he'd suggested for me to watch the launch from, whether I had trouble finding this restaurant. I'd forgotten this about him since Family Day, the way he seems to feel responsible for everything I experience here at the Cape. Not only the launch itself, but also things like weather, the behavior of other space fans, the service I encounter in restaurants and hotels, and the performance of the space shuttle program itself. I get the impression that if today's launch had scrubbed, as it seemed for so long that it was going to, Omar would have apologized and taken it upon himself to make it up to me in some way.

While we wait for our food, we browse through news stories on our phones about the launch. I read one tidbit out loud to Omar: STS-133 had the longest vertical flow (170 days) since STS-35 in 1990, still the record-holder at 183 days.

"Oh yeah, I remember that one," Omar tells me. "That was *Columbia.* My father was involved in fixing the tanking problems. It actually rolled back to VAB, demated, and went back into OPF to start all over again. Then it had to roll back to VAB a second time because a hurricane was going to come through. That one seemed cursed there for a while."

"For this mission, I wondered whether they were going to roll back *Discovery* and demate it," I say.

Omar grunts noncommittally, and it occurs to me that he might know something about this that he's not supposed to tell me. I don't want to sound as though I am prodding him to break a confidence.

Omar has his video camera with him, and he shows me the footage he shot from the VAB parking lot. It's impressive: in his camera's frame, the stack is much bigger than what I saw today, the controlled explosion of the solid fuel much sharper and brighter. It's a completely different experience, a different launch. I try to hide my jealousy.

We eat mediocre Mexican food and I drink two beers. I probably should stick to one, but I've had a long day, I'm relieved that everything has gone as planned, and I'm falling for the celebratory post-flight atmosphere. Omar considers getting a beer but keeps ordering Cokes instead. Now that I'm a little tipsy, I ask Omar a question I've wanted to ask him for a while: I ask him about the masculine envy Norman Mailer experienced at the launch of Apollo 11. I tell him that, like all space writers, I am asked from time to time whether I would go up on the space shuttle if I had the chance. I tell him I'm not sure what to say because in reality, I think I would be terrified.

"Still, you'd have to go if you had the chance, right?" I asked. "After all, the track record is pretty good." 98.5 percent of space shuttle missions have returned their crews safely; the statistics get even better if you count Mercury, Gemini, and Apollo.

Omar pauses. "That's something I think about a lot. I grew up wanting to go. Now that I work there, I've seen everything that goes wrong as they're preparing to launch," he says. "All the stuff they catch and fix."

I know what he means. One faulty part, one procedure not executed correctly. What destroyed *Challenger* was the failure of a simple rubber O-ring, like you have in your faucets. What destroyed *Columbia* was a dent on one of the tiles.

"But they catch them and fix them, right?" I ask. The astronauts themselves don't know all the details about problems found on the orbiter and the other components. They are busy training for their own roles; they have to trust that the engineers and technicians are doing their jobs.

"They'd only have to miss one thing," Omar says. He pauses, smiling broadly. "But I'd still go."

If the shuttle continued flying a hundred more missions, statistics dictate another one would probably be lost, maybe to something equally mundane. In 1967, the crew of Apollo 1 was killed in a training exercise on the launchpad. The plan to go to the moon went on without too much controversy, but now, it seems, we no longer have the stomach for burying astronauts. After *Challenger,* the space agency was criticized for undervaluing safety in favor of budget and scheduling pressures; after *Columbia,* the board tasked with investigating the disaster recommended that crew safety become "the overriding priority" in NASA's next space transportation system, "rather than trade safety against other performance criteria, such as low cost and reusability, or against advanced space operation capabilities." This requirement would make spaceflight slower, more expensive, and less ambitious—exactly the opposite direction from what proponents of heroic-era lofty goals demand.

On the way out of the restaurant, we pass a small clump of people wearing brightly colored badges that read "NASATweetup." The badges display the NASA logo and the person's Twitter handle, indicated by the leading @ sign. Omar points them out to me as if they are celebrities, but he doesn't approach them.

"Those are the people chosen for the NASATweetup," he tells me. When I look confused, he explains. "NASA started doing it for the last few launches. They choose 150 people who follow NASA on Twitter and give them special access to the launch. They get to meet astronauts and stuff like that. A few weeks ago I saw a bunch of them when they got to go inside OPF. They looked like kids in a candy store."

When I was here for Family Day, I learned to refer to the hangars where the space shuttles are maintained between missions as "OPF," not "*the* OPF," as I had been doing.

"*I* got to go inside OPF," I brag needlessly.

Omar smiles. "Yeah, you did."

Outside, Omar tells me that he recognized the Twitter handle of a woman who had traveled from Australia for the previous launch attempt but couldn't afford to return for this one. The space community on Twitter took up a collection for her, and a few locals offered her free places to stay. This is a great example of the fellow feeling that exists among the hard-core space enthusiasts online—they give each other money, are welcome in one another's homes. Omar is clearly delighted to see the Australian woman has made it here. When I ask why he doesn't approach her and congratulate her in person, he shrugs and says she looked like she was busy talking to her friends. Omar's shyness is a lot like my own, I realize. He likes people and wishes the best for them. He is willing to e-mail strangers (as he did me after he read my book) or to reach out to them on Twitter, but to walk up to a woman in a restaurant and introduce himself is another matter, farther than he is willing to go. I am moved all over again that he made the bold gesture of inviting me for Family Day.

Omar has tried to impress upon me how awful the traffic will be tonight, especially heading west toward Orlando, which is where I'm going. He's explained that a lot of NASA people choose to live in Merritt Island because it's the only town on the same landmass as the Kennedy Space Center, the only one from which a car can reach the gates of the Kennedy Space Center without having to cross a body of water using one of the causeways, which clog up unspeakably after launches. The epic traffic is largely due to the bottlenecking of these causeways, and Omar points out that the one and only motel in the town of Merritt Island, the Clarion, while not luxurious, would save me half an hour to forty-five minutes prelaunch and inestimable hours afterward, when up to a million people will be trying to get off Merritt Island at once.

"Good tip," I say. "That will be my new Florida home."

Omar suggests that in order to kill time we go to Barnes & Noble and look around in their space book section. This is only the second time Omar and I have met in person, and it's already the second time we have wound up perusing books together. As a writer I tend to find myself in bookstores or libraries wherever I visit, but it's unusual to meet a nonwriter who seems to share the same instinct. We find the Space area within the Science section, and as with the Visitor Center gift shop book section, Omar seems to have read every book in the place. He points books out to me, I point books out to him. I show him Norman Mailer's *Of a Fire on the Moon,* recently reprinted in a coffee-table version with huge glossy photos.

As Omar pages through the book, I try to tell him about Norman

Mailer, about how the book came to be written. I tell him that I find
Norman Mailer unbearable, but also quite brilliant. I tell him about
the things Norman Mailer saw and described that no one else did, like
Wernher von Braun's speech at a Titusville country club the night before the launch of Apollo 11 or the cold drink machine at the Press
Site whose malfunction became an extended metaphor for American
technology and arrogance. Omar and I flip through the book, talking
about which of the Apollo-era images we have seen before. Only one
of them is new to Omar, an aerial shot of the launchpad with Apollo/
Saturn stacked and pointing at the sky, tiny workers visible on the
gantry. Omar looks at it for a long time before putting it back. Then
he picks up another book he's read, a history of the space shuttle, and
shows me his father's name in the acknowledgments. Frank Izquierdo.

"Your dad's name is Frank?" I ask. "That was the name I gave the
dad who worked at KSC in my book," I remind him.

"Oh yeah," Omar says. "I'd forgotten about that. Coincidence,
right? My father's real name is Francisco."

I'm more surprised by the coincidence than Omar seems to be. I
try to remember why I chose the name Frank for the father. I wanted
him to be a little bit square, a nerdy, old-fashioned hardworking
dad. And I wanted him to be honest, dependable—*frank*—a man of
his word.

Omar has to work early in the morning, so we say our good-byes.
I'm going to hang around in the bookstore for a while, since the traffic
getting off the island has probably not let up.

"See you for 134?" he asks after we hug.

"Yes, 134," I say, happy to have a next launch to look forward to
in a couple of months.

I stay in the bookstore's café area, making notes from the day,
until it closes at nine o'clock. Surely traffic has let up by now, I think,
four hours after launch, but when I get onto the 528 causeway leading
back to Orlando I find it's still a parking lot. People are getting out of
their cars to walk around on the grass, drink beer, and hang out as if
they were tailgating, exactly as they were twelve hours ago. When we
finally do start moving again, it's at a creep. Toward eleven, I finally

pass the spot from which I watched the launch earlier today. Now that seems like a lifetime ago.

In the morning, as I am leaving town, I decide to drive back inland along a different route in order to try to better understand the confusing geography. I have written a book set here, but in that book the child protagonist has only a loose understanding of the Cape beyond the fixed sets of her backyard, her school, and the Kennedy Space Center. In order to write this place from her point of view, I had to gain only as much of an understanding as she would have. On my second visit since finishing that book, I still don't feel confident I know where things are. I still don't understand why everything is called something other than what it is, why the same names mean two or three different things. Confusing naming practices are often associated with areas closed to outsiders, but the Space Coast has been welcoming tourists almost as long as it has been home to space families. The names have to do with the elusiveness of the place itself, my working theory goes, the way the land and the freshwater and the seawater all blend into each other in unexpected ways. The way water seems to be on all sides at all times, though none of these areas quite meet the definition of an island, just as in Omar's video of the launch the fire plume of *Discovery*'s engines blends complexly into the steam beneath it, so that it's hard to tell whether any one point is fire or steam. The way the marshiness of the terrain makes one piece of land either an island or a peninsula, the same spot brown on some maps and blue on others. The way the isolation of this place defined it until the rockets came in, and how quickly it's grown since. It's a community of transplants and immigrants. These are big towns now, with traffic and shopping centers and miles and miles of strip malls, but before Omar's generation very few people could say they had been born and raised here. Almost no one knew it as their native place.

I drive across the causeway spanning the Indian River to Cocoa, a dense little town that feels like it's been here longer than the others, maybe because it doesn't seem as touristy. Then north to Titusville. Everyone in the area makes fun of Titusville, but I can't really see how it's different from anything else around here—it's strip-mally and a little run-down, but so are the other towns. The streets are lined with motels with space-themed signs, as they are in Cocoa Beach and Port St. John and everywhere else. I suppose every area needs one town to make fun of.

I cross back to Merritt Island using a different causeway, and rather than heading toward the gate of the Space Center I take the turn for the Merritt Island National Wildlife Refuge. This place is beautiful in a prehistoric kind of way, wetlands with palmettos and slash pine, everywhere the sounds of alligators and frogs, exotic-looking birds touching down and taking off again. Across the Mosquito Lagoon, the Vehicle Assembly Building and the launch towers stand sentinel on the horizon, a reminder of why all this is here. I've visited this refuge a couple of times before, and every time I come here I envision the landscape as an inch-for-inch replica of what Ponce de León found when he landed here in 1513. There are few places like this left on either coast, places where you can imagine the European explorers encountering this land for the first time.

I've been reading about Juan Ponce and about Captain James Cook, whose ships *Discovery* and *Endeavour* were the namesakes for two of the space shuttle orbiters. On his first voyage, Cook established an observatory in Tahiti to record the transit of Venus across the sun. He was the first to circumnavigate New Zealand, took possession of Australia for Great Britain, and became the first European to visit Hawaii. After his second voyage, he was already famous and could have rested on his laurels, but instead he kept looking for an excuse for another expedition. He set off for his third and final voyage in 1776. Legend holds that the Hawaiian natives mistook him for a god, though this has been disputed; these same natives stabbed him to death and preserved his remains as they preserved their chiefs'. Cook wrote that he intended to go not only "farther than any man has been before me, but as far as it is possible for a man to go."

Reading about their voyages, I keep thinking how strange it is that these grand vague ideas of discovery and endeavor actually become, when you look at them closely, weirdly specific stories of weirdly specific people, adventures that take place at particular moments and under certain pressures. These were actual human beings who climbed into actual boats for actual reasons, many of those reasons being less grand and lofty than the names of their ships. Juan Ponce and James Cook and the others wanted to be rich, or to impress people, or to escape something at home, or to make a name for themselves. Taken as a whole, their achievements have less of a feeling of grandeur than of something like coincidence: if the conditions that made their trips advantageous hadn't come about when they did, someone else would have made the trip at another time, and the contact between cultures would not be exactly what it was, the New World would not be exactly what it is. The story would be a different one.

I get back in my car and drive across the causeway to Cocoa Beach. There is a motel here that was once owned jointly by the seven Mercury astronauts, the place they stayed when they came to town to race their hot rods up and down A1A and laugh at the local sheriff and get drunk around the pool. That motel, when I stop in, is now owned by a chain. The lobby has no space memorabilia, no indication that the first Americans to go to space owned it, slept here. When I ask the young woman behind the counter, she acknowledges it's true but doesn't seem particularly energized by the fact. She looks young enough that she was probably born after *Challenger;* the Mercury astronauts are probably older than her grandparents, their accomplishments prehistoric and irrelevant.

The drive home to Tennessee is easier and quicker than the drive down—the trip home always seems faster, I suppose. On the way to Cape Canaveral two days earlier I'd passed through Florida entirely in the dark, but coming back I get to see the outskirts of Orlando and the swampy landscapes of central Florida. Many billboards advertise upcoming rest stops and their free orange juice. I know from reading John McPhee that the orange juice will be the same concentrate one buys at any grocery store in Knoxville, or in Minnesota, or in Siberia. Other billboards denounce President Obama. Still others implore me in more and more urgent terms not to have an abortion.

To pass the time, I listen to audiobooks—I get through the latest well-reviewed literary doorstopper and start another. I stop for lunch somewhere in south Georgia. At sunset, as a gorgeous orange light is filling my car and everything else, I notice myself: I'm sucking on a milkshake, tearing down the highway at eighty miles per hour, singing along to a pop song I'd never heard until several days ago, thinking about where to stop for dinner. For today, I don't have to worry about my son's nap schedule or answer my students' e-mails. I can stop wherever I want without accommodating someone else's preferences. I can listen to trashy music or talk to myself or think, just sit quietly in the hushed luxury of my own secondhand car, the landscape of Georgia whistling by outside the window.

I hear the "Firework" song again. "Baby you're a firework / Come on, show 'em what you're worth / Make 'em go, 'Oh, oh, oh,' / As you shoot across the sky-y-y."

I pull into my driveway in Knoxville late that night, and my house is already dark. I carry my bags in as quietly as I can. The house is tidy, the dishwasher humming and sloshing, my husband and son asleep, seemingly undamaged by my absence. I kiss them both and crawl into bed exhausted, still smelling of the swamps of Florida, the red dirt of Georgia, smelling of fast food and all the diesel fumes of all the truck stops of the Southeast. I'd feared making this trip, had felt it a necessary inconvenience to transport my eyeballs and brain down to the launch site to be able to say that I had personally witnessed the event myself. Now, having experienced unexpected and complicated things, having felt the heat and having smelled the smells, I see what it means to actually go to the Cape, to make the drive covering every inch between my driveway and the causeway, to get dirty, get drunk, get sunburned, and pee in the bushes. It was important to feel the light of the launch against my own face, its vibration pushing against my clothes. I'd thought I had to be there in person in order to get the real story; in fact, by being there, I—a tiny bit—changed the story.

Before I'm awake the next morning, my phone buzzes with an incoming text. I roll over in bed and squint at the screen with one eye. The text is from Omar.

> Good morning. Home safe?

I smile. Only Omar.

> Yup, I tap out with my thumbs. Got in at 11pm. Lots of traffic around Atlanta.

Soon, we will make plans to go to the launch of STS-134, the last mission for *Endeavour.* Mark Kelly has announced that he will remain on the crew as its commander. It's scheduled for No Earlier Than April 19, 2011.

Space flight is a dream, and dreams do not have to be entirely real in order to motivate behavior.

—Howard E. McCurdy, *Space and the American Imagination*

CHAPTER 4. A Brief History of the Future

March–April 2011

I'm sitting in my office at the University of Tennessee the Monday after I return from the launch of *Discovery,* still sunburned and sleep-deprived from the trip. It's hard to believe I'm going to do the same thing at least two more times. I've plugged my phone into my computer to upload the images from the trip; as they flow by on my screen, I'm startled by how many pictures I've taken. A picture of my odometer as it clicked over to forty thousand, one of a sign welcoming cars to Merritt Island that reads WHERE DREAMS ARE LAUNCHED!, one of a huge peach-colored full moon hanging low in the sky, the kind of moon that must have made a tempting target for the newly transplanted spaceworkers of the sixties.

As the photos upload, I start preparing to teach my next class, Writing Creative Nonfiction. I've built into the syllabus a unit I call A Brief History of Creative Nonfiction, in which we spend a few weeks reading Truman Capote, Gay Talese, Joan Didion, John McPhee, Hunter S. Thompson, James Agee, Tom Wolfe, Norman Mailer— important writers who were working in that moment in the sixties when literary journalism converged with a thread of creative writing and the genre we now call creative nonfiction was born.

On the syllabus for tomorrow are selections from Tom Wolfe, who is rightfully credited with being one of the founding fathers of creative nonfiction by helping to define the New Journalism. I open the file and flip through pages covered with my notes from previous semesters. I stop on a random page from *The Right Stuff.*

> The passion that now animated NASA spread out even into the surrounding community of Cocoa Beach. The grisliest down-home alligator-poaching crackers manning the gasoline pumps on Route A1A would say to the tourists, as the No-Knock flowed, "Well, that Atlas vehicle's given us more fits than a June bug on a porch bulb, but we got real confidence in that Redstone, and I think we're gonna make it." Everyone who felt the spirit of NASA at that time wanted to be part of it. It took on a religious dimension that engineers, no less than pilots, would resist putting into words. But all felt it.

Flip a chunk of pages.

> That was what the sight of John Glenn did to Americans at that time. It primed them for the tears. And those tears ran like a river all over America. It was an extraordinary thing, being the sort of mortal who brought tears to other men's eyes.

Flip.

> At night some sort of prehistoric chiggers or fire ants—it was hard to say, since you could never see them—rose up from out of the sand and the palmetto grass and went for the ankles with a bite more vicious than a mink's.

As I read, I reach down and scratch at my ankles, the raised red spots where the invisible bugs got me while I waited on the causeway. Flip.

> There was no such thing as "first-class accommodations" or "red-carpet treatment" in Cocoa Beach. The red carpet, had anyone ever

tried to lay one down, would have been devoured in midair by the No See'um bugs, as they were called, before it ever touched the implacable hardcracker ground.

I've taught excerpts from *The Right Stuff* many times, and it always leads to a useful discussion. My students respond to the audacity of Wolfe's voice, and as the semester goes on they remember him as a key example of what we mean when we use the adjective *voicey*. It makes me proud when my students can identify little echoes of this voice in David Foster Wallace, in John D'Agata, in Susan Orlean. This semester I've also added to the syllabus the first chapter of Norman Mailer's *Of a Fire on the Moon,* which we will be discussing tomorrow as well. I've always talked about Norman Mailer's role in defining literary journalism and thus creative nonfiction, but not until this semester have I tried to teach an example of his work. He is generally more resistant to excerpting than most. I'm curious what students will think of the differences in the ways Wolfe and Mailer write about spaceflight; for all the similarities that come with the era and the subject matter, the differences between them are stark. For one thing, Wolfe is obsessed with *character,* clearly believes that character is at the center of everything, and he creates dozens of characters big and small: astronauts, engineers, gas station attendants, astronauts' wives, reporters, even chimpanzees being trained for spaceflight. For Mailer, the only real character in the book is Norman Mailer; even the astronauts are there only as archetypes upon which to project his own ideas about himself.

I look over the pages of Mailer's I've assigned for tomorrow. His sentences are dense, paragraphs long and wandering, scenes structured by free association rather than anything like theme or plot. I fear that my students won't get him, that I might be the only reader who could fall in love with prose like this. For instance, about the moment of launch:

The flames were enormous. No one could be prepared for that. Flames flew in cataract against the cusp of the flame shield, and then sluiced along the paved ground down two opposite channels in the concrete. . . . In the midst of it, white as a ghost, white as the white of Melville's Moby Dick, white as the shrine of the Madonna in half the churches of the world, this thin slim angelic mysterious ship of stages rose without sound out of its incarnation of flame and began to ascend slowly into the sky, slow as Melville's Leviathan might swim, slowly as we might swim upward in a dream looking for the air.

On my computer's screen, more photos and texts flow by. A row of cars glinting in the hot sun on the 528 causeway. A heron perched on the roof of my car in the parking lot of a fast-food restaurant. Launch pad 39A shimmering in the heat across the Banana River. Already it seems long ago.

On Tuesday afternoon, I walk into the classroom where my Writing Creative Nonfiction class meets to find that students have already arranged the chairs into a circle. They are chatting about the readings rather than about the weekend's football and parties, a good sign, and they seem to be saying positive things. When I call the class to order, the students seem eager to share their impressions. My most talkative student raises his hand first.

"It was cool that both of the writers brought out their own personal feelings about what they were seeing," he says. "They didn't try to be objective, and I'm starting to get why that's a good thing."

"Right, that's what Tom Wolfe said in his definition of the New Journalism," I say. "He felt that objectivity was no longer going to be a useful standard."

"I thought it was interesting to see two different writers talking about the same moment," another student says. "The way they write about it is so different, you'd never know they were in the same place at the same time."

"Well, they were in the same *place,* at Cape Canaveral, but not at the same *time*," I correct her. "Wolfe was writing about the Mercury era, the first astronauts to travel in space in the early sixties, and Mailer was writing about the missions to the moon, in the late sixties and early seventies."

Blank faces.

"But the Russians had already gotten to the moon first, right?" my most talkative student asks.

I'm opening my mouth to respond when another student cuts in.

"Of course not, *we* won the space race. We got to space first."

"Actually, you're both wrong," I say, and everyone laughs. I laugh too, but I'm a bit shocked. These are the most basic facts, the ones I would have thought everyone would know.

"Let's get back to the structure of these chapters," I say. "We've been talking about the New Journalism and Tom Wolfe's idea that we should write in scenes wherever possible. What are some places in *The Right Stuff* where he chose *not* to do that?"

But as we go on discussing Tom Wolfe and Norman Mailer and the New Journalism and the way in the sixties everyone thought they were reinventing everything, the optimism embodied in redefining literature once and for all, the optimism of sending human beings to space, two things become clear to me: my students did not grow up with the same idea of the sixties that I did. Maybe because their parents were born too late to remember that era as their own, as my parents do. Maybe these kids didn't grow up with stories about how great the sixties were, how much better than any decade that dared try to follow. The phrase "the sixties" for them conjures not an emotion or a set of values, but only a vague idea of fashion, music, a historical event or two, the same useless window dressing I get when I think of "the twenties" or "the eighteen fifties." Whatever ideas my students have about the sixties, their ideas of spaceflight are not attached to the sixties as a historical era, as they are for my elders and for me.

The next time my Writing Creative Nonfiction class meets, I get to the classroom fifteen minutes early. I'm intrigued by my students' ignorance about spaceflight, and I'm hoping to get the chance to learn more from them without cutting into our official class time. As students file in, I put a few questions on the board:

> *What year did the first human being travel in space?*
> *What nation achieved this first?*
> *What year did the first human being land on the moon?*
> *What nation achieved this first?*
> *How many human beings have walked on the moon total?*
> *What year did the space shuttle first fly?*
> *What is the furthest the space shuttle can go from the earth?*
> *What percentage of the federal budget goes to NASA?*

As I write, my students perk up and look curious.

"*Don't* look these up on your phones," I order them, because I know this will be their first instinct. They dutifully lock their screens and place their phones facedown on their desks, even more intrigued now.

"You don't have to participate in this discussion," I tell them, "because it has nothing to do with our class. But this is something I'm curious about, if you're interested."

They lean forward.

"Let's start with the first one," I say. "What year did the first human being travel in space?"

The United States got to space first, in 1956. Humiliated, the Soviets put forth a new and arbitrary goal: to put a man on the moon. They accomplished this feat in 1962; NASA didn't get the first American (John Glenn) to the moon until 1965. He traveled there on the space shuttle, a vehicle that is capable of voyages beyond the moon to Mars and Jupiter, up to 40 million miles into outer space. The most recent mission to the moon was in 2001—in the decades the space shuttle has been going to the

moon, over 400 people have walked on its surface. NASA gets 20–30%
of the federal budget.

This account was provided by one of my undergraduate students, and as far off the mark as it is, the wildness of its guesses is typical of the group's responses. Only a minority of my students can correctly place the sequence of "firsts," that the Soviets got to space first, after which Americans got to the moon first. I'm not looking for correct dates here, only the correct order; the number of students who knew the correct *dates* for these events was one.

My students have an invariably positive, even affectionate, opinion of NASA, even if they aren't entirely sure what the scope of NASA's mandate is, or how old it is. In this respect NASA has shown itself to be one of only two government agencies (the other is the FBI) that consistently has a positive public image. Former NASA administrator Dan Goldin once said of his agency that it was "the one organization in American society whose sole purpose is to make sure our future will be better than our past."

A lot of my students think American spaceflight started in the forties or fifties. Many believe women have walked on the moon. Some think American astronauts have traveled to other planets. But to me, these are not the worst misunderstandings. Much more troubling is the extent to which they conflate the two eras of spaceflight into one big lump. When students are asked when the space shuttle first flew, they tend to give the same dates that they gave for the first human spaceflight—in other words, they seem to think there has only ever been one space vehicle. My students don't understand that there was a significant change between the heroic era and the shuttle era, separated by years and a great leap in technology and fanfare that was very moving to little children in the early eighties. I'm left with the disconcerting fact that they don't actually know what the space shuttle *is*. And if they think the space shuttle has already been going to Mars since before their parents were born, why would they agree, as taxpayers, to pay billions for the first *actual* mission to Mars?

I tell my students that when I missed class last week, it was because I was at the Kennedy Space Center to see *Discovery* launch. They are impressed, though I have to explain that *Discovery* is not *the* space shuttle, but one of three. I tell them that this mission is *Discovery*'s last, that when *Discovery* returns to Earth it will be sent to the Air and Space Museum. My students' mouths fall open. They had no idea.

"So—we won't be going to space anymore?" one student asks.

"American astronauts will still travel to the International Space Station, but they'll have to hitch a ride with the Russians, on their Soyuz spacecraft."

Some of my students actually gasp with horror. They had no idea. They wear the outraged expression of people who feel they should have been consulted. But then I tell them that *Discovery*'s construction started in 1979, making it a thirty-two-year-old vehicle. My students, most of whom were born in the early nineties, are dismayed to hear this. Thirty-two sounds pretty old to them. The space shuttle *should* be retired if it's that old, they feel, but we should have a newer spacecraft to replace it with. They are shocked that we don't.

"So what are the answers?"

They are all looking at me. I wish I could get this kind of attention from them when I'm trying to get them to map out the structure of an essay, when I'm trying to explain what a comma splice is.

I look at my watch. Seven minutes before class starts. We talk through some of the answers: Only twelve people have walked on the moon. All of them were white men, all of them American. The space shuttle can only go to low Earth orbit, 240 miles above Earth. As I go on, students express bewilderment at how much less has been accomplished than what they had thought. They are embarrassed that they didn't know the facts, but they also seem indignant that their optimistic narratives have not come to pass.

In one way it's touching. I hadn't known to expect this credulous faith in their own country's relentless conquering of space. This faith is supported, no doubt, by the wildly exaggerated beliefs most people hold about NASA's funding: a multiyear survey asking Americans to guess what percentage of the federal budget goes to NASA regularly turned up an average of over 20 percent, a percentage reflected in my students' guesses. Worse: the Americans polled who guessed the correct category (0–1 percent) were, in some years, outnumbered by those who chose "over 50 percent." I would like to repeat this for emphasis: a significant number of adult Americans walking among us believe that NASA receives *over 50 percent of the entire federal budget*.

I give my students the real numbers. "NASA gets 0.4 percent of the national budget," I tell them, "and that's been true for most of its history. Most of you said around 20 percent—you should know that 20 percent is more than the entire *defense* budget. Last year NASA's total budget was less than the cost of *air-conditioning* for troops in Iraq. The bank bailout of 2008 cost more than the entire fifty-year budget for NASA."

My students sneak looks at each other. Can this be right? It's hard to comprehend numbers in the billions. When people talk about the cost of spaceflight, they usually refer to it in terms of a project that, whatever its inspirational qualities, is not an investment that will pay off financially. Yet in my reading I recently came across a surprising quote from Lyndon Johnson—he once remarked that the information gained from satellite photography alone was worth "ten times what the whole program has cost." Before the space program had made satellite spying possible, gaining information about our enemies' military capabilities was difficult, costly in money and lives, and often unreliable. Inaccurate data led the American military to overprepare to meet threats that turned out to be exaggerated or nonexistent. "Indirectly," historian Howard McCurdy explains, "space research enhanced the funds available for domestic development." NASA's public image might be even more positive if it were generally known that the space program might in fact have paid for itself.

When my students are given the sad facts and asked why they gave such outlandish answers, they shift their feet and look embarrassed. But one brave woman gives an interesting response.

"I knew we went to the moon in the sixties," she explains, reddening, "so I assumed whatever we're doing now with all the technology we have is—like—*better* than that." It's true, technology does generally work that way. If your parents had big slow expensive computers, you get fast cheap portable computers. If your parents got to go to the moon, you get to go to Mars. It's sound enough logic, if innocent of the realities of public policy.

As frustrating as my students' misunderstandings are, I can't say I blame them. People my own age aren't much better informed. We didn't get to watch that one small step for a man live on TV, can only view that footage now through layers of history and cliché. MTV's re-appropriation of Buzz planting the flag, the bits and images used again and again to symbolize, variously and contradictorily, HISTORY and THE FUTURE. It's boring to hear other people tell their dreams, and people too young to remember the moon shot have grown tired of listening to this one. Encumbered by such dreams myself, I squint at the footage brought back from the moon landings, and I have to agree that we who are watching from 2011 can't ever really see what those innocents who watched those events unfold in real time saw, what it looked like to watch while the dream came true.

It's close to three years after Neil and Buzz's giant leap for mankind, April 1972. Two men bounce along together, almost skipping, exuberant and unstable as toddlers in their bulky space suits. This is Apollo 16, NASA's sixth mission to the moon, and while the journey to the moon will never become routine, it is no longer regarded with the same breathlessness and wonder as it once was. The number of people who turn out to see the launches on the Space Coast has steadily shrunk, as have the TV audiences. Politicians have started to wonder aloud why we need to keep going to the moon when the race with the Soviets, ostensibly the reason for doing all this, is over. NASA's budget is in steep decline. I won't be born for another four months.

Today, John Young and Charlie Duke are walking on the moon.

Far ahead of them, mountains stand stark white against the deep black of the sky. These men have work to do here on the Plain of Descartes, but they enjoy themselves as they work. You can see it in the way they jump higher than is strictly necessary, you can hear the glee in their voices through the crackling of the static between the moon and Houston. Even without looking up the video online, you can picture their low-gravity antics: you've seen it many times. Envision the astronauts bobbing along gently in their white space suits, their lightheartedness in strange contrast to the alien hostility of the terrain, in contrast to the risk of death all around them, the risk of death ahead of them on their way back home. You aren't concerned for them; you already know they'll get home safely.

As they work, John Young and Charlie Duke chat happily with each other, with their crewmate Ken Mattingly, alone in lunar orbit, and with Mission Control in Houston. In the course of a daily news update, the astronauts learn that Congress has just approved a budget for fiscal 1973. This budget includes funding NASA has requested to get started on its still-hypothetical space shuttle program. When he hears the news, John Young remarks, "The country needs that shuttle mighty bad. You'll see." He doesn't know yet that he will command the very first space shuttle mission, and he also doesn't know how frustratingly long it will take to get that shuttle flying. He can't guess the mixed history the shuttle will live out, the way it will be doomed by compromises even before it rolls out to the launchpad for the first time. He can't know that two shuttle disasters will kill fourteen of his fellow astronauts, forever changing the history of American spaceflight.

It is this moment I want to describe to my students who don't understand the difference between Apollo and shuttle. This moment, a moonwalker reacting with joy on the surface of the moon because the shuttle era has officially begun, is the seam between the two.

After one last moonwalk, John Young and Charlie Duke climb back into their lunar module, secure their haul of new moon rocks, and fire the ascent rockets to lift them up to orbital rendezvous with Ken

Mattingly and the command module. After a four-day journey back to Earth, the crew in their capsule splash into the Pacific Ocean and are greeted aboard the USS *Ticonderoga* with the same patriotic fanfare with which every American astronaut has been welcomed home. But when I study those photographs now, I can see a wistful, bewildered look in the eyes of the astronauts, a look that can be seen in the eyes of the current crop of American astronauts. It's a look of being grounded, of being trapped on the surface of the home planet. A look of wanting to go up in the bird, though they had only just returned. A masculine envy of their own selves.

When we think about the Apollo project now, we think of it as being a time when all Americans were united behind a project they could take pride in. The fact is that Americans were slowly falling out of love with Apollo right from the beginning. Even before Neil, Buzz, and Mike made it to the moon, only about a third of Americans thought the moon project was worth the cost. At the same time, a clear majority of Americans throughout the sixties said they *approved* of Apollo; in other words, uneasiness about the cost of spaceflight has always been paired with widespread positive feelings about spaceflight. This contradiction has made NASA the site of one of the deeper ambiguities of American culture: spaceflight is an achievement we take great pride in, paid for with our own money, over our objections.

Hugely wasteful; hugely grand. Adjust the focus of your eyes and the same project goes from being the greatest accomplishment of humankind to a pointless show of misspent wealth.

None of my students have heard of Wernher von Braun or the German rocket program. Von Braun ran the rocket design facility for the Third Reich at Peenemünde, where he was responsible for the development of the V-2 rocket, the first human-made object to enter space, a weapon used to bomb Allied cities. At the end of the war, von Braun and his team surrendered to the United States and managed to immigrate here in order to resume their work on rockets. Von Braun's membership in the SS and the Nazi party would haunt him, and throughout his life he would have to answer to new charges about what he knew and what he was responsible for, especially having to do with the slave laborers forced to construct the V-2. As popular a public figure as he was in the United States, von Braun could never entirely get away from the specter of the concentration camps, and even at the moment of triumph for his Saturn rocket, his adopted country couldn't quite forget his past. Von Braun maintained all his life that he only wanted to build rockets for the peaceful exploration of space, and that he worked on weapons only because doing so allowed him to continue his research. The evidence seems to bear this out—in researching his biography of von Braun, historian Michael J. Neufeld uncovered documents that show von Braun resisting joining the SS as long as possible, even after he had become director at Peenemünde. Though when it became clear that his failure to join would not be overlooked, von Braun did join the SS and was seen wearing the uniform on a number of occasions, including in several surviving photographs. Some survivors later accused him of overseeing beatings and executions of prisoners, though historians question whether this was a case of mistaken identity.

Von Braun himself has always denied that he had anything to do with violence against prisoners, or that he knew the extent of their mistreatment. Of course, he knew his rockets were being built by prisoners, and to some this is enough. To many, though, surprisingly many, von Braun's crimes can be if not forgiven at least *contextualized*. When Oriana Fallaci met him, she described his large frame, his "heavy paunch, the florid complexion of a beer drinker," his handsome face. She describes his Prussian accent: he "manages to make the softest words sound hard: such as *Moon*."

As he talks he stands erect like a general addressing a stupid recruit and his smile is so cold that it seems more like a threat than a smile.

118 | CHAPTER 4

Odd: by all rights he should be unlikable and yet he isn't. For half an hour I made myself dislike him. To my utter astonishment I found myself feeling just the opposite.

As an Italian who worked for the Resistance and lost a great deal in the war, Fallaci is well positioned to articulate certain grudges, to argue that von Braun was an opportunist and a murderer. But she finds she can't. "Although I am one who doesn't forget," she writes, "I find it dishonest and unfair to deny von Braun what is von Braun's, to leave him out of a tale of this kind." She points out that Enrico Fermi and Robert Oppenheimer made the atom bomb that killed civilians in Japan. Is von Braun different?

When Fallaci asks von Braun whether he would go to the moon himself, he answers that he'd go in a second. (Neufeld's biography reveals that this has been his desire since childhood, that the dream of space travel is what led him to develop rockets in the first place.) "Maybe they'll put up with me on flight number 10," von Braun muses to Fallaci, "like you put up with a grumbling old uncle, to make me happy." When the space shuttle emerged as the spacecraft to follow his Saturn V, with its lesser physical demands on astronauts, von Braun speculated it might be an appropriate vehicle for an older spacefarer to travel on, and indeed NASA may have let him, as they indulged John Glenn in a flight on *Discovery* at age seventy-seven, but by the time the shuttle was ready to fly, von Braun was dead, from pancreatic cancer, at age sixty-five.

Apollo 17, the last mission ever flown on von Braun's Saturn V, is remembered largely for a photograph the astronauts took of Earth once they were far enough away to see the whole thing. Nicknamed the "Blue Marble," the image was the first to show the entirety of Earth illuminated and suspended in space. Carl Sagan called the photograph an "icon of our age." Africa can clearly be seen, and the white cloud cover over Antarctica swirls like a delicate lace. The image is one of the most widely distributed photographs ever taken—next time you see an image of the whole earth in any context, look closely: it's probably the Blue

Marble. The image has even been credited with the rise of the environmental movement in the seventies. A few years ago, I met Jack Schmitt, a geologist who flew on Apollo 17 and walked on the moon. There is some debate over which of the astronauts actually snapped the picture, but Schmitt told me it was him, and I believe him. There is a large framed copy of the photograph hanging on the wall in my son's room, with an inscription Schmitt wrote for him: "To Elliot, and the future."

It's hard to imagine what it was like for the crew of Apollo 17 to splash down, board the aircraft carrier, strip off their space suits, and write up their reports. They had spent their adult lives preparing for this adventure, they had accomplished it, and no one was planning to go back again. The moon rocks they brought back, including the one I have touched in the Air and Space Museum, would be the last to come back for generations. No one has gone to the moon since, and it would be nearly as difficult for us to try to re-create their trip now as it was to accomplish it then.

The space shuttle is a far more advanced vehicle than was Apollo/ Saturn, but because it lacked the pure thrust to get any farther than low Earth orbit, it felt like a step backward to many Americans. The next vehicle should go *farther* than the previous one, it seemed obvious. After discovering the New World, Columbus did not take a renewed interest in the area around the Mediterranean. Yet the public had tired of the expense of Apollo even before the missions to the moon had gotten started. After a brief resurgence in interest caused by the drama on Apollo 13, Americans went back to caring less and less about Apollo, saying in larger numbers that it was pointless and too expensive. A scaled-back space vehicle funded partly for its ability to get military and commercial satellites into orbit—a reusable shuttle with a large payload bay—was the only one that had a chance of gaining the approval of Congress. As it was, the shuttle's funding was the subject of constant wrangling and severe cuts over the years of its development, and it was in danger of being axed altogether multiple times.

Unlike average Americans, though, rocket engineers saw the space shuttle concept as a huge step forward. If they could build a spaceship the way they wanted to, not with the Soviets breathing down their necks but with the time to build it properly from the ground up, what would that spaceship look like? It would look more like a space plane. It would look *elegant*. It would be capable of carrying different types of payloads, not only human beings. And it would be reusable. "When I was a kid reading *Buck Rogers,* the spacecraft all looked like bullets or saucers, with sweeping fins and fancy tail skids," said astronaut Michael Collins. "We are beginning to see Buck's dream emerge in the squat but elegant space shuttle."

The concept of reusability had been a fantasy of engineers from the beginning—rather than building expendable rockets that would be abandoned in space or burned up in the atmosphere, NASA wanted a vehicle that could launch like a rocket, fly in space, and land like an airplane on a runway. "There's no way that you can make a railroad cost-effective," explained a NASA representative, "if you throw away the locomotive every time." After some maintenance on the ground, a reusable spacecraft could be loaded with new cargo and a new crew of astronauts, to be launched again. An ideal (and, it turns out, entirely unrealistic) turnaround time on the ground was two weeks. The urgency of Apollo, the before-the-decade-is-out deadline, had ruled out anything but the quick-and-dirty approach of attaching hastily designed capsules to rockets of the type that had been developed as weapons. Now that that deadline had been met, rocket engineers had time to go back to their childhood fantasies of spaceflight, their science fiction dreams.

Most people don't realize that since the time of Apollo we've been in a feedback loop: as a nation, we elect representatives who thwart NASA, and then we blame NASA for its lack of vision. There is a simple and frustratingly predictable pattern: first NASA comes up with an exciting and ambitious long-term plan for getting to Mars, or for getting back to the moon, or for building a space station, or for traveling to an asteroid. Once there is a plan on the table, it is scrutinized and called too ambitious, redundant, unrealistic, or ridiculous. Always it's called too expensive. One instance of such a vision was Wernher von Braun's plan for an expedition to Mars, presented to the Senate Space Committee in 1969. He impressed the committee by announcing that on precisely November 12, 1981, two spacecraft would leave Earth for Mars simultaneously. The plan was serious, well thought out, technically sound, and incredibly expensive. It went nowhere. Another example was the Vision for Space Exploration endorsed by George W. Bush in 2004, which called for an extended human presence on the moon. Mostly these long-term plans are rejected by Congress altogether, but once a generation a plan is approved.

In that rare instance when a plan is approved, it's always in a scaled-back way, always a compromise of the original lofty vision. Most importantly, it's always structured in such a way that a future Congress will have to put up the majority of the money, making the whole thing feel precarious at best. Why will a future Congress and president make political sacrifices to fund a project they won't get credit for in the minds of the public? Congress is a group of ever-changing politicians who answer to constituents of the present, not a fantasy for the far-off future.

But then of course the scaled-back, cheaper vision is opened up for national ridicule. *Why doesn't NASA dream bigger?* Americans complain. *Why aren't they pushing out farther? They're playing it safe, they've lost their vision, lost their way.* Once we're done criticizing the plan, we will start to love it, because spaceflight is fun, and because this is all we've got. But then (in the case of shuttle) some of the technical compromises Congress demanded in order to save money will lead to accidents, and NASA will be blamed again, this time for its lack of attention to safety.

There are four warring interests in spaceflight: ambitiousness of vision, urgency of timetable, reduction of cost, and safety to astronauts. These can never be entirely reconciled. In the sixties, urgency and ambitiousness were the driving factors, and because this was understood and accepted, the massive cost and risk were accepted as well. We now seem to be at a moment when reduction of cost is paramount, with safety coming in a very close second. This being the case, we should not be surprised that ambitiousness and urgency have had to be set aside altogether. But it's ludicrous to claim, as I often hear people do, that "NASA has lost its vision." NASA has lost support, not vision.

Wernher von Braun's plan for Mars was complex. Getting astronauts to a planet 140 million miles away is even more difficult than getting them to the moon; to travel that far, one would have to construct a much larger space vehicle than could be built on Earth. The best way to assemble such a large vehicle would be to do so in low Earth orbit, using an orbiting space station as a base of operations. And in order to construct a space station, one needs a smaller launch vehicle— ideally a reusable shuttle—to haul the pieces of the station, and then later pieces of the Mars transport, up to Earth orbit. NASA's plan was for a reusable shuttle with which to construct an orbiting space station with which to construct a large interplanetary spacecraft. As enthusiasm waned toward the end of Apollo, funding became scarce, and most politicians found it expedient to set themselves apart from the expense of spaceflight without going so far as to close down any NASA sites or major contractors, many of which were located in the states and districts of important members of Congress. So NASA got only the budget for the shuttle. By all accounts, it was lucky to get that much. Apollo 17 was the last mission to the moon, launched in December 1972. Meanwhile, Apollo 18, 19, and 20 were unceremoniously canceled, their crews left earthbound until the space shuttle would be ready to fly. Soon NASA's budget was only one-third what it had been at its peak.

When President Nixon approved the plan for the space shuttle in 1972, he released a statement:

> I have decided today that the United States should proceed at once
> with the development of an entirely new type of space transpor-

tation system designed to help transform the space frontier of the 1970's into familiar territory, easily accessible for human endeavor in the 1980's and 90's. . . .

The new system will differ radically from all existing booster systems, in that most of this new system will be recovered and used again and again—up to 100 times. The resulting economies may bring operating costs down as low as one-tenth of those [of] present launch vehicles.

If you get the chance to talk with a modern-day NASA engineer or manager, don't mention that one-tenth figure unless you want to see her beverage come out of her nose. It's not NASA's fault that the projection never came true—with the generous resources of the Apollo era, they probably could have done it.

Students of space policy might wonder why in the seventies, with the goals of Apollo accomplished, the government didn't simply shut NASA down entirely. The agency had been created to accomplish a very specific task and had accomplished it. But Caspar Weinberger, who was then deputy director of the Office of Management and Budget, warned Nixon that ending NASA would lead to claims that "our best years are behind us." He said, "America should be able to afford something besides increased welfare, programs to repair our cities, or Appalachian relief and the like." This is another great example of the ways in which spaceflight can be made to seem a paragon of, or negation of, any political ideology. But Weinberger's argument won: Nixon did not want to be remembered as the president who shut down a source of national pride, the president who canceled the future. No president does.

As historian Howard McCurdy puts it, Nixon's "need to maintain political support in aerospace states such as California and Texas contributed to his decision to maintain the human space flight effort, but so did his sense that NASA oversaw one of the few remaining technologies of optimism at that time."

The Apollo project had put Nixon in an impossible position—everyone knew the vision had been Kennedy's, and so the credit would go to his memory regardless of what president was in office at the time the goal was accomplished. Yet Nixon had no choice but to continue support for Apollo, as canceling the program would mean making the billions that had already been spent wasted money, not to mention disappointing everyone.

Writes historian Michael Neufeld:

> Nixon's behavior toward the space program in 1969–70 was disingenuous. He was quick to associate himself with the astronauts and the triumphs of Apollo when it was politically convenient, and he was equally quick to slash the budget of NASA when choices had to be made between agencies.

Neufeld points out that NASA saved the last Apollo mission from being canceled "by cutting a secret political deal with the White House to postpone it until after the November 1972 presidential election." Presumably, this last launch would be the cause of some hand-wringing and soul-searching about the end of spaceflight and the shortsightedness of politicians, just as we are seeing in this present moment, and Nixon did not want those lamentations to become part of his opponent's campaign.

This starts to clarify why a person like Buzz Aldrin would praise President Obama's cancellation of Constellation as a courageous move. It's easy to let a plan limp along, slowly starving to death via budget erosion; it takes some boldness to declare the project dead, thereby accepting the ire of people who support the project, or any spaceflight project.

Pity those of us who were children in the flightless years of the late seventies, when the space shuttle was under construction but took forever to emerge. Pity the dreamy little kids who wanted to be able to aspire to spaceflight but had no actual American astronauts to emulate. The space shuttle's design had been approved, but it had not yet appeared. We had to imagine it. My children's books about space from the seventies are filled with conceptual paintings, the type from midcentury trade show magazines, in which the colors are strangely muted. Brushstrokes are visible in the clouds, in the flames from the hypothetical rockets, in the hair of the hypothetical astronauts. The artists' rendering portrays the futuristic and imaginary nature of the space shuttle, and it evokes a futuristic nostalgia, to look at these pictures now that the shuttle is being retired.

In that era of budget defensiveness, even the books for children tended to highlight NASA innovations that had proven themselves useful here on Earth—weather satellites, metal alloys, advances in microchips. Velcro always gets a special mention. I want to shout backward into the past: Stop emphasizing the Velcro. *People don't care that much about Velcro.* People care about the unutterable awe of American heroes stabbing into the heavens on columns of fire. But it's too late: in the midseventies, the first orbiter, *Columbia,* is still years away from rolling out to the launchpad for its maiden flight. And from where I write, *Columbia* has already burned up into pieces all over Arizona and Texas.

NASA engineers had wanted a two-piece spacecraft that would be fully reusable—one piece a booster whose sole purpose would be to get the other piece, the orbiter, off the ground. Both segments would land like planes and would be able to fly again and again. The space transportation system envisioned by engineer Max Faget looked like two airplanes piggybacked, stacked upright for launch. But this concept would have been expensive to design and test, and once the budget started to decline, NASA shifted its goals downward to a reusable orbiter and two booster rockets for the first stage. The boosters would carry the shuttle to a certain altitude and then drop off, with built-in parachutes to soften their landing in the Atlantic. The rockets could then be reused, a key part of the proposal, though as historian Howard McCurdy points out, "Flight engineers were understandably nervous about reusing rocket engines that had been dunked in salt water and were discouraged that they had lost their airplane-like first stage."

Then the decision was made to use solid fuel in the booster rockets, rather than a more easily controlled liquid fuel, again to save cost. This series of decisions in essence wrote the fate of *Challenger,* which would fall victim to the specific weaknesses of the solid rocket boosters—that they can't be shut down if something goes wrong.

Predictions from the seventies about how often the shuttle could fly, and how cost-effective it would be, seem insane to us now in their optimism. A launchpad technician I know recently e-mailed me an image that had been used to promote the space shuttle concept in the seventies—it showed an orbiter, looking much like the ones we know, being maintained and reloaded for a new flight. A simple staircase has been rolled up to it, with a jumpsuited worker doing some light repairs. As it turns out, the orbiters need a much more elaborate hangar, the Orbiter Processing Facility, in which the spacecraft can be hoisted up to have the tiles of its underside repaired while workers on levels above attend to the engines, payload bay, orbital maneuvering system, and other components. The caption to this ludicrous image estimates that each orbiter can be turned around in two weeks. In reality, the shortest turnaround ever was eight weeks, and the average was measured in months. To be self-sustaining, the shuttle project would need to launch at least twenty-five times a year, with most missions being dedicated to the Department of Defense or customers paying to launch commercial satellites. This was a pace that might have been possible had the turnaround times been anywhere near what was predicted, but the compromises on the shuttle's design had led to more complicated and costly maintenance procedures. In reality, the most shuttle launches NASA ever accomplished in a single calendar year was nine, in 1985—far short of the magic number of twenty-five. New regulations recommended by the *Challenger* Commission slowed the pace of flights, and the *Columbia* Accident Investigation Board imposed even more. In recent years, the record for most launches in a year was five, in 2009. The fact that shuttle was meant to be self-sustaining and never was made the promise of new space projects even murkier.

When I arrive at our classroom the following week, my students are already there, ready with their questions. They've gotten into the habit of these space discussions before class starts.

Why can't we go back to the moon now? they want to know. *Can't we just rebuild the rockets from the sixties?*

Did we really go to the moon? How can we be sure it wasn't a hoax?

What is NASA doing with all the money if they're not flying the shuttle anymore?

Why *are we stopping?*

As a writing professor, I don't often get the experience of imparting empirical knowledge to my students. I almost never get to explain to them things that I know to be true that they don't yet know. I never get to *lecture.* And while it goes against my idea of my own strengths as a teacher, I find that it's a pleasurable experience to be listened to as an authority on facts rather than always being a facilitator of discussions in which no one is necessarily holding the right answer.

I tell them why going back to the moon would be almost as challenging now as it was in the sixties. The plans for millions of pieces of hardware are scattered among the storage facilities of dozens of contractors all over the country, if not lost altogether—not to mention the issue of the software, which would have to be re-created from the ground up. The deep, hard-earned knowledge of the problems involved, and how to solve them, locked in the minds of engineers now in their eighties and nineties or gone altogether.

"So what about the hoax?" an impatient student asks without raising his hand. "Do you believe it's true that they went?"

"I do," I answer.

"Why?"

Because Buzz Aldrin told me so, I think of saying.

"I'd like to hear what you believe first," I say instead. "What *you've* heard."

My students say they are not sure what to think. Many of them have heard enough of the "evidence" for the hoax to put them in the "serious doubts" category, but they are not among the True Believers of conspiracy. (Bart Sibrel—the man who sued Buzz Aldrin for punching him in the face—has said that he would bet his life that astronauts have never walked on the moon, and I believe he is sincere.) The conspiracists make some good claims, my students explain, and they have never heard anyone answer them.

I tell my students my favorite answers to the conspiracy theories—Michael Collins's point about four hundred thousand people keeping a secret for forty years, the one about the moon rocks. I have others. I have explanations for the various pieces of "evidence" my students have heard. But underlying all of this for many of my students, I know, is an assumption that a government agency can't have accomplished something so awesome. They are proud of their country, but not of their government. Apollo would seem to run against so many popular understandings about government, about government bureaucracy, about government spending. All of us were born after Watergate. In so many ways it's easier to believe the whole thing was a lie. That would better fit what they have been told.

"You have to weigh the evidence for yourselves," I tell them. "But don't assume it can't be true just because it's cool. Sometimes people manage to pull off cool things. We are allowed to enjoy them."

"Why *are* we stopping, then?" a student wants to know. "Why are we not going to space anymore?" Such a simple question, one I should be able to answer as easily as the others. But it's not. This is a question that intelligent and well-informed people can argue about. It's a question with layers and contradictions, a question that depends how far back you want to go in history, how technical you want to get. A question that depends on what you believe about big concepts like Human Nature and the American Spirit.

"There are a lot of reasons. It's maybe easier to answer why we went in the first place and then to talk about why those forces have weakened or disappeared. But at the simplest level, we're stopping because the *Columbia* Accident Investigation Board called for it in 2003."

A student who is normally quiet raises her hand.

"Was there one that blew up?" she asks. I'm taken aback for a moment that this knowledge seems so uncertain to her. Was there one that blew up? I don't know whether she's talking about *Columbia*, which was lost when she was thirteen—or *Challenger,* which was lost when *I* was thirteen.

Columbia was the first space shuttle completed, the first to fly, and as such it will for many Americans forever be The Space Shuttle. We first laid eyes on it when it rolled out of a hangar in California in spring 1979. In the footage shown on the news, it was nighttime, and lights played over the orbiter. *Columbia* backed out of the hangar then straightened itself, the huge metal bells of its three main engines pointing at us, the tail fin rising above. When it turned, its long white flank became visible for the first time, *NASA* and the orbiter's name inscribed on its side. A great cheer went up among the crowd of assembled aerospace workers.

After years of waiting, space fans were finally able to lay eyes on the world's first true spaceship, the first real step forward in spaceflight since the Saturn V. America's space plane. Even though work on *Columbia* had fallen way behind schedule, NASA managers decided to send it on the journey from California to the Kennedy Space Center as scheduled. The work would be completed in Florida. The most visible of *Columbia*'s deficiencies was its thermal protection system: over and over the procedures for attaching the tiles securely to the orbiter's skin had failed, and not all of the tiles were in place when *Columbia* rolled out. Temporary fake tiles were attached for the journey.

Crowds of people were invited out to watch and cheer *Columbia*'s arrival at Kennedy Space Center. But, as it turned out, the glue on the temporary tiles failed, and the tiles loosened in transit. Many people's first look at *Columbia* was the humiliating spectacle of the new orbiter shedding black and white tiles like confetti behind her, tiles we had been told were necessary to the survival of the ship and crew. Frank Izquierdo, who was standing on the runway for the welcoming ceremony at Kennedy, still shakes his head ruefully when he relates this story. "She looked like a dog after a big fight," he told me. The space shuttle project was made to look ridiculous at best, a failure at worst. As was NASA. As was the idea of continuing to fly in space. It would be another two years before *Columbia* would finally be ready for flight, and that image would remain in many people's minds throughout that time.

When I first saw *Columbia* roll out of the Vehicle Assembly Building on TV as a third-grader, the launch vehicle was an ungainly appealing sight, a lash-up of orbiter, external tank, and solid rocket boosters. I had never seen anything like it. The orbiter, the space plane, clung to the external tank affectionately, like a baby animal to its mother.

Columbia first took to the sky on April 12, 1981, flown by Apollo veteran John Young and pilot Robert Crippen. The launch was a success, and more journalists came out to KSC than had appeared there since Apollo 11. John Young, who was fifty, became the hero of the transition story—he had not only walked on the moon on Apollo 16, but before that had flown with Michael Collins on Gemini 10. His presence symbolized that shuttle was a natural and logical vehicle to follow Apollo-Saturn, and his age implied that the task of flying the shuttle was different from that of flying an Apollo mission—a man well into middle age could safely do it.

The shuttle encountered problems on each of its four test flights, but it was declared operational and began flying missions with full crews and cargo, most often commercial satellites. A second orbiter, *Challenger,* made its maiden voyage in 1983. From the start, the idea of the shuttle had been an idea for a *fleet,* with the reliability that comes with multiple identical vehicles. One orbiter could be prepared for flight while another was in space and yet another undergoing repairs. Ultimately, the fleet was to consist of five orbiters, taking astronauts and cargo to space with a regularity more like a commercial airline's than the risky one-off ventures of Mercury, Gemini, and Apollo.

The space shuttle *Challenger* was named for HMS *Challenger,* a

British Royal Navy warship that in 1872 undertook the first global marine research expedition. HMS *Challenger* sailed the world, making the first thorough survey of the oceans and discovering forty-seven hundred previously unknown species; the expedition is credited with giving rise to the field of oceanography. In preparation for the expedition, HMS *Challenger*'s guns were removed and its interior outfitted with laboratories, an operation that will strike some as reminiscent of the swords-to-plowshares process of converting missiles into rockets for the peaceful exploration of space.

In its three years of use, space shuttle *Challenger* flew more often than any other orbiter. No doubt there is a technical reason for this, but to young space fans it felt as though NASA simply *liked Challenger* the most. To me, *Challenger* will always be a bear cub, or some other kind of mammal—maybe a sweet and solid dog of unpretentious pedigree. *Challenger* is the fuzziest, friendliest of the orbiters, its edges somehow more rounded than the others', yet also the most dependable.

Some of the bright cheer and innocence of the eighties sticks to it—I suppose because *Challenger* is the only orbiter that resides forever in the eighties—or perhaps it's the innocence of my childhood. Maybe I'm getting some interference from Christa McAuliffe's personality, her bubbly motherly sweetness, since the name *Challenger* is forever connected with her fame, and her death.

On *Challenger*'s second flight, Sally Ride became the first American woman to fly in space. Its third mission flew the first African American astronaut, Guy Bluford, and on its fourth mission *Challenger* landed at Kennedy Space Center rather than the lake bed at Edwards Air Force Base, the first time a spacecraft landed back at its launch site. A third orbiter, *Discovery*, was added in 1984, the same year two women went to space together for the first time. In 1985, the fourth orbiter, *Atlantis*, made its first flight.

In all, twenty-four missions launched and landed successfully between April 1981 and January 1986.

We said good-bye to *Challenger* first. It broke up in the skies above the Kennedy Space Center seventy-three seconds into flight on January 28, 1986, at 11:38 a.m.

If you were born between 1968 and 1980, you were probably in school that morning. If you went to a public school, chances are decent that you watched the events of that day unfold live. The year before, NASA had run a contest for a teacher to fly in space, the first step of what was to be an ongoing civilian-in-space program. The teacher chosen for the flight was Christa McAuliffe, a likable social studies teacher from New Hampshire. Because of McAuliffe's inclusion on this mission, NASA had made special efforts to make this launch available to schoolchildren, including arranging for many public schools to receive a live feed. No national networks outside of the Space Coast area carried the launch live, so it's one of the ironies of the day that the only people to have witnessed the disaster in real time on TV were children, those least prepared to deal with what they saw.

We watched in school multipurpose rooms, sitting cross-legged on the floor. We watched in classrooms, bored, staring at TVs on rolling carts, the blinds drawn against the glare of the morning. We watched the seven astronauts emerge from their quarters, single file, waving to a rising cheer and the flashes of cameras, watched them climb into the van that would take them to the launchpad. I was in the eighth grade, and starting to understand that it wasn't cool to get visibly excited about something like a space shuttle launch. For my friends and me, any disruption to the normal school day was a fresh opportunity to make an elaborate show of being unimpressed.

I didn't happen to be in a classroom with a TV during the launch that day, though other classrooms in my school carried the live feed. I didn't hear what had happened until lunchtime, less than an hour later, when kids who had been watching the launch live were busy spreading the news. I remember feeling shocked but not particularly traumatized, as so many people my age say they were. I didn't know until later that my favorite astronaut, Judith Resnik, had been on board *Challenger*. I didn't know yet what far-reaching consequences this seemingly simple explosion would have. No one did, I guess.

We spent the rest of the school day watching the footage of the explosion replay over and over on TV. It was odd, seeing the launch from the start, because every time it seemed as though *this* time it might get off okay. Even the most cynical of us couldn't help but respond to the poetry of countdown, to the *three—two—one—*. Even the coolest of us looked up at that sudden flash of light, held our breaths at the moment of ignition, the strange fire and shudder. At *liftoff*, the bolts detached, and for a second we could imagine the thunderous thrust of the rockets. For one long minute, the shuttle rose on a fat column of puffy steam.

Then the white *pop* in the sky. Something unscripted had happened—though it took a long time for the voice of the announcer to acknowledge it. Not until the next day was it clear that there was no hope that the crew might have survived. A lot of people, telling this story now, describe seeing a fireball on their televisions and knowing instantly that the crew was dead. But if you watch the unedited footage again, you might remember that feeling of uncertainty and dread as pieces slowly rained down from an altitude of eight miles, tracing fingers of white contrails across the bright blue Florida sky.

At school that day, some kids were visibly upset, crying or burying their faces in their crossed arms on their desks, but a more common response was blankness, a weirded-out adolescent *whatever*ness. Some kids went straight to malicious laughter and making up *Challenger* jokes. (What kind of grades did Commander Scobee get in flight school? Below sea level! What do the *Challenger* and a penguin have in common? They're both black and white and kinda cute, but neither one can fly!) Widespread tears were reported among teachers and principals. Some teachers made efforts to explain what had gone wrong, though no one on that day fully understood what had gone wrong; no one would for many months. Some teachers shut off the televisions and changed the subject, leaving the task of explaining the unexplainable to our parents. Other teachers tried to draw larger lessons, to talk about mishap and risk and death. My brother's fourth-grade math teacher had the children flip to the page in their textbooks about astronaut Ronald McNair, one of a series of biographies intended to show children examples of women and minorities who use math in their jobs. Under his name was printed "1950–   ," and my brother and his classmates followed their teacher's instructions to carefully write "1986" in the blank space.

We wouldn't know it for a while, but that explosion marked the beginning of the end of American spaceflight. Mission STS-51L had been plagued by many slips and scrubs, the most frustrating of which had been the day before the launch. A special tool used to close the hatch to the crew compartment had broken off, and technicians had been unable to remove it within the launch window. If *Challenger* had taken off that day, a day much warmer than the fateful January 28, the rubber O-ring in the right solid rocket booster probably would not have stiffened with cold, and burning gases probably would not have escaped to detonate the external tank. Engineers, already aware of the O-ring problem, might have had a chance to fix it before the next attempt to launch in unusually cold weather. The space shuttle program might have moved forward as was intended, with the Department of Defense continuing to use it to deploy spy satellites. A second launch and landing facility might have been built, as planned, at Vandenberg Air Force Base in California. Flights might have continued at a steadier pace, and the shuttle might have made itself more useful, might have earned more of a place in the national consciousness. A Congress and a public more convinced of the shuttle's accomplishments might have been more likely to fund the next steps in spaceflight—a habitat on the moon, a trip to Mars. Instead, the space shuttle has quietly wound down without any spacecraft planned to follow it.

Frank Izquierdo was in Launch Control for *Challenger*'s last launch. When he tells me about it twenty-six years later, his memory seems precise and undistorted by emotion. Flight controllers dress up in suits and ties on launch days, partly a tradition of respect, but Frank also mentions that he was always glad to wear long sleeves and layers in the Firing Room, which was kept very cold to keep the computers safe. By the time the cryo tanks were being filled, Frank was chilled to the bone as well. When I ask Frank what it was like in the Firing Room that morning, he answers by telling me the facts—what happened in what order—rather than talking about emotions.

"First we lost comm," he says. "Then we lost data. We were all looking at our screens trying to make sense of what we were seeing."

"How long was it before you knew it hadn't been caused by the main engines?" This is a polite way of asking how long it was before he knew the accident hadn't been his fault. The engines were the most complex component, thought to have the highest risk of failure, and many people had assumed at first they were to blame for *Challenger*.

"It wasn't too long," he recalls. "They figured it out by looking at video and still images rather than telemetry. I'd say it was days rather than weeks."

I comment that Frank must have been relieved to learn that the disaster had been caused by a faulty solid rocket booster and not one of his engines. But in his memory of that time, this distinction doesn't seem to be nearly as relevant to him as I would have guessed.

"We all worked on shuttle," he explains. "I worked on one part of it for a while, and then I'd be given more responsibility, and the parts I was responsible for would change. But we all worked on shuttle. We all worked to keep the astronauts safe."

Months later, the presidential commission tasked with investigating *Challenger* issued its report. The cause of the explosion had been the solid rocket boosters, whose faulty design combined with the unseasonably cold weather in Florida to create a catastrophic failure. A picture in the paper showed Richard Feynman, a physicist who had worked on the Manhattan Project, smirking and holding up a piece of O-ring he'd been soaking in ice water to show that it became brittle. Sally Ride, also on the commission along with Neil Armstrong, sat a few seats away, looking pissed. She'd trusted her life to *Challenger* twice.

Only recently, since her death, has it come to light that the key piece of information about the O-rings had been supplied to another member of the commission by Sally Ride herself.

The commission's report also revealed that the crew cabin had remained intact after the explosion, that the astronauts had been alive, though not necessarily awake, for the two minutes and forty-five seconds it took them to fall back to Earth. This revelation struck us children as horrifying, yet it somehow made sense. We'd already grown used to that portrait of the seven smiling astronauts standing for TRAGEDY rather than ADVENTURE. We'd seen updates about Christa McAuliffe's family, her two small children readjusting to life without a mother. We had already come to realize that the adults in charge of making the world run smoothly actually had no idea what they were doing.

Challenger changed Americans' perceptions of spaceflight irrevocably. Shortly after the disaster, a poll found that 47 percent of Americans reported their confidence in NASA had been shaken. Two years later, only one-third of that group indicated that their faith had been restored. If the first disaster during a launch had taken place during the heroic era, people might have understood the astronauts' deaths to be a sacrifice in the name of progress. This certainly seemed to be the case for the Apollo 1 fire. But the disaster-free launches NASA ran from 1961 to 1986 gave people the sense that astronauts' safety should be guaranteed. Losing a crew during the shuttle's operational period seemed a worse failure, a worse betrayal of trust, than losing a Mercury capsule might have. Though the investigation into *Challenger* didn't end the space shuttle program, as some feared it would, American spaceflight would never entirely recover.

Discovery was the return-to-flight orbiter in 1988, and though the shuttle was still associated with a new sense of danger, people soon got used to the idea that things had been fixed. Another successful period followed, from 1988 to 2003, during which fewer missions flew, many of them devoted to delivering components of the International

Space Station. The overly ambitious pace of the early eighties had been found to be partly to blame for *Challenger,* so the idea of making the shuttle pay for itself was officially abandoned.

As the oldest of the orbiters, *Columbia* was a bit heavier than the others—it missed out on a technological breakthrough involving stronger and lighter alloys—and as a result *Columbia* somehow always seemed bumbly, a chunky older sister forever dropping crumpled tissues from her sleeves. The fact that in coming years *Columbia* had a disproportionate number of delays compared to the others did nothing to contradict that dundering image.

Because they were lighter, *Challenger* and *Discovery* were always the ones to fly high-profile missions taking heavy and important cargo to space. *Columbia* became, unofficially, the science-mission orbiter. Predictable, reliable, unadventurous. It doesn't seem right, then, that *Columbia* was the one that gave way to structural weakness, the heat of reentry sneaking itself between the tiles and pulling the ship apart over Texas on February 1, 2003, killing all seven crew members aboard. Debris was strewn across three states.

Maybe losing *Challenger* taught us how to say good-bye to space shuttles and their crews. Or maybe it was because the terrorist attacks of 2001 fell in between, forever readjusting our scale of horror. Either way, there was much less fanfare, much less hand-wringing, when we lost *Columbia.* *Challenger*'s disaster had been so dramatic, breaking up visibly in the sky during launch, during those two minutes when everyone was watching, tracking the bird through the clear Florida sky. Far fewer people turn out to watch landings; far fewer people were there with their faces turned up expectantly for *Columbia.* Even for those who were there, the only sign of *Columbia*'s demise was its absence. *Columbia* was supposed to land that morning, and simply did not.

Norman Mailer says of the Apollo astronauts, operating with the risk of their own deaths, "Like all good professional athletes, they had the modesty of knowing you could be good and still lose." He was fascinated with the possibility of Neil Armstrong and Buzz Aldrin dying on the moon. On the one hand, the loneliness of that final resting place was terrifying to contemplate; on the other, Mailer considered the prospect of the souls rising—as so many who have had near-death experiences describe—rising faster, more cleanly than those earthbound, into a "transpostmortal insertion to the stars."

As with *Challenger,* an investigation followed. Sally Ride became the only person to serve on the investigation boards for both *Challenger* and *Columbia.* As was expected, the *Columbia* Accident Investigation Board (CAIB, pronounced "cabe" by insiders) found that the immediate cause of the disaster was a chunk of foam falling onto the tiles and that the organizational cause was a pattern of dismissing problems too easily, the "normalization of deviance" as Diane Vaughan put it so memorably in her study of *Challenger.* When a shuttle flew with a known issue and came back safely, the tendency among managers was to assume that the issue was not in fact a risk, using the previous success as "evidence." "Try playing Russian roulette that way," Richard Feynman remarked after *Challenger.* CAIB found that after a short period of vigilance, the same error of thinking had crept back into NASA decision making. The board stated in the report that "the causes of the institutional failure responsible for *Challenger* have not been fixed."

The return-to-flight mission after *Columbia* was on *Discovery,* as the return-to-flight mission had been after *Challenger.* This one was commanded by Eileen Collins, the first woman to command a shuttle mission and one of only two women ever to do so. I remember seeing the front page of the newspaper the second day of that *Discovery* mission; a large color photograph showed the full black underside of *Discovery* pointed at a satellite to have its tiles examined, a new protocol demanded by CAIB. The tiles were found to be undamaged, and *Discovery* returned home safely, as has every shuttle to fly since then.

I keep thinking that *The Dream Is Alive* was a portrait of the space shuttle at its most hope-filled, and it is. But when I look up the date of the film's release, I discover that the earliest I possibly could have seen it was June 1985. Six months after the film came out, *Challenger* exploded and one of the film's stars, Judith Resnik, was dead. I'm not sure I ever got to enjoy this golden period of shuttle history that I've come to associate with my childhood. It may be that by the time I had any understanding of shuttle at all, *Challenger* was already lost, and that was the beginning of the end.

My students think spaceflight is cool. They are openly jealous that I got to see a launch. As we talk through the counterarguments to the hoax conspiracy theories, my students seem relieved to be able to believe in the triumphs of the heroic era; spaceflight is one of the few legends of the past they can feel an unambiguous pride in. They are saddened that shuttle is being shut down and would like to know whom to blame. Yet they misunderstand the vehicle's capabilities and estimate insanely high numbers for its cost. Will they hang on to the new numbers I have given them and a new idea that a government agency has achieved a lot with a little?

We're always being told unkind things about this generation of Millennials—that they are annoyingly attached to their devices and social networks, that their sense of entitlement leaves them without any work ethic, that their helicopter parents have made them helpless to care for themselves or others. This has not been my experience of them. Like young people of any generation, they think they are the first to experience everything. Like young people of any generation, they lack a sense of history. They are alarmingly vague about the events that seemed so earth-shattering to their elders, but so was my generation and so was my parents'. The ignorance is as unchanging as the outrage, as the belief that we were smarter when we were young. We were not. I had thought my students would have at least a sketchy idea of what their country has accomplished in space, and I had worried that they might be too cool to care about it. I was wrong on both counts. In other words, despite how much things have changed, not much has changed.

The space shuttle project never did get us any closer to Mars, but it deployed more than half the cargo ever carried to space and sent three hundred fifty-five people into orbit. Shuttle allowed repairs on satellites that could be fixed only by human hands, including repairs to the Hubble Space Telescope, an instrument that has changed our view of the universe. Shuttle pieced together the International Space Station bit by bit over twelve years and carried thousands of experiments small and large for investigators ranging from National Science Foundation–backed scientists to elementary school children. The ISS alone is cited by many space advocates as having made the whole shuttle project worthwhile. The orbiting laboratory has been occupied nonstop since November 2, 2000—in other words, November 2000 was the last time all human beings were on the surface of the earth at once.

Is $209 billion a lot of money for the entire space shuttle program, or too little? Is 0.4 percent of the national budget way too much for NASA, or way too little? In comparing the two eras of American spaceflight, I've heard it said that Apollo was a mission in search of a vehicle while the space shuttle was a vehicle in search of a mission. This comparison is generally meant to be at the expense of the space shuttle, though I have never understood why shuttle has to suffer from the observation. Or rather, assuming that the comparison is an insult to shuttle reveals the speaker to be a heroic-era space fan who values "firsts" over all else. My parents' generation tends to take it as an article of faith that setting a goal ("let's go to the moon") and then slapping together an odd-looking agglomeration of incredibly expensive single-use components to reach that goal was inherently cooler than designing a reusable and upgradable space vehicle from the ground up. Fewer people grasp the achievement of shuttle, suitable for many possible uses, some of which had not yet been dreamed of when *Columbia* was first being assembled.

Consider that the people who know best how to feel about the space shuttle might be the people who worked on it every day. I have heard spaceworkers call the shuttle "a magnificent space vehicle," "an elegant space plane," "the most complex human invention ever built," and "the most beautiful thing I've ever seen." I have always wondered whether the space shuttle's workaday name robs it of some of the wonder it deserves. A "shuttle" is what you take from an economy parking lot to an airport terminal, not a beautiful machine. A name pulled from mythology, like Mercury, Gemini, or Apollo, might have better told us how to feel about it.

At any rate, the people who knew the shuttles best, the workers at Kennedy, tend to talk about individual orbiters and call them by name—they know what was accomplished by *Endeavour*, what was accomplished by *Discovery*. They believe these spacecraft are the best things that have ever flown, and they are proud to have helped make them fly.

The ground trembled. . . . These artificial clouds unrolled their thick spirals to a height of 1,000 yards into the air. A savage, wandering somewhere beyond the limits of the horizon, might have believed that some new crater was forming in the bosom of Florida, although there was neither any eruption, nor typhoon, nor storm, nor struggle of the elements, nor any of those terrible phenomena which nature is capable of producing. No, it was man alone who had produced these reddish vapors, these gigantic flames worthy of a volcano itself, these tremendous vibrations resembling the shock of an earthquake, these reverberations rivaling those of hurricanes and storms; and it was his hand which precipitated into an abyss, dug by himself, a whole Niagara of molten metal!

—Jules Verne, *From the Earth to the Moon*, 1865

CHAPTER 5. Good-bye, *Endeavour*

STS-134: May 16, 2011

On May 16, 2011, nearly three months after the launch of *Discovery*, my phone alarms me out of sleep at 4:00 a.m. I wake and wonder where I am for a few seconds in this strange room with its cheap slick bedspread, its seventies-era brown color scheme, a smell of cheap air freshener barely covering cigarette smoke, faint mildew, and underneath that, the salt of the ocean.

This is the Clarion Hotel in Merritt Island, Florida, the place Omar told me about last time. I haul myself out of bed, turn on the TV, and start dressing and organizing my things by its light. Like Norman Mailer before me, I have had only two hours of sleep before heading to the Space Center. I did not create this similarity on purpose, but I decide to embrace it. Sleep deprivation, like waiting itself, is part of the launch experience. I check the status of the launch: the countdown is continuing, and the weather is 70 percent go. It's now T minus five hours.

This mission had been set for April 19 when I was here last for *Discovery*, but that date had changed to April 29 because of a conflict with a Russian trip to the International Space Station. I did not want the launch date to be April 29. I was scheduled to be at a conference at NASA Headquarters in Washington, DC, a meeting of space historians I had managed to worm my way into by proposing a paper months before. As the date approached, I kept one eye on the calendar, hoping the launch attempt would slip. I told people I "had a feeling" the launch would be postponed, but what I meant by that was I hoped very much that it would be. I hassled Omar constantly about how things were looking and whether it still seemed the 29th would be the day. He replied diplomatically each time—this launch had already slipped multiple times, which made it seem entirely likely that it would slip again, but we couldn't know what would happen until it was announced.

When April 29 stayed on the launch manifest for a while, and especially when the mission passed its flight readiness review, I panicked. On the 27th, I headed off to the space history conference in DC, thinking maybe I could write about going to two of the three last launches. Maybe my missing the last launch of *Endeavour* could somehow be smoothed over, or made into some sort of metaphor. Maybe there was a way, rhetorically, to make that work. I was going to have to think of one because I couldn't miss the conference, and I also had no intention of abandoning this last-launch project.

The conference in DC, titled "1961/1981: Key Moments in Human Spaceflight," was cosponsored by NASA and the Smithsonian National Air and Space Museum. According to the call for papers I had stumbled across on the NASA website, the conference was meant to "bring together scholars, practitioners, and the interested public to consider the place of human spaceflight in modern culture." I liked the idea of parlaying my obsession with sixties writers' treatments of spaceflight into a chance to visit NASA Headquarters, meet space historians, and learn more about the history of the space program. A few months earlier I'd considered myself something of an expert on the subject. Now I was only learning how much I didn't know, and that made me want to meet the people who knew more.

NASA Headquarters is noticeably different from the other NASA sites I had visited. It is a normal-looking office building in downtown DC rather than an outsized experimental and training facility (Houston) or a spaceport (Kennedy). On the first morning of the conference, NASA administrator Charles Bolden addressed us, and while his speech mostly consisted of general remarks about the importance of history, of understanding where we have been in order to envision where we are going next, he also told a story about meeting President Obama not long before that made me sit up in my seat.

"I stood in the Oval Office," Bolden told the assembled attendees, "stood square in front of the president, and I asked him, 'Mr. President, do you believe in human spaceflight?'"

It was a bit thrilling, the idea of the NASA administrator, a former astronaut himself, going toe to toe with the president of the United States. Not long ago, the idea that both men in this dialogue would be African American would have sounded unbelievable.

"And the president looked me in the eye, and he said, 'Yes, I do.'"

We all clapped furiously. This is a great NASA administrator anecdote in the way it implies a faith in spaceflight, an intention to move forward, without any actual commitment or, especially, budget. But even we space historians and space curators and scholars of many disciplines, we who should know better than anyone, seem to lack any built-in resistance to this anecdote. We want very much for General Bolden to have confronted the president, want very much for the president to have confirmed his commitment to human spaceflight, even if we haven't seen much evidence of that.

During the two days of the conference, I went to as many presentations as I could, gave my own paper on representations of spaceflight in literature, and met many of the historians whose work I had been reading. On the last day, I got up early to catch my flight home. I spent the day in airports, obsessively refreshing the NASA app on my phone, hoping to get some news of the *Endeavour* launch. I learned that Gabrielle Giffords had made the trip from Houston and would be watching from the roof of the Launch Control Center. President Obama had come to Cape Canaveral with his family, and they too would be atop Launch Control. Still, I hoped for a scrub, ideally a long delay that would buy me some time to finish my semester and get final grades in. At 12:20 p.m. I got my wish: problems had been discovered with the auxiliary power unit fuel line heater. Hundreds of thousands of people, including the president and his family, left the Cape in disappointment.

Launch was rescheduled for No Earlier Than May 2, then May 8, then May 10. In the coming week, the target launch date slipped again to May 16 at 8:56 a.m., then held there. I started to make tentative plans.

On the morning of the 15th, the day I made the drive from Knoxville, I got a weather update from Omar by text: Weather is good, 70% chance acceptable.

I smiled down at my phone, was about to start tapping out a response, when I got another text:

My grandpa came into town, he may not come tomorrow cause it's so early, so today he said he'd let me know if he's coming with us. If he's not then you're in. Sorry it's so last minute

Grandpa? As far as I knew, all of Omar's extended family was in Puerto Rico, so this grandpa must have come a long way, and unless he was planning to come back in a couple of months, this was going to be Grandpa's last chance to see a space shuttle launch. None of this boded very well for my chances of getting in to the employee viewing site, and I began making peace with the fact that I would probably be watching from a public spot, maybe Space View Park in Titusville this time. Maybe Omar could get me in for the last one.

I drove all day. This time, I had a sense of how long seven hundred miles would take, and I knew what I-75 had to offer. As with my last trip here, I kept thinking I should listen to audiobooks and return phone calls, but once I was in motion I remembered how pleasant it was to let my mind go blank. I ate junk food and drank sugary drinks all day, listened to music for many long miles. There's something pleasing about the accomplishment of the miles ticking by on my odometer by the hundreds, seeing the changing landscape pass with the day. An unusual sense of satisfaction in getting out of my car in a state different from the one in which I climbed into it, finding palm trees, birds, and bugs, finding the land has a different smell, the air grown humid. The sun high in the sky at a truck stop outside Atlanta, then the sky washed with pink as the sun starts to dip at a gas station south of Cordele.

In the evening, I was eating dinner at a Cracker Barrel in Valdosta and reading a book about the Apollo project when my phone buzzed. Omar.

Ok you're in!

Alone at my table with my pancakes, I clapped my hands over my mouth, then smiled at the truckers seated around me. Some of them smiled politely back.

Text you bout when to meet later. Gonna be eeeaaarrrlly

I texted Omar back that I would be wherever he wanted me to be, at whatever time.

This turned out to be his parents' house, at quarter to five in the morning.

I was going to get onto NASA grounds.

When I pull into Omar's neighborhood before dawn, I switch off my headlights so as not to wake his neighbors. The houses are like the ones I took pictures of when I was researching my novel—square one-story houses with tiny yards and big swimming pools. Before I can ring the bell, Omar's dog senses me and starts barking. Then Omar steps out wordlessly into the dark, looking as tired as I feel. We get into my car and head north.

Since I was here last, an engineer named James Vanover committed suicide by jumping from the gantry at pad 39A, where *Endeavour* was being prepared for launch. Like many employees of long standing, Vanover had been offered an early retirement package. Many considered this preferable to taking their chances waiting to be laid off, as nearly everyone at Kennedy will be eventually. Vanover had accepted the offer, then reconsidered and tried to revoke his decision but was told he could not; he would have to leave NASA. James Vanover had worked on the space shuttle project since 1982. I didn't ask Omar, when I first read about the death, whether he knew Vanover—I figured it might be more appropriate to ask in person. Now, sitting beside him at quarter to five in the morning, I know I won't. It's only a twenty-minute drive to the main gate of the Kennedy Space Center; we pass the DAYS TO LAUNCH sign, which now bears the huge white numeral 0.

At the south gate to the Kennedy Space Center, we show a guard our papers, and he leans in to greet us, smiling. After he waves us through, we drive through miles of darkened tropics, alive with insects even in the dark. We reach an intersection clogged with vehicles. A trail of red brake lights ahead of us marks a string of stopped cars. Guards are holding up traffic in both directions.

"It's the astronauts," Omar tells me, as if this were no big deal. We see a string of helicopters fly overhead along the road from west to east, after which a convoy of vehicles comes down the road, mostly dark SUVs. At the convoy's midpoint: an old silver Airstream trailer emblazoned with the NASA logo. I know this vehicle from pictures and movies—all space fans do. It's the Astrovan, carrying the astronauts from their crew quarters to the launch pad. Six people are going to space today.

Once the Astrovan has passed, Omar and I continue on. We pull into the parking lot of the Headquarters Building, one of the many nondescript low-slung midsixties office buildings at the Kennedy Space Center, where we wait, idling in the dark, for Omar's father to emerge. The parking lot is full, even at this hour. I've been hearing about Frank for a long time but have not yet met him, and I'm curious what he'll be like. Before too long we see a figure emerge from the main entrance and approach us.

Like all mechanical engineers, Frank dresses neatly—a polo shirt, khakis, tidy hair, and glasses. As we transfer our stuff to Frank's SUV, Omar makes the introductions. Frank is as friendly as his son, but he seems unsure what to make of me, a married woman his son met on the Internet, traveling alone with vague plans to write about the end of shuttle, about the end of his life's work.

We park in a field of grass pressed into service as a parking lot. As I circle around the back of the SUV, I notice that Frank has a special license plate with an image of the space shuttle on it that says CHALLENGER · COLUMBIA across the bottom. We carry lawn chairs and tripods to the viewing area; the Vehicle Assembly Building, as it always does, looms over everything. We settle in for the wait—T minus three hours.

When I ask Frank about his work, he is reticent at first, as engineers tend to be when they are talking to nonengineers. He gives simple, nontechnical answers to my questions: *I've worked on the main engines and on procedures for tanking fuels.* I know from Omar that Frank has been in Launch Control for a number of launches, including *Challenger*'s last, and part of me wants to ask him about that: *At what point did you realize something had gone wrong? How did you feel when you realized the astronauts were dead?* Instead I ask him about the more mundane aspects of his work.

I've found that all it usually takes to draw out an engineer is to ask a couple of technical questions and then remain calm while listening to the answers. Most people tend to take on a blank, frightened look as soon as they realize that a technical explanation is under way; if you can resist giving this reaction and simply listen, your engineer will open up and tell you everything you ever wanted to know.

Soon Frank is telling me about the complexities of tanking cryogenic gases, the leak check procedures he developed. His eyes light up as he tells me an anecdote about erratic readings on a mass spectrometer. With some prodding, Frank describes to me the first shuttle launch, a test flight of *Columbia*. The launch had been delayed for months and years as unexpected problems with the shuttle system emerged and branched into multiple new problems, some of which Frank helped to solve. Now, finally, the day had arrived when the shuttle was ready to take to the sky. He had been given a pass to watch from the Turn Basin site, but security was so lax in those days that he drove his family all the way up to the VAB, and held one-year-old baby Omar up to the horizon, trying in vain to interest him in the show.

Like Omar and everyone else I've met here, Frank has nothing negative to say about the decision to end the shuttle program, about NASA, or about his own work here. If he is upset that the spacecraft he's spent his life working on is being mothballed before its time, he will not betray a hint of that disappointment—at least, not to me, not today.

T minus two hours. Omar and I go for a walk. This area is known as the Turn Basin site because it edges up against a human-made body of water known as the Turn Basin, an extension of the Banana River that allows the external tanks to be delivered by barge directly to the Vehicle Assembly Building. Attached to the VAB is the Launch Control Center, the building where I saw the mission patches with the missing dates on Family Day. It's a building with huge windows facing the launchpads, the building from which launch directors and their teams of engineers have controlled every launch since Apollo 4 in 1967. On the roof of the Launch Control Center is the viewing area where the astronauts' families gather for launches. Since *Challenger,* the families have been removed from the general spectators—never again will the deaths of astronauts play out on the faces of their families on the front pages of newspapers. This morning, Gabrielle Giffords is sitting up there with the other crew families to see her husband launch into space. Omar has heard that she is in a wheelchair, wearing a helmet to protect her head because her skull has not been entirely rebuilt, and that she is sitting behind a privacy curtain so no one takes pictures of her in this state.

Down here at the Turn Basin, there is a set of bleachers, but most people have brought lawn chairs or blankets to sit on for the wait. It's still full dark, and generators roar to maintain floodlights. A few children run around; others sleep in their parents' laps. Some people line up for the snack truck and to look over the offerings at a mobile gift shop offering souvenirs. I've noticed that space vendors are extremely effective at anticipating and meeting any possible demand for space-related swag—T-shirts, hats, pins, postcards, plush toys—including on this field of grass early on a Monday morning.

T minus one hour. Once we are settled in lawn chairs with our coffee, I ask Frank, "How many of the space shuttle launches have you seen?"

He pauses modestly for a moment.

"All of them," he answers.

"*All* of them?"

He nods. "Well, I live nearby. And I work here, so it's not too hard."

Sure, but—*all* of them? One hundred and thirty-four, as of today. Night launches, day launches, scrubbed launches, delayed launches. Launches in 100-degree weather, launches in mosquito season, and launches that require spectators to get up in the middle of the night only to wait for hours. Launches called off at the last second before liftoff due to weather or mechanical problems, single missions that took a half dozen attempts to get off the ground. *Challenger*'s last was one of these.

It occurs to me that if I were a different sort of person I would really dig in now. I would ask him what the space shuttle means to him, how he feels about this era coming to an end. But I don't press. Neither did Norman Mailer, incidentally—he only rarely reports asking a direct question of a specific person. We could chalk this up to laziness, or to an understanding of the linguistic banalities and evasions of astronauts and scientists. Or it may be squeamishness about asking people to reveal emotions they may not have revealed to their spouses, or even to themselves. Frank Izquierdo has dedicated his professional life to the space shuttle. It is his life's work, his family history, his migration story. Like Ponce de León, Frank Izquierdo made the trip from Puerto Rico to Florida knowing this place would become his new home. He knew this was the place where his children would be born, the site of his life's work. Whatever he feels deep in his heart about the end of this project, I feel certain he wouldn't tell me even if I asked.

Instead, I ask him more about something he'd mentioned earlier, about how he developed procedures to check for leaks during fueling.

"When I first got here, I spent a lot of time talking to the engineers who had worked on the Saturn Vs. The hardware wasn't exactly the same, but they still had a lot of experience that helped me."

I express surprise that Apollo engineers were still around in the space shuttle era, considering the long lag between projects.

"Oh, sure. We called them the graybeards. They stayed around to pass on what they had learned firsthand. It was crucial for us to be able to get their input on things. Saved us a lot of trial and error."

"I think it's too bad," I say cautiously, "that you won't be able to pass on your knowledge to the people who come along to design the next thing." I'm reminded of instances of lost knowledge in history—a civilization inventing a device, or navigating an ocean, or curing a disease, and then forgetting how, leaving their descendants to struggle through it all over again, sometimes multiple times. The truth is that Frank's generation of space workers will very likely be retired, moved away, or gone from this earth by the time the next big spaceflight project is under way, if there is one at all. In computing the costs of a huge engineering project, the cost of this loss is hard to quantify— the cost of knowledge hard-won over a lifetime that could have been passed on to another generation and won't be. This is maybe the biggest waste of all, bigger than the waste of the orbiters themselves, which everyone agrees still have useful life left in them. And it cheats Frank out of the engineer's great love: explaining to others the things he has figured out.

Frank nods. "Yeah, it's too bad," he says lightly, as if a waiter has told him the restaurant has run out of his first choice of entrée.

We watch our phones and listen to our radios and wait.

As the sun starts to come up, Omar mentions that his girlfriend, Karen, is making her way over to join us. She came in on another Turn Basin pass with a bunch of friends in an RV. I've been hearing Omar talk about Karen for a while now—she was on base when I was here for Family Day back in September, but on that occasion, too, she was bringing in a carful of friends on her own badge and we never quite managed to be in the same place at the same time. Karen is a space-worker like Omar, which makes sense; the job seems to be so demanding, and Merritt Island such a company town, it's hard to imagine how spaceworkers could hope to meet anyone any other way. Karen works in the same position as Omar; other than that, I don't know much about her except that she owns and rides horses. Omar often posts pictures of the horses' antics on Facebook.

When Karen makes her way over to us, I see that she is in her early thirties, about Omar's age, with sandy blond hair and tanned skin. She's friendly, but a little more reserved than Omar. We shake hands, and I'm relieved to see that she seems relaxed around me. I wondered at first how she would feel about her boyfriend spending time with me when I'm here and keeping in touch with me when I'm not. But as I've gotten to know Omar, it's become clear that he has a lot of friends of both genders and that neither of them think that's a problem. While Frank and Omar work on setting up their cameras, Karen and I chat about the weather and chances for launch today. She tells me about her photography hobby—she likes to take pictures of the shuttles and facilities here. She flips through some of her favorites on her iPad, and I tell her she has a great eye for color and proportion. The shuttle and its gantries are in many of the images, of course, but many of her photographs feature the wildlife here. This place is a photographer's dream. After a while, Karen goes back to the RV to watch the launch with her friends. We're getting close to T minus nine, and it's time to choose our final viewing sites.

Endeavour was built to replace *Challenger*, largely from spare parts, making it the only orbiter that would not have existed if not for the destruction of another. As such it is the youngest orbiter, and when it is retired after this mission it will have flown twenty-five flights to *Discovery*'s thirty-nine and *Atlantis*'s thirty-three. Like *Discovery*, *Endeavour* was named after one of the ships in Captain James Cook's eighteenth-century fleet, and the British spelling came with it. *En-deavour*'s odd name and complicated origins set it apart from the others, as does its relative youth. Though it's been flying for eighteen years and has some high-profile accomplishments to its credit (it flew the first Hubble servicing mission and the first mission to assemble the International Space Station), *Endeavour* still seems a new and slightly peculiar addition to the family—a quirky cousin from another country, a foreign exchange student with a strange accent.

I'd thought seeing *Endeavour* launch from the Turn Basin site, watching it with the NASA workers and their families, might be even more jubilant than what I experienced on the causeway with *Discovery*. But I should have guessed from my talks with Frank and Omar that the reaction here would be more subdued. There are very few first-timers; everyone here knows how to watch a launch. At T minus sixty seconds, Omar and Frank take the lens caps off their cameras and recheck the shots they had lined up. They both take deep breaths, plant their weight squarely on both feet, then look behind them to make sure they aren't blocking my view.

"It's cloudy," Omar frets. He's seen launches called off this late due to weather.

But at T minus six seconds, the main engines light up, exactly as they are meant to, and at zero, *Endeavour* begins to rise.

The light emanating from a space shuttle launch is different in color, quality, and intensity from any other kind of light. Photographs and videos can only approximate it, can only serve as a souvenir to the odd sensation, the combination of beauty and near-painfulness of that specific brightness in the sky. And this launch of *Endeavour* is the brightest I've seen so far, in part because this is closer than I've ever been, but partly because a low blanket of cloud cover bounces the light back at us. And the sound—the engine's roar is deep and loud, satisfyingly rumbly.

People around us cheer. A woman to my right shouts her encouragement: "Go! Go!" Frank, Omar, and I stand and watch silently, the light and the noise and the vibration pressing back against us. None of us cheers, none of us cries. We watch it go up and up for about fifteen seconds; then it punches through the opaque cloud cover and is not seen again. A few minutes later, we discover that people in airplanes were startled to see *Endeavour* emerge on their side of the clouds. Their pictures show up on Twitter before we leave the Turn Basin.

Later in the day, we also learn that Gabrielle Giffords, from her vantage point atop Launch Control, reported that her overwhelming emotion was relief when her husband and his crew achieved orbit.

Good-bye, *Endeavour*.

When *Endeavour* is gone, we admire the steam trail it leaves behind. One thing I had never known to expect before experiencing space shuttle launches in person: the steam trail itself is an unusual object in the sky, a solid-looking vertical fluffy sculpture, and for the few or many minutes it lingers, depending on the speed and direction of the wind, spectators like to observe it and discuss its quirky behavior, the unearthly shadows it casts.

Frank and Omar set about dismantling their tripods while I pack up the lawn chairs. The steam trail remains, but we are keen to get to the car and beat some of the traffic. On our way through the parking area, we pass a family wearing matching T-shirts that read THANK YOU SHUTTLE! AMERICA'S WINGS TO THE FUTURE. We pass a car with a custom license plate that reads NDEAVR. Seated in Frank's Suburban, we creep forward in a flood of other cars.

Outside the gates of the Space Center, we see mom-and-pop souvenir shops displaying GO ENDEAVOUR signs. We pass a McDonald's with an enormous space shuttle mockup on its Playland structure. Banks, nail salons, more palm trees. A roadside vendor with a pile of cantaloupe displays a hastily hand-lettered sign: SPACE MELONS.

The people who live in these towns around the Space Center have known for a long time now that the space shuttle is coming to an end. No one I've met down here will speak a word of self-pity, or any regret over having devoted their lives to the project of sending people to space. To an individual, they are positive about their time with NASA and positive about the future.

But this region is called the Space Coast for a reason. Before NASA chose Cape Canaveral as its moon port, almost no one lived here. Cocoa Beach, Florida, for instance, saw a 1,000 percent increase in population between 1950 and 1960. This region does not seem to offer any other way to support the thousands of people who work at the space center or who depend on the business of those workers and the tourists the launches bring, the many thousands who have migrated here over decades, generations. These are people who know how to do one thing, and do it very well: maintain and fly a fleet of spacecraft. Some spaceworkers, when they're feeling sanguine, offer each other the analogy of the seventies—the people who didn't give up and stuck around for the eight-year lapse, Frank's graybeards, were the ones who got the chance to work on shuttle. But in that situation there was already another spacecraft in the works; it had already been designed, and its funding approved, before the end of Apollo. Spaceworkers in 2011 who say they want to wait for the next era of spaceflight are not only going to wait for a spacecraft to become operational, as the spaceworkers in the seventies did; they are also waiting for it to be fully funded. How much longer than eight years might that take?

———————————————

Frank goes back to work for the day; Omar and I have breakfast at a Steak 'n Shake. As always, there is a festive atmosphere in the packed restaurants right after the launch, a patriotic and fun-loving common cause. People smile and make eye contact when we recognize each other by sunburn and memorabilia.

A lot of people are wearing bright red T-shirts from the Visitor Complex gift shop commemorating the last launches that say: I WAS THERE. The hard-core space fans who have been here before, the people who are now showing up for a launch because it will soon be too late, the only vaguely interested who came along but have now caught the fever and wear the lovesick look of the newly converted. All of us are already anticipating a moment when all this will be in the past, will be a chapter in history. The risk, the messiness, the work, the specific brightness of the fire from the main engines, the way its sound bounced off the VAB and back at us—all this will be robbed of its reality. *I was there.* We are already preparing ourselves to tell the next generation, those who will doubt whether any of this happened, those who are bored and don't care, that we saw it with our own eyes.

As we are finishing our eggs, I tell Omar about how Norman Mailer said the Vehicle Assembly Building is the ugliest building in the world from the outside and the most beautiful from the inside. I think Omar will find this interesting because he spends a lot of his time inside the VAB. But he looks confused.

"You mean, the other way around?" he tries to correct me. Omar tells me how dirty and disused certain areas of the VAB are, areas I didn't see on Family Day, that have sat empty or been pressed into service as storage since Apollo.

"I think he means when you just walk in and look up for the first time," I explain. I don't mention that I wept when I walked in there myself, that I stayed several paces behind him and the others so they wouldn't see.

"I guess I can see that," Omar concedes.

We drink our coffee and compare the photos in our cameras, and I decide not to bring up my theory that, though the VAB was designed with nothing but function in mind, its form reflects with utter clarity the purity of its ambitions. That sometimes out at the edges of human expression it's hard to tell whether what you're looking at is ugly or beautiful, stupid or brilliant.

When we finish eating and go outside, the cloud cover has cleared and the sun seems too bright, as if someone has turned it up beyond the point that cloudlessness and proximity to the equator can logically provide. The Florida sun often seems this way to me, and I keep thinking I'll get used to it. Instead, I am always squinting, despite my sunglasses, and always manage to get a sunburn through the SPF 50 I copiously reapply throughout my days here.

Omar has to go to work for the rest of the day, so we hug and say our good-byes until the launch of *Atlantis,* the last one, in the summer. I will head back to Knoxville at first light.

I go back to my hotel and take a nap. When I wake up again I have the weird feeling that this is the real morning, that the predawn events never happened, that I never woke and dressed and went to the Kennedy Space Center and witnessed a spacecraft leaving the earth with six astronauts aboard and then ate eggs and toast with my friend Omar. These memories all seem weak, provisional, like the trailing details of a dream that you won't remember if you don't tell them to someone. It makes me panicky. I get into my car and drive back to the Barnes & Noble, where I sit in the café section with a giant coffee and scribble frantic notes until the store closes. I have to write down what I've seen today before it slips away.

Within a few hours, Omar has uploaded his video of the launch to YouTube and posted a link on Facebook. It makes me a bit self-conscious of my own postmodernity to take a break from writing my impressions of the launch in one app in order to watch Omar's video of the same event in another.

At first the video shows a nondescript shot of horizon with a little bit of gantry and a little bit of a pole from a satellite uplink van, with the squiggly cord tracing its length. If you know where to look, you can see the tip of the launch vehicle next to the gantry, the tip of the external tank tinged gray-orange, while everything around it is misty gray. The overcast sky makes everything flat and boring. No people are visible, a minor miracle given how many spectators were out there this morning, and given that Omar and his father didn't make any particular effort to get their equipment up above everyone else's heads. They would never do that, I know, as doing so would be inconsiderate of the spectators standing behind them.

Soon after the video starts, Omar's voice can be heard saying, "Thirty-nine seconds." He must have seen this on his phone; no NASA announcer can be heard. Around his voice, lots of people chatter. When I press my earbuds hard into my ears, I think I can hear my own voice speaking to Frank, then laughing—but I can't be sure it's me.

Then I hear Omar talking quietly, and at first I can't make it out but then I do: "Let me get out of your way, there." I remember the moment: he's talking to me. He hadn't been standing in my way at all, of course.

The camera's frame starts to shake subtly. Then a steam cloud starts to emerge above the trees. The main engines have ignited. The voices of the crowd start to lift, hesitantly—they aren't sure at first whether they are seeing what they think they are seeing. But then the tip of the external tank starts to rise, to separate itself from the gantry. Within a few seconds, it's lifted itself far enough that we can see the whole of the launch vehicle rising in the air—external tank, *Endeavour,* the twin solid rocket boosters, and the impossibly bright light emerging from beneath the stack. The steam cloud spreads itself majestically underneath, and soon *Endeavour* is gone, has disappeared past the top of the camera's frame. The bright plume continues behind it, fading into the ever-fattening steam column that billows up beneath it. The camera does not tilt up to follow *Endeavour* into the sky; Omar has told me that he prefers to use a fixed camera on a tripod to catch the start of the launch, but that he wants to be able to watch it himself rather than trying to follow it squinting through a viewfinder. This makes sense to me. The launch will be thoroughly photographed and filmed from every angle by professionals with better equipment. The people who come out here to see it in person, I agree, should experience it with their own eyes.

In Omar's video, the crowd lifts their voices, sounding a little incredulous, then a little frantic, as though it is their enthusiasm and nothing else keeping *Endeavour* on its path straight up. I watch the video, leaning in to my laptop, then watch a few more clips that YouTube suggests based on that page, different views of the same launch, some from professionals working for NASA TV or for news outlets, some shot by amateurs. Omar's appears to be the only amateur video shot from the Turn Basin, at least so far.

I remember how, when I was here for the last launch of *Discovery* in February, the video that Omar had shot from the VAB parking lot filled me with envy. But now, in a weird way, this video makes me feel envious too, even though I was there with him, was standing right at Omar's elbow, right at the camera's vantage point, as this video was being made. There is something about the way the video fixes the event in a frame that makes it possible to understand it, describe it, in a way I haven't quite been able to for any of the three launches I've now seen in person. Somehow, the lived experience is prone to slippage, confusion, interference from the thoughts and recollections passing through my mind and the distractions—the people all around with their irrelevant sounds and expressions. The way things smelled, a sudden gust of wind. All of the things I could see and half-see beyond the narrow scope of the camera's frame. I watch Omar's video over and over. And while I wouldn't trade, for anything, the experience of being out there this morning, I'm also aware that I wasn't really able to *describe* this launch, to understand what makes it different from the others, until I could watch *this* version, the version anyone with Internet access can see, that dozens already have seen, all over the world.

The next morning, I drive home to Knoxville. There is only one shuttle launch left.

> [There must be] some secret pleasure taken in the magnified luxury of treating all the workers at the Space Center to the pleasure of watching their mighty moonship edge along the horizon from morning to dusk, or even more spectacularly at night, with lanterns in the rigging, like a ghost galleon of the Caribbean! The beginning of the trip to the moon was as slow as the fall of the fullest flake of snow.
>
> —Norman Mailer, *Of a Fire on the Moon*

CHAPTER 6. A Brief History of Spacefarers

STS-135 Rollout: May 31, 2011

When the Kennedy Space Center was constructed, it was with the knowledge that incredibly large objects, skyscraper-sized objects, were going to have to be moved about the landscape like children's toys by some means that had yet to be invented. The Mercury rockets had been simply set to vertical at their launchpads on Cape Canaveral, but the new facilities for the Apollo project were going to have to be more elaborate. First of all, the moon rockets would need to be assembled indoors, and that indoor space, which was the Vehicle Assembly Building, had to be separated from the launchpads by at least three miles for the disconcerting reason that an explosion at the launchpad would destroy everything within that radius; NASA managers understandably hoped to minimize the losses in case of such a disaster. But this separation of three miles between assembly building and launch pad meant that the assembled Apollo-Saturn, a spacecraft taller than the Statue of Liberty, would somehow have to be moved across three miles and up a steep incline, an unimaginable engineering challenge. The world's most powerful ground vehicle would have to be invented, and it would have to be capable of keeping the enormous spacecraft perfectly level. The vehicle that resulted, the crawler transporter, is one of the components of the space program that would be remarkable on its own but can disappear among the other astounding and record-setting innovations that surround it.

The crawler transporters survived the transition between Apollo and shuttle. In the shuttle era, the space shuttle launch vehicle is assembled atop a mobile launch platform, the enormous metal structure we saw in the VAB on Family Day eight months ago. The presence of the word *mobile* in the name is misleading; the platform looks like an oil rig, like a building, like a permanent structure that isn't going anywhere. Each one weighs 8.2 million pounds by itself, 11 million pounds with a space shuttle assembled on it, even more once the shuttle's external tank is filled with fuel. Once the shuttle is stacked on the MLP, the crawler transporter slides up underneath the platform and shrugs the entire stack up onto its shoulders before rolling it out to the launchpad three miles away.

For the first rollout at Kennedy, for Apollo 4 in 1967, spaceworkers were encouraged to bring their families to see the show. Rollouts have sometimes been open to workers and their guests, but they haven't always been big events, since they often took place in the middle of the night and were not well lit. This year, with the end of the program in sight, NASA has started inviting workers to bring their families again and has brought out massive spotlights to make the stack visible. Tonight I'll be among them for the last rollout in shuttle history.

It's only been fifteen days since the launch of *Endeavour,* which is still on orbit and is due to land tonight at 2:35 a.m. In the meantime, *Atlantis* has been mated with its external tank and solid rocket boosters for its last flight; this process takes place in the VAB, a dramatic ballet of engineering in which the orbiter is hoisted up into the air using a crane built into the ceiling, then lowered with incredible delicacy onto the external tank. Omar was there in the VAB to see the stacking process, which takes eight to ten hours. Tonight the assembled vehicle will roll out of the building and out to the launchpad. Omar has invited me to join him and his father and some friends for yet another "last." After checking with my husband, I'd agreed and flown out.

On launch days, hundreds of thousands of people show up and vie with one another for hotel rooms, seats in restaurants, and launch viewing sites, but today will be different. Rollouts are open only to NASA employees and their families, so my visit will not coincide with the visits of hundreds of thousands of other tourists; I'm getting to see the Space Coast as it is most of the time for the people who live here. Because the causeways won't be clogged with traffic, I have a wider range of options and don't have to stay on Merritt Island, at my Florida Home. Instead, I'm staying in a hotel in Cocoa Beach for the first time. A beachfront room here during an off week costs the same as the unglamorous Clarion during a launch.

This morning when I wake up in that hotel room in Cocoa Beach, I am disoriented, at first, to hear the ocean. I dress and step out onto the beach, blinking at the white-hot sun. A few families are already setting up their blankets and umbrellas and coolers and rafts and Frisbees. The surf is calm, and children are wading in to stand waist high and shriek while they splash water onto each other. Out on the horizon I can make out an enormous cruise ship, one of the many that leave from Port Canaveral on their way to the Caribbean, moving almost imperceptibly slowly. Watching it embark is like a form of meditation. I breathe in the saltwater air with my toes in the surf, snap a picture with my phone to prove I've been to a beach, then get in my car and head toward the Space Center.

I drive through Cocoa Beach along the tacky stretch of A1A. Tom Wolfe says of Cocoa Beach that it "was so Low Rent that nothing on this earth could ever change it. . . . Even the beach at Cocoa Beach was Low Rent." In stark contrast to the unspoiled green flats of the Space Center on Merritt Island, there is nothing beautiful about Cocoa Beach along A1A. Not the surreal sculpture of a surfer balancing on a concrete slab of wave, not the chain hotels done up in pastel colors, not the souvenir ships with multicolored signs advertising SHELLS (who *buys* shells?) and WOMEN'S BIKINIS (who else buys bikinis?) and BEACH TOYS and SUNSCREEN. Not the fake tiki lounges left over from the early sixties when the Mercury astronauts first came here for their training and tests and launches, those old-school crewcut astronauts who declared the Cape a "no-wives zone" and called the young women who followed them back to their motel rooms "Cape cookies."

I cross the Banana River on the 520 causeway to reach the Kennedy Space Center from the south and pass through Merritt Island. I take the turn for the Kennedy Space Center Visitor Complex. You can't miss the turn: it's marked by a life-size mockup of the space shuttle launch vehicle. The Visitor Complex boasts a museum, a rocket garden, an IMAX theater, a beautifully preserved Saturn V housed in its own hangar, a seriously well stocked gift shop, and an attraction called the Shuttle Launch Experience that I've never done because I'm always here alone and I'd feel stupid getting on an amusement ride by myself. Once you're in the Visitor Complex, you can board a bus to take a tour inside the working part of the space center, including the Vehicle Assembly Building (only as far as the parking lot) and an observation gantry overlooking the launchpads. Most tourists leave here thoroughly propagandized about spaceflight and their nation's role in it.

The Visitor Complex has become so familiar to me, I decline the map the ticket seller offers me. I know where the vintage space suits are displayed, where to find the diorama of local wildlife, where the least-used bathrooms are, where to buy ice cream without waiting in a long line. Omar has been hoping to join me after he runs some errands, but he keeps texting me about delays. Finally he decides that he won't have time to join me after all, texting me by way of explanation:

Goin to buy some hay now

Hay? It takes me a moment to remember that Omar's girlfriend, Karen, owns horses, and that Omar helps out with their care. I text him back:

21st century transport by day, 19th century transport by night

Omar's response:

Karen just LOL'd

Later, I sit on a bench in the Rocket Garden by myself, eating an ice cream cone in the beastly heat. Behind me squats the enormous silver base of the Atlas rocket, gleaming in the sun like a piece of metal sculpture. It's easy to forget, unless I look straight up, that I am sitting among rockets. Tourists swirl around me, reading the plaques and taking pictures. A tour guide, a paunchy white man in his fifties, tests his microphone and encourages visitors to gather around. A few families wander over; I remain on my bench but listen, curious. The man clears his throat loudly into his microphone, a signal that he is ready to begin.

"Welcome to the Kennedy Space Center Visitor Complex Rocket *Garden!* I would like to tell you about some of the important and historic rockets we are proud to have on display here in the Rocket *Garden!* This right here is the mighty Atlas *rocket!*" His delivery is odd, deadpan, punctuated with an emphasis at the end of each sentence, as if someone has encouraged him to vary his tone.

"The Atlas was first developed as an intercontinental ballistic *missile!* Or ICBM! Perhaps you've heard of *those!* How many of you have heard of the Atlas *rocket?*" A few uncertain hands wander up. No one wants to be called on.

"The Atlas rocket ran on a mixture of liquid oxygen and a type of kerosene known as RP-*one!* The Mercury astronauts trusted the Atlas with their lives when they climbed into their capsules perched at the top of these mighty *rockets!*" A practiced pause. I wonder whether the tour guide is paid by Delaware North, the company that runs the Visitor Complex, or whether he is a volunteer. He has the affect of an enthusiast, an evangelist.

"Can you *imagine*—!" and here he gives a gesture toward the top of the rocket, ten stories, while his gathered listeners shade their eyes against the bright Florida sun to dutifully tilt their faces up—"Can you imagine what it felt like to those seven astronauts who trusted their lives to this mighty *warrior?*"

"Four, not seven," I whisper into my ice cream. The first two Americans in space flew on Redstone rockets, not Atlas; also, one of the Mercury astronauts, Deke Slayton, had been grounded for a heart condition. That left *four* who trusted Atlas with their lives. I feel a moment's self-satisfaction—I will report to my husband later that I knew a fact this tour guide did not—but then I wonder, what kind of person takes pleasure in correcting a tour guide, even if she does so too quietly to be heard? I've kept telling myself that I'm not one of the hardcore space people, that I am somehow different from them because I'm a writer, because I would not have come here just for my own enjoyment. Maybe this was true at one point, but I'm starting to question how different I really am.

Omar has told me to be at his parents' house at 6:00 p.m. so we can head over to the rollout together in Frank's SUV. When I pull into his neighborhood, I recognize the house, the same house where I'd picked him up for the launch of *Endeavour.* On that morning it had still been dark, so I didn't get a very good look at it and hadn't gone inside. It's a small white house on a cul-de-sac. Today I park, knock on the front door, and am greeted by Omar and a small white dog who goes so insane with barking that he has to be put out back.

Inside, the house has an open floor plan, all cream-colored carpet and tile, opening out toward a pool. Omar introduces me to his mother and his grandmother. His mother, Angie, is a small dark-haired woman who smiles politely and shakes my hand, then disappears into the kitchen again. Omar has told me that his mother is not much interested in space and that she hasn't been to any shuttle launches other than the very first one in 1981—this in stark contrast to her husband's record of 134. When Omar tells me this detail about his mother, I remind him that in my novel, the main character's mother has also boycotted all the shuttle launches after the first, while the father takes his space-obsessed child to every launch. "That *is* weird," Omar agrees. It pleases me when things I made up turn out to be true for someone. I think about a line from a letter Hemingway wrote to F. Scott Fitzgerald about character—"make it up so truly that later it will happen that way."

Omar and I sit in the living room catching up while we wait for his other friends to arrive. He tells me about having escaped another round of layoffs; he's been told he will keep his job for at least a few more months. He shows me his new laptop and clicks through some photos he and Karen have taken recently at the Space Center. One of Karen's shows a launch vehicle stacked on the pad, photographed from the crawlerway; she has arranged the shot so that some of the crawlerway's pebbles are visible at the bottom of the frame, looking huge and marbled and distinct, while behind them the stack looms like futuristic architecture.

"That's gorgeous," I say. Part of what we are admiring, when we admire the image, is the vantage point itself. Most photographers, even those who get press credentials from NASA, would never get the chance to take a picture like this. The launchpads are among the most tightly restricted sites at the space center. It's one of the things that keeps Omar working here as long as they will let him.

Omar's friends Kris and Dayra show up, and we all pile into Frank's Suburban. I met Kris at Family Day; Dayra is a friend of Omar's from the University of Central Florida. I'd forgotten, until I'm chatting with her about the classes she and Omar took together, that Omar was a history major.

At the checkpoint, Frank shows the guard his badge. The two men share a joking exchange that makes it seem as though they've met here many times before. We pass through the gate, and the geography changes abruptly into the straightaway of Kennedy Parkway with the green wetlands on either side of us. The early-evening sunlight makes everything golden, and the Vehicle Assembly Building is lit up like a religious destination. The others don't interrupt their conversations, but I stop talking to look out the window at it. I was here only two weeks ago, but I'm surprised by how pleased I am to see the VAB again. This is my fourth visit within eight months, but I never seem to get used to the sight of it. If anything, I become more emotionally involved with it the closer we get to the end. I snap a picture through Frank's windshield and post it on Facebook. "Are you back there again already?" a friend from graduate school comments under the picture. "Or do you *live* in Florida now?"

As we pull into the grassy area where cars are parking in neat rows, we pass a bus whose front sign reads PRESS. When I peer inside, I can see row after row of white men in their fifties, some of them balancing large tripods in the aisle. I feel a surge of jealousy, as I did when I passed the Press Site on my first visit here with Omar.

"Press," I point out to the others in the car. "Those guys think they're better than me."

"You should try again for the next NASATweetup," Omar says. He had reminded me faithfully of every deadline for the selections for spots to see launches from up close. He doesn't enter them himself, he told me once, because as a badged employee he already gets better access than most, and he feels he should let someone else have a chance.

"I don't think I'm on Twitter enough to get chosen," I say. The selection process is supposed to be random, but the people who are chosen tend to have suspiciously high numbers of followers. "I'll keep trying, though."

"You should try again for regular press credentials, too," Omar says. I've complained to him that after being turned down a number of times I had become frustrated and given up trying. But he's right—it wouldn't hurt to try again.

We pile out of the SUV and follow Frank and Omar to a good spot in the field. They know from past rollouts where the best place is to stand.

Once again, I'm standing in a grassy field at the Kennedy Space Center with Omar and Frank, the Vehicle Assembly Building filling the sky as a backdrop, waiting for something to happen. The sun is setting, and people mill around us excitedly, chatting and buzzing with anticipation, like every other time I've been here. Classic rock plays over giant speakers. Children chase each other, some of them dressed in tiny flight suits and helmets. Reporters and photographers wander among the crowd, getting shots of the kids playing and asking people what they think is the significance of today's event.

Frank, Omar, and I are standing not far from where we stood for the launch of *Endeavour,* fifteen days ago. That day, people had been finding good spots with a clear view to the northeast, toward the launchpad, but today we are facing west, toward the massive doors of the Vehicle Assembly Building. The launch vehicle will emerge from the VAB, roll along the crawlerway directly in front of us, and then head off toward the launchpad. It will move so slowly, about half a mile an hour at its fastest, that we will have plenty of time to take it in while it moves this short distance.

One of the enormous VAB doors has already been opened, the seven metal panels folded vertically up on each other to reveal a sliver of the stacked launch vehicle. Bleachers are set up out here for spectators, as always, but more people are sitting on blankets, walking around, and visiting the booths that have been set up with snacks and drinks and (of course) space souvenirs. Most people have gathered at the rope barrier marking off a safe distance from the crawlerway. The setting sun is lighting everything up rose gold—the VAB, the clouds in the distance, the NASA families with their binoculars and their American flags and their cameras.

The rollout is scheduled to start at 8:00 p.m., but at five after, ten after, we still haven't detected any movement. Omar has brought his work radio with him, and from it he learns that the crawler transporter has a hydraulic leak. The rollout is going to be delayed at least fifteen or twenty minutes.

We watch the VAB doors and wait.

After we learn that the hydraulic leak will cause a delay, Dayra and I go for a walk while Frank and Omar set up their tripods. We stop by the snack booth to buy bottles of water, then notice a clump of people who seem to be gathering excitedly near the bleachers, lining up. We drift over to see what's going on.

"It's an astronaut!" Dayra gasps. A moment later I spot the figure she's pointing to: a woman wearing the bright blue flight suit that turns an otherwise normal-looking person—in this case, a woman in her thirties with curly brown hair—into a celebrity and a figure of fascination. People are clamoring to get autographs and pictures taken with this astronaut, whose name patch reads AUÑÓN.

"Let's get pictures with her!" Dayra says, and, grabbing my arm, steers me into the line. I tell Dayra I suspect this astronaut is from the new class chosen in 2009. This group is unique among astronaut classes in that they were hired knowing they would not get to fly on an American spacecraft. They will be assigned to missions on the International Space Station, which they will reach via the Russians' Soyuz spacecraft. The 2009 class is the first group of astronauts for whom fluency in the Russian language will be a necessity.

When we reach the front of the line, the astronaut greets us. We clutch her hand in turn, then take each other's pictures with her. Up close, I can see in the astronaut's eyes that she is a bit overwhelmed by all the attention. Her expression, while friendly, is a bit bewildered.

Dayra asks her if she's been to space.

"Not yet," the astronaut answers with the practiced smile of someone who has answered the same question a hundred times today. Both Dayra and I know enough not to ask her when she will. She doesn't know. She might not be assigned to a mission for years, and the waiting, though part of the job, must be excruciating. Dayra and I thank her before starting to walk away. A little boy is already offering her a space shuttle book he wants signed.

"Good luck!" Dayra calls over her shoulder to the astronaut, who smiles back. As we rejoin our group, I realize what I saw in her expression: she is out here at a space shuttle rollout, answering questions about the space shuttle, but she knows she will never get to fly on a space shuttle, that they will all be sealed up in museums by the time her training is complete. I've never before met an astronaut who hasn't been to space. An astronaut candidate, but not a space-flown astronaut. An earthbound spacefarer. You'd think the limited opportunities for astronauts would dampen the appeal of the position, but in this last round of astronaut hiring, NASA counted more applications than it has ever received. There are still a great number of people who just want to go to space, who are willing to dedicate their lives to that chance.

Since I saw it roar into space fifteen days ago, *Endeavour* has had a busy schedule. As all shuttle crews have done since *Columbia*'s demise, the crew of *Endeavour* made it their first order of business to inspect the condition of the tiles using a camera at the end of the remote manipulator arm. Some damaged tiles were found on the underside of the orbiter, but upon closer inspection they were cleared for reentry. *Endeavour* docked with the International Space Station on day three of the mission, and a traditional welcome ceremony was held between the six-person crew of ISS and the six crew members of *Endeavour*.

The combined crew unloaded new components of the International Space Station and unpacked supplies from *Endeavour*. Crew members did a total of four spacewalks to install new equipment on ISS and to service existing equipment. On day eight of *Endeavour*'s time in space, three of the six ISS crew members—Dmitri Kondraytev of Russia, Paolo Nespoli of Italy, and Cady Coleman of the United States—finished their six-month missions, and after the others had gone to sleep for the night, the three of them crawled into their Soyuz spacecraft, detached from Station, and fell to Earth. On day twelve of the mission, astronaut Mike Fincke surpassed Peggy Whitson's record as the American astronaut with the most time in space, 377 days.

In between doing their work, the crew also spoke with Pope Benedict XVI, four hundred students in an elementary school in Arizona, the Italian president, students and faculty members at the University of Arizona, PBS, NPR, ABC, CBS, CNN, NBC, AP, Reuters, Gannett, the Voice of America, and Fox News.

Today, May 31, is day sixteen of *Endeavour*'s mission. The astronauts have undocked *Endeavour* from the ISS, and they have spent most of today testing the shuttle's systems, stowing equipment, and going over plans for deorbit and reentry. They will start the deorbit burn tonight at 1:29 a.m. and, assuming all goes well, land here at the Kennedy Space Center at 2:35 a.m.

It's easy enough to follow all these goings-on on the NASA site, or on other sites like Spaceflight Now or Space.com. What's harder is to guess what it feels like to the crew to know that they are doing many of these things for the last time. The following shuttle mission, which will be the last one for all time, will not include any space walks because of the smaller crew size and limited training time. So all the little rituals of shuttle space walks—sleeping in the airlock to purge their bodies of nitrogen, donning the space suits piece by piece, opening the airlock and stepping outside—all these are happening for the last time. The ISS crew will be able to do space walks to maintain the station as necessary, but never again will astronauts slip out the air lock of a space shuttle orbiter to float and work in space.

"It's ready," Omar announces. He has continued to monitor his work radio, and apparently people are saying to each other that the hydraulic problem has been fixed and that rollout is about to start. We direct our attention toward the Vehicle Assembly Building door, where still no movement can be detected.

"I think I see it," says Frank at length. He is watching the VAB through binoculars. He politely hands them over to me, and I look too; the eyepieces are still warm from his face. At first I think his claim that the shuttle is moving was wishful thinking, but then I think I see it too. I choose a frame of reference, a girder just inside the door, and watch to see whether the space between the girder and the right-hand solid rocket booster is shrinking. I think it might be. I hand the binoculars back.

Behind me, a few space fans start clapping and hooting, the way people at rock shows do to let each other know that they were the first to notice the band stepping onstage. The noise catches the attention of the people around us, and soon everyone has stopped their conversations to concentrate on the open door. The rollout has officially started at 8:42 p.m.

Atlantis is definitely moving now; the stack is visible in the doorway, no longer behind the threshold, as it was a minute ago. We watch and watch, and now the stack is mostly outside the doorway. People continue to clap and holler. The sound of the crawler transporter is monumental, like hundreds of heavy-duty tractors running at once, which, I guess, is more or less what it is. In the footage I've seen of rollouts, the sound of the crawler has always been left out or minimized, but in person the deafening rumble is inescapable. The stack is also preceded by a diesel smell that, like the engine noise, I should have known to anticipate but somehow did not. A toxic cloud like the idling of a hundred eighteen-wheelers wafts over the crowd. It occurs to me, not for the first time, that a lot of people who might normally object to the climate-change impact of the space program choose not to think of it in those terms, simply because it seems *less* stupid and wasteful than so many of the other ways in which large amounts of resources are consumed or, in this case, large amounts of carbon dioxide released.

As the stack gets closer to us, Frank and Omar get to work snapping pictures of it. It's still not full dark out yet, and enormous xenon lights are bathing the shuttle in an unearthly white that is quite beautiful to the naked eye but hard to photograph. I take a couple of pictures of it, but, as with launches, I don't make any real effort to capture it.

The stack is nearly directly in front of us after moving for about fifteen minutes, and it's only at this point that I notice there are a handful of *people* riding on it. Mostly men, mostly dressed in the jeans and T-shirts of technicians, they are riding on the mobile launch platform. Some of them walk up and down, waving to the crowd. A few of them seem to be working up there, seem to be actually checking on the equipment and monitoring the base of the stack. But most seem to be along for the ride—standing at the railing, or sitting on lawn chairs facing out at the crowd, waving at us as if the mobile launch platform were the biggest float in a small-town parade.

"There are *people* on it," I say to Omar. By now, I reflect, he has probably gotten used to me making incredibly obvious statements in his presence. He never gives me a hard time about it.

"Yep," he confirms. "The crawler was built to keep the Saturn Vs steady, so it's gotta be a pretty smooth ride." It's true that none of the people standing and walking appear to be unstable on their feet. The ride is probably much smoother than it would be on a flatbed truck.

Seeing the stack go by this slowly, I notice things I have never seen before. From here I can see clearly the struts that attach the orbiter to the external tank, with explosive bolts in between to blow the tank free once it's empty. The way the tiles hug the graceful curve of the orbital maneuvering system pods. The way the orbiter's name, *Atlantis,* was clearly painted onto the orbiter's flank by hand rather than using decals or stencils. This isn't the closest I've ever been to an orbiter—that would still be my visit to the Orbiter Processing Facility on Family Day, when *Endeavour* was so close I could read the serial numbers on its tiles. But I've never seen an orbiter this close up when it's stacked upright for launch, and neither have most people. Even space nuts who come out for every launch only get to see the stack from miles away.

"Want your picture with it?" Omar asks, as he always does. We snap each other's pictures without trying too hard to get great shots. Our cameras can't really capture the spectacle of the bright white ship, the warm orange tank, the gray grumbling crawler, all against the black sky of night. We want pictures that show our own faces only so that we can tell people that we were here.

Norman Mailer's description of the rollout compares the slowly moving launch vehicle to a "ghost galleon of the Caribbean." I've always thought that description sounded fanciful, and because Mailer was never here for a rollout himself, it was easy to assume that his speculation may have been overly romantic. But it's true there is something nautical about the way the thing creaks along, the multiple levels of walkways and stairways and signs and safety equipment and flags, the little lights hanging all over it, the way a crowd has come to see it off. The people standing and sitting at the railings are waving to us like old-timey travelers embarking on a cruise, as if the crawler trans-porter were an enormous cruise ship leaving port and the Kennedy Space Center a calm blue sea. They are close enough that we can read their expressions, but they are inexorably separated from us—not by their distance, but by their trajectory. They are on their way to some-where, and we are stuck here.

Like so many things we wait so long to see, the rollout is both fast and slow. We stand there a long time marveling at it, long enough to re-sume our conversations, long enough to post to Twitter, long enough to notice some of our fellow space fans again, to notice what they are doing and wearing and saying to each other out here in the floodlit dark, long enough to return our attentions a second and third time to the massive stack and to realize that it is past us now, and now show-ing us its back side, and now definitely on the wane. Some observers leave as soon as the crawler is well past, some while it was still quite visible, but the Izquierdo party stays until only the lit stack is still visible in the distant vicinity of launch pad 39A, the glowing white of *Atlantis*'s back and spread wings. The crawler underneath has dis-appeared in the dark, so the ghost ship seems to move by itself, imper-ceptibly slowly, out to its destination still a couple of miles, and many hours, away.

After dropping off Frank, we head to dinner. Omar asks that we go to a place with a TV in the bar so he can keep an eye on an important basketball game, so we choose an Applebee's. While we wait for our food to arrive, Dayra asks Omar and me how we met. Omar and I look at each other bashfully for a second, conscious of how the telling will seem to spin the meaning of our friendship.

"Well, Margaret wrote a book about *Challenger*," Omar begins, "and I read it."

"Wow, you wrote a *book*?" Dayra repeats. Somehow in all our chat-ting today I'd mentioned that I'm a professor but not that I'm a writer.

"Then Omar wrote me to tell me about the errors I made," I continue, ribbing him.

"I wrote to say I liked it," Omar corrects. "And you had very few errors, considering."

"Later I found him accidentally on Facebook," I explain. I tell them about the group called "If You Oppose NASA in Any Way I Will Punch You in the Face." Everyone laughs and agrees that that is *so Omar*.

Our food arrives, and we eat in companionable silence. Everyone's food is covered with cheese. Whenever something exciting happens in the basketball game Omar is watching, a table of three young men near us erupts in cheers. Omar sails a friendly comment their way, and soon they are exchanging banter and predictions about the rest of the season. Omar has made yet more new friends.

That night, I'm sleeping in my motel bed in Cocoa Beach when the sound of the space shuttle *Endeavour* entering the atmosphere rips through the air with a sonic boom. It's like nothing I've ever heard before—not exactly a sound, more like a low-level molecular event—and, as Omar told me it would happen, I know exactly what it is the moment I hear it. I almost feel as though I knew the split second *before* I heard it, the way dreams can seem to predict events in the waking world. The sonic boom: a disturbance to the air caused by *Endeavour* traveling toward Earth faster than the speed of sound, breaking through the sound barrier twice, once with its nose and once with its wings. *Boom-boom.* I look at the clock and it's 2:30 a.m., right on time.

I know from my reading that *Endeavour* has broken the sound barrier at an altitude of sixty thousand feet and won't touch down for another five minutes. The mission won't officially be over until *Endeavour* comes to a full stop at the end of the runway at Kennedy. *Wheel stop*, they call it, the official end of the mission. Journalists are out there right now, maybe some of the same journalists on that press bus I saw at the rollout, waiting at the Shuttle Landing Facility to take pictures of *Endeavour* gliding in and touching down. I feel faintly jealous of them. There is always someone who will get to see more.

When I get home I look up the current corps of astronauts on the NASA website and click through their smiling portraits in their blue flight suits, looking for the one I met at the rollout. I find her easily enough: Serena Auñón. The bio on her page says that before being selected as an astronaut she worked for NASA as a flight surgeon. She lived in Houston, Texas, and Star City, Russia, caring for astronauts and cosmonauts on their way to missions to space, having gone through one of the country's few residencies in aerospace medicine. When I Google the term "aerospace medicine," I'm taken to a page that informs me that while other branches of medicine deal with ab normal physiology in a normal environment, flight surgeons deal with normal physiology in an abnormal environment.

Astronauts are hard to get hold of when they are about to go to space or have recently returned, but an astronaut candidate from the most recently selected group who has yet to be assigned to a mission is easier to secure a interview with. After filling out a form online with the Astronaut Office's media liaison describing who I am and what sort of interview I'm trying to get, I receive an e-mail back telling me when to call for a phone interview with Serena.

The call for applications for this new class of astronauts went out in 2007. That announcement was forwarded to me multiple times by friends as a joke, suggesting that I should apply, though I lack the ad's most basic requirement, a degree in math or science. It's hard to imagine what it would be like to join the astronaut corps at a time when the only American spacecraft is being retired, to join the ranks of astronauts who have flown on shuttle and to know they would never get to fly on it themselves. This is the first class of astronauts who know they will not launch from Cape Canaveral; they will wait, probably for years, to get to fly with the Russians to the International Space

Station. What would it be like, I wonder, to compete as hard as previous classes of astronauts have to get a spot, but for the spot to be such a compromised one?

One of the things that makes the job title *astronaut* different from other jobs is that it existed in the collective imagination for centuries before it was ever actually anyone's occupation. In the second century CE, Lucian of Samosata imagined travelers going to the moon and fighting a war with its inhabitants. In Jules Verne's immensely influential 1865 novel *From the Earth to the Moon,* the word *astronaut* is never used, but three men seal themselves into a metal capsule in order to fly to the moon. Many of the details Verne came up with were so outlandish as to invite ridicule if they had not become reality a hundred years later in the Apollo program, including a launch from Florida and a safe splashdown in the Pacific Ocean. Verne's three space travelers behave in some ways we now associate with astronauts—they solve problems that arise on their mission, analyze new information they observe outside their windows, and do calculations to figure out their location and speed. On the other hand, they indulge in non-astronaut-like behaviors such as getting drunk, becoming histrionic about unexpected problems, and expressing doubt about the meaning of their journey, about whether they should be doing this at all.

One of the first uses of the word *astronaut* to refer to a human traveling in space was in Neil R. Jones's short story "The Death's Head Meteor" in 1930.

> The young astronaut entered the space flyer, closed the door, and was alone in the air-tight compartment just large enough to accommodate him. On the instrument board before him were dials, levers, gauges, buttons and queer apparatus which controlled and operated the various features of the craft. He turned on his oxygen supply and his air rejuvenator so that the air could be used more

than once, after which he shoved his starting lever forward. The craft raced suddenly off the roof and into the cloudless sky above the vast city of the twenty-sixth century.

Jones was probably as surprised as anyone to learn how soon his new word became an actual job title, only twenty-nine years later. In between, during World War II, the first actual rockets emerged. This was the beginning of a new era in which the astronaut became a consistent character to tell stories about, if still speculative. Though the rockets weren't ready to safely contain humans, their streamlined hulls brought with them a clearer image of the astronaut fantasy. Part fighter pilot, part frontiersman, the helmeted spaceman climbed into sleek machines and left Earth in the black-and-white television shows of the fifties. In 1954, Walt Disney created *Man in Space,* a series intended to promote his new Disneyland, which was set to open the following year. In the opening shot of the series, Walt himself speaks into the camera. "One of man's oldest dreams has been the desire for space travel," he tells us with an avuncular twinkle. "Until recently this seemed to be an impossibility."

Man in Space gives a brief history of rockets, complete with a racist cartoon of the first Chinese rocket builders. This historical overview is politely evasive about the German rocket program, referring to the V-2 rockets as "forerunners to space travel" rather than as instruments used to rain death upon our allies in Europe. Wernher von Braun, the German rocket engineer responsible for the V-2, gives a talk about multistage launches. Von Braun is movie-star handsome and looks disturbingly like a textbook illustration of what Hitler's anthropologists meant by the term *Aryan.* His English is extremely fluent, but his unmistakable German accent must have sounded jarring to an American audience not all that many years after the war.

Man in Space dramatizes the experiences astronauts were expected to encounter, especially the experience of weightlessness. "How will man's subconscious mind react," the cartoon voice-over asks, "to his first experiences with space travel? Will he not suddenly be aware of his precarious situation trapped in a tiny metal box floating through the incomprehensible nothingness of space? We do not know."

The idea of the astronaut evolved significantly in 1959, the year the Mercury astronauts were chosen. Crew-cut, Caucasian, and confident, most were veterans of World War II or Korea or both. They were all husbands and fathers. They embodied the contradictions embedded in the American masculine ideal: they were military men (rule followers, patriots) on the one hand and test pilots (steely-eyed maverick cowboys) on the other. Their names tripped off the tongue: Carpenter, Cooper, Glenn, Grissom, Schirra, Shepard, and Slayton. They were handsome and daring. Asked at their first press conference whether they would be willing to launch into space tomorrow, they all raised a hand. Some of them raised two. Even for those of us who hadn't been born yet then, in many ways what we imagine when we say the word *astronaut* is still those seven men.

Stories about astronauts are stories about risks. It is precisely the risks they take that make us admire them, that makes the wonders they encounter so wondrous. Tom Wolfe started writing about the Mercury astronauts after he met some of them at the last Apollo launch; in a foreword to *The Right Stuff*, Wolfe describes his motivation for writing the book: to understand what gave the astronauts the courage to undertake such daring missions. "What is it, I wondered, that makes a man willing to sit on top of an enormous Roman Candle . . . and wait for someone to light the fuse?" The answer, as Wolfe constructs it, is the so-called Right Stuff. He uses an extended analogy with the ancient concept of single-combat warfare—the strongest combatant from each army would fight each other one-on-one. By doing so, the single-combat warrior took the burdens of an entire war upon himself, risked death so none of his countrymen would have to. At the same time, the single-combat warriors were "revered and extolled, songs and poems were written about them, every reasonable comfort and honor was given them, and women and children and even grown men were

moved to tears in their presence." More than the best and the brightest, more than role models, the Mercury astronauts embodied the best
we were capable of. Astronauts still do. They are our avatars for our
dreams of spaceflight, for our dreams of escaping Earth.

Tom Wolfe defines the Right Stuff:

> The world was divided into those who had it and those who did not.
> This quality, this *it,* was never named, however, nor was it talked
> about in any way.
>
> As to just what this ineffable quality was . . . well, it obviously
> involved bravery. But it was not bravery in the simple sense of being
> willing to risk your life. . . . No, the idea here (in the all-enclosing
> fraternity) seemed to be that a man should have the ability to go up
> in a hurtling piece of machinery and put his hide on the line and
> then have the moxie, the reflexes, the experience, the coolness, to
> pull it back in the last yawning moment—and then to go up again
> *the next day,* and the next day, and every next day, even if the series
> should prove infinite.

Yet Wolfe describes a growing concern among the astronauts: they
were accustomed to testing themselves and besting one another through
their flying, but the Mercury capsule itself would require no piloting.
We tend to forget from our vantage point in history that even as the
astronauts were chosen there was still controversy over whether space
travel should involve humans at all. Robotic spacecraft could send
back scientific data at half the cost, pragmatists pointed out; public
opinion on the issue was divided. In 1960, President Eisenhower refused NASA's request to fund the first steps in the proposed Apollo
program—a three-man spacecraft and a rocket powerful enough to
get to the moon—because his Science Advisory Committee had informed him that the motives for a moon shot involving astronauts
were "emotional compulsions." If this seems like a laugh line now that
we know Apollo was in fact funded and did in fact carry out its missions successfully, it's useful to keep in mind that this analysis was
also pretty accurate.

The debate over whether it's important for humans to go to space is a debate about the dream lives of taxpayers. The scientists and engineers didn't see the point of sending astronauts, but the people who romanticize spaceflight—the ones who want to see their science fiction fantasies come true—felt in their geeky hearts that sending astronauts to space, seeing human protagonists for our stories of leaving Earth, was in fact the whole point. And those geeks won. Jules Verne's *From the Earth to the Moon* was devoured, and loved, by Tsiolkovsky, Oberth, and Goddard, the three geniuses who developed rocketry more or less simultaneously and in isolation from one another; it was also read and loved in childhood by Wernher von Braun, who developed the rocket that actually achieved the goal. Viewed from more than a century on, the most outlandish bit of invention in Verne's novel is the idea that a flight to the moon could be funded entirely by a subscription service—regular citizens all over the world voluntarily paying into the project with no hope of being paid back.

The Mercury Seven were so deluged with media requests for their time that they signed contracts with *Life* magazine for the exclusive right to their personal stories. *Life* paid them half a million dollars, a great deal of money for astronauts who were still living on military salaries, and gave them the added benefit of letting the astronauts and their managers at NASA control the story that reached the public. The *Life* contract did as much to cultivate and burnish the image of what it means to be an astronaut as anything else NASA did. One of the reporters for *Life* later admitted:

> I knew, of course, about some very shaky marriages, some womanizing, some drinking and never reported it. The guys wouldn't have let me, and neither would NASA. It was common knowledge that several marriages hung together only because the men were afraid NASA would disapprove of divorce and take them off flights.

As Wolfe describes it, the risks of single-combat warfare earned the astronauts certain privileges ("every reasonable comfort and honor"), and drinking and womanizing were among them. Historian Margaret Weitekamp writes, "Such macho excesses did not worry NASA decision makers. The space agency viewed this particular kind of manhood as part and parcel of the talents NASA needed."

I read *The Right Stuff* for the first time while I was researching my first novel. When I went back to the book before interviewing Serena Auñón, I found a note in the margin, in my own handwriting, that I didn't remember writing: "A man is the opposite of a woman, and he is also the opposite of a monkey." It was in a chapter about the astronauts' medical testing at the Lovelace Clinic in Arizona. A monkey was going to make the first flight, attacking the definition of astronauts from one side; simultaneously, the definition was being attacked from the other side by women pilots who were demanding to know why they couldn't be included in the space program.

A strange precedent had been set in the early days of the airplane—promoters had encouraged women to learn to fly and to do so publicly, with the idea that seeing a woman in lipstick and heels climb into a cockpit and fly away would encourage the public to think of aviation as easy and safe. As a result, there was an unexpectedly high number of very qualified women pilots around the time the Mercury astronauts were chosen, and some of the women wanted to go to space. A small group organized themselves to approach NASA.

The women were experienced pilots. Many of them had broken records; some had broken the sound barrier. Their efforts to get NASA to recognize them as potential astronaut candidates were met with evasion. When the women managed to gain access to the same rigorous physical and psychological testing the Mercury Seven had gone through at the Lovelace Clinic, thirteen of them passed. Some of the women beat records set by the men. By doing so, these thirteen women managed to create enough pressure that a congressional hearing was held to address the question of women joining the astronaut corps. In July 1962, only a few months after his triumphant orbital flight, John Glenn testified at the hearing and argued against the inclusion of women in space with a remarkable piece of circular logic:

> I think this gets back to the way our social order is organized really. It is just a fact. The men go off and fight the wars and fly the airplanes and come back and help design and build and test them. The fact that women are not in this field is a fact of our social order. It may be undesirable.

Margaret Weitekamp notes that Glenn's assertion of essentialism ("it is just a fact") is at odds with his attempt to justify and explain these roles—not to mention his willful ignorance of the women testifying at the same hearing who did, in fact, "fly the airplanes."

Six of the seven Mercury astronauts got to fly in space, each of them setting a record or achieving a "first" of some kind. (The seventh, Deke Slayton, would get his chance on the Apollo-Soyuz Test Project in 1975.) Once the moon program was under way, five more classes of astronauts were chosen and trained. As their numbers grew, it became harder to keep track of their names and faces, as it had been possible to do when there were only seven. But the word *astronaut* still meant the same thing, and in July 1969 everyone knew the names of the three men who were on their way to the moon to fulfill Kennedy's challenge.

The seventies were a dead period in the history of the American astronaut. Two projects were cooked up to use leftover Saturn V rockets that had been assembled before Apollo was canceled: Skylab and the Apollo-Soyuz Test Project. But no new astronauts were recruited between the class introduced in August 1969 and the new batch presented to the public in January 1978, over eight years later. By that time, the Mercury Seven were past fifty years old. This was during a period you may recall being associated with a "malaise" (though President Carter never actually used that term), a post-Vietnam distrust of anything having to do with the military or government. What it would mean to be an astronaut in this era would have to be different from what it meant for the Mercury astronauts.

The new class of astronauts introduced in 1978, soon dubbed the Thirty-Five New Guys, was the largest astronaut class ever chosen and was profoundly different from the classes that had come before. The TFNGs were introduced at a press conference at Johnson, and their uniqueness as a class was apparent from the moment we set eyes on them. With larger crews of up to seven on each flight, the shuttle did not require that all astronauts be able to fly the spacecraft, removing the official barrier that had kept women out of the astronaut corps. Some of the new astronauts were doctors or scientists, some were women, and some were African American. One was Asian American. Two were Jewish. NASA had never had a policy against minority astronauts (just as it had not had a policy specifically prohibiting female astronauts), but the group of military test pilots from which potential astronauts had been drawn had included almost no minorities.

For a bit of perspective: at the same time the Mercury astronauts were being chosen, a nine-year-old African American boy was being asked to leave his town's whites-only public library in Lake City, South Carolina. Fourth-grader Ronald McNair refused to leave until he could check out the books he had chosen, prompting the librarian to call the police. McNair eventually earned a PhD in physics from MIT, was selected in the astronaut class of 1978, and flew in space for the first time in 1984. He was killed in the space shuttle *Challenger* disaster in 1986. The library where he was once denied service is now named for him.

The women astronauts were a late-seventies dream of second-wave feminism with their graduate degrees in science and engineering, their feathered hair and lip gloss. I thought they looked fantastic. Rhea Seddon even looked a little like my mother, with her blond flip and her petite frame. My mother had been one of the first women to graduate from her law school; Rhea Seddon was a surgeon and would be one of the first women to go to space. The role of astronaut, the role that defined masculinity like none other, was now open to young women, young *mothers,* even. To some people this meant an important barrier had fallen, as when as a few years later Sandra Day O'Connor would be appointed to the Supreme Court, and a few years after that

Geraldine Ferraro would run for vice president. To many, the fact that space travel was now a challenge women were capable of facing meant that it was no longer exciting. Weitekamp: "the very presence of women in orbit would indicate that space no longer remained a battlefield for international prestige." Wernher von Braun, asked about female astronauts in the sixties, had joked that the men in charge were "reserving 110 pounds of payload for recreational equipment."

This is the odd thing about the shuttle era: it wasn't only that the ranks of astronauts were infiltrated by women, nonwhites, nonmilitary, and nonpilots. It wasn't only that the astronauts were now numerous and anonymous. More than that, the vehicle itself changed the nature of what it meant to fly in it. A vehicle that can only go to low Earth orbit, can come back safely to land on a runway, exactly as you and I do at our local unexciting airports, diminishes, for some, the entire meaning of spaceflight. Stories about astronauts are stories about risk. So if we imagine the risks to have changed, the astronauts had to have changed as well.

As the program has gone on, thirteen more classes of astronauts have been chosen since that groundbreaking class of 1978, for a total of 335 American astronaut candidates altogether. Viewed another way: of all the American astronauts in the history of NASA, 55 were accepted into the corps during the Mercury/Gemini/Apollo "heroic" era, and 266 were accepted during the shuttle era. Yet if you can name any of them off the top of your head, they are probably heroic-era astronauts, with the possible exception of Sally Ride, the first American woman in space.

Part of what it means to be an astronaut today is that the "firsts" are all used up. Not only the first human in space, the first to orbit Earth, the first spacewalk, and the first to walk on the moon—these were all in the history books before Serena or I was born—but the demographic firsts as well. Serena Auñón is a Hispanic woman, but when she goes to space she will not be the first woman in space, the first astronaut of Hispanic descent in space, or the first Hispanic woman in space. Nor will she be a first for any of these categories to live on an orbiting space station. If she were to one day set foot on the moon, of course, she would be achieving any number of firsts (including first astronaut to walk on the moon who was born after the most recent moonwalk), but there are no plans for this under way. Maybe it's a good thing for this crop of astronauts that they don't have to go to space as representatives of demographic groups anymore—what sort of pressure did it put on Sally Ride not only to prepare for her own responsibilities on her mission but also to bear the burden of representing all female humans in history? When Serena goes to space she will bear no such burden; her every move will not be scrutinized as a data point in an argument about whether certain types of people can or can't be astronauts. It's been established that they can. She can go as herself.

More than 3,500 people responded to the 2007 call for applicants for new astronauts. That pool was first culled for those who didn't meet the basic requirements, then winnowed again. Semifinalists were brought to Houston in groups for interviews and medical tests. The finalists were brought back again for even more interviews. The screening process has put increased emphasis on psychological fitness since the scandal caused by Lisa Nowak, the astronaut who drove from Houston to the Cape with intent to harm the girlfriend of a fellow astronaut. NASA hopes to avoid future embarrassments like this one by identifying applicants with psychological problems, but everyone seems to agree that it's impossible to predict who will and who will not crack under the pressure.

The day of my appointment to talk to Serena Auñón on the phone, I type up a tidy list of questions to ask her. At the appointed time, I hang a sign on my office door warning people not to knock on it, then dial the number I was e-mailed by the Johnson Space Center media liaison. A few rings, then someone picks up.

"Good morning, Astronaut Office?" a friendly female voice answers. This is a delightful way to answer a phone, I think, but I don't say anything about it out loud. I'm suddenly taken back to Oriana Fallaci's description of the Astronaut Office in 1967:

[A] very long corridor with a lot of doors, each opening into the office of a new astronaut. Each door is generally wide open so that you can see the astronaut sitting at his desk surrounded by papers and pencils—say about twenty pencils to each astronaut. Why the astronauts should have so many pencils no one has ever been able to explain to me.

I mention my appointment with Serena, and the woman puts me through. Serena answers on the first ring. She seems comfortable on the phone, more at ease than when I saw her at the rollout.

"I'm going to be eating my lunch while I talk to you," she announces with a smile in her voice. "So excuse me in advance if I make chewing sounds in your ear." Even as an astronaut candidate who hasn't been assigned to a flight yet, she is already on a busy schedule learning the systems on the ISS and the Soyuz, training for spacewalks in the underwater mockup, and studying the Russian language intensively. Serena is warm and friendly when I explain my nebulous-sounding project. "My mom is a novelist too," she tells me, "and her name is also Margaret. So I'll give you the benefit of the doubt."

I start out by asking her what made her want to become an astronaut. Serena answers that she was inspired by watching shuttle launches as a child and that when she told her parents she wanted to be an astronaut, they didn't laugh at her. Her father encouraged her to study engineering, as he had. So she did, earning a bachelor's degree in electrical engineering, then went on to medical school and then to work as a flight surgeon for NASA. Serena tells me she didn't make any choices specifically in order to make herself a more appealing candidate to be an astronaut; she says that at every stage she chose to follow her passion.

I ask Serena whether there are personality traits that she and her fellow recruits have in common. I mention the Right Stuff stereotype and the way it seems to cling to the job.

"Honestly," Serena says, "the biggest thing I've found is that they're all so down to earth it will shock you. You wouldn't know walking in the door that this person has flown on the ISS. They are sisters and brothers and moms and dads and have all the same interests that other people do, like going to movies and going to sporting events." She allows that while in the sixties NASA was looking for military pilots, the astronaut corps is now made up of "scientists, researchers, physicians . . . now when we look at flying to ISS, they really look at how people perform in extreme environments, how well they're able to handle their own weaknesses, how people get along. That's what they're looking for." In other words, NASA is no longer looking for the badass loner maverick cowboy; it is looking for team players, people who can keep from getting on each other's nerves.

Serena tells me that every new astronaut is assigned a mentor when he or she arrives at Johnson Space Center in Houston, an experienced astronaut who can help gain entry to the sometimes-bewildering NASA culture with its alphabet soup of acronyms.

"That's interesting," I answer. "If it's not inappropriate, can I ask who your mentor is?"

"Oh, sure. It's Doug Hurley," she says. Doug Hurley is a Right Stuff type Marine pilot who is scheduled to fly on *Atlantis*'s last mission. It's interesting that she was assigned a mentor who was not a woman, not a minority, and not a scientist, despite there being plenty of astronauts in the corps who would meet one or more of those criteria. Maybe it means that things have progressed to a point where these factors are not as prominent as they once were, that Serena and Doug are well matched in terms of personality, or that they knew each other from Star City when Serena was his flight surgeon. "He's someone I trust," Serena says with genuine warmth in her voice.

I wonder what John Glenn thinks of this turn of events in the history of the astronaut, that getting along with others is now prized over lightning-fast reflexes or superhuman daring, that Serena's place in the astronaut corps is so unremarkable that Doug Hurley, a Marine pilot like himself, would be assigned to mentor a nonpilot Hispanic woman, and that the two would be great friends. Later, I would read that when Doug Hurley's wife, Karen Nyberg, flew her own mission to space, a six-month stint on the International Space Station, Hurley took care of their son. He shut down reporters' attempts to define his parenting as an unusual or excessive burden—he pointed out to the Houston *Chronicle,* "Every other man up on the space station has children, too. Why is it different for her?" Yet as published, the piece focuses on his burdens over her accomplishments and bears the subtitle "Mr. Mom."

"So, I have this question I've been asking as many people as I can," I tell Serena. "What does it mean that we have been flying American spacecraft in space for fifty years and now have decided to stop?"

Serena pauses. Then she sighs heavily into the phone.

"Yeah, that's a tough question," she says. "It's true that this is a weird time. This is a gap when we don't have an American vehicle. It's the first time we've really had to reeducate people about the space station. Now that shuttle is retiring, we are hearing more about the ISS, and maybe that's a good thing.

"I find myself explaining to people a lot what the state of our space program *is,*" she says. "People think that NASA is shutting down, or that Johnson Space Center is shutting down."

"I've heard visitors say that at the Cape," I say. "People show up and are surprised the facilities are still there."

"Right," Serena says. "It's like people thought shuttle was all there was. Now that shuttle will be gone, we'll have the chance to let people know what else we've been doing all this time."

"That's true," I say grudgingly.

"Look, it may be kind of sad, but we are ending this program successfully," she points out. "People should be proud of that."

We are proud of that, I tell her. I know this from seeing the people who show up at launches, the simple joy they take in seeing spacecraft leave Earth. At the same time, this statement hinges on a definition of success I'm not sure everyone would agree with.

Most Americans probably couldn't name a single active astronaut. Yet there is still something about the way an astronaut looks in a blue flight suit. Fit, fearless, competent. Ready to take on the burdens of our dreams. When I ask Serena about the flight suit, what it's like to put it on and go out to meet the public, she laughs.

"It's true, the flight suit does energize people," she says. "And our job is to inspire. What helps inspire *me* is knowing that kids of today know what that blue flight suit means, and they care. It's hope and promise of the future, and hopefully it symbolizes someone they can look up to."

I decide to ask Serena something I have always wondered.

"What's it like," I ask her, "when you're in a bank or getting your taxes done, and someone asks you what your occupation is, and you get to say 'astronaut'? Is that the best thing ever?"

Serena laughs happily and at first seems to be at a loss as to how to answer. I go on.

"I mean, it's like, when someone asks you what your job is, answering 'I'm Batman.'"

Serena laughs some more, and I'm about to apologize for putting her on the spot when she finally replies.

"It *is* pretty cool," she says. "I'm not going to lie. Every time I say it, I get to remember it's true, and maybe at some point it will get old, but—it hasn't yet."

When we talk about the future, Serena repeats the standard-issue Charles Bolden talk about how commercial ventures will be up and running by 2016–17. I am as skeptical as always about whether SpaceX or any of the other space startups can achieve human spaceflight on anything like the time frame we are being promised. Yet I have to admit this happy talk sounds better coming from a member of the astronaut corps than it does coming from a politician. Serena has put everything at stake hoping for the happy talk to come true, and at least for the time I'm talking with her, I feel it can come true too.

I didn't have much of a relationship with the Mercury astronauts at first. Even as I started writing my *Challenger* book, I found the shuttle astronauts more accessible, more human, more like people I knew. Part of this appeal was that some of the shuttle astronauts were women, but also that they did things like juggle and do somersaults, clowned around in weightlessness. They seemed to have a sense of humor about it all. They took the time to enjoy it. The Mercury astronauts were all military pilots, laconic and square-jawed. They'd been given a tough job to do and they did it with machine-like precision. They brooked no goofing off.

It wasn't until I was well into my research, well past the Right Stuff stage and into individual accounts, that I started to see the Mercury Seven as individuals and thus started to love them. Gus Grissom was the one I understood first, with his engineering degree and his hang-dog expression always recognizable among the others. John Glenn, of course, has a boyish bow-tie appeal and a charismatic kind of intelligence. Gordo Cooper, Scott Carpenter, Deke Slayton. One by one I started to be able to pick them out and started to call them by their first names. Soon I know the Gemini and Apollo astronauts as well. Neil Armstrong has a goofy sincerity. Gene Cernan has a tough visage right out of a spaghetti western. Michael Collins lends a folksy, humorous light touch to the most serious or technical of discussions. Alan Bean exudes gratitude for his adventures more than the others and has a huggable grandpa quality. And so on. I understand that I don't actually *know* these men at all, that the simple caricatures I have made of them in my head are not the same as actual human beings. But still it's irresistible to indulge in this kind of hero worship, because this is precisely their job.

When I think back on how those first six women astronauts looked to me as a child, I remember a fierce admiration that's hard to describe. It has a lot to do with the possibilities of competent femininity. This was only a few years after *Star Wars* came out, after all, and infected a generation of girls with the role model of Princess Leia. In that scene when we first see her, when her spaceship is being boarded by storm troopers, she steps out of the shadows warily, holding a blaster muzzle-up beside her head. Baby-faced, with that strange sleek hairdo picking up red alarm lights, her face in a serious glower. Her lip gloss is perfect. She is beautiful, and she is ready to commit violence in pursuit of values larger than herself. I saw that again when the women astronauts were introduced. I remember the first time I saw them, in some footage on the evening news, all of them leaning against a fence. They looked fantastic.

A few years later, the space shuttle documentary *The Dream Is Alive* I saw at the Air and Space Museum showed me Judith Resnik sleeping in space. In that film, she no longer looks uncomfortable, as she had leaning against the fence. She smiles at her male crewmates and somersaults in space. She no longer wears lip gloss, but she doesn't have to. Her femininity is no longer as marked as it once was; already it's no longer as remarkable. She belongs in space, it seems to the children watching her for the first time—at least, until she dies on her way to space in 1986.

I've been talking to my fellow Americans about what they will miss about spaceflight, and I'm gratified by how many people share my simple love for the astronauts, both the famous ones and the obscure ones. A lot of women my age remember those first six and the way they seemed to open up possibilities for all of us. When I talk to people about the astronauts, about the end of American spaceflight, they want to know whether the shuttle is really ending, whether anything can be done to save it, as I asked Omar the first time I met him for Family Day. I find it depressing to have to explain to these people why nothing can save it now. And I hadn't realized how much, even now, people still hope it could be saved.

[The astronauts] would get in their cars and go barreling into Cocoa Beach for the endless, seamless party. And what lively cries and laughter would be rising up on all sides as the silvery moon reflected drunkenly on the chlorine blue of the motel pools! And what animated revelers were to be found!   —Tom Wolfe, *The Right Stuff*

And out on the beaches and the causeways and river-banks, another audience was waiting for the launch. America like a lazy beast in the hot dark was waiting for a hint in the ringing of the night. . . . In bed by two in the morning, he would be up by four. An early start was necessary, for traffic on the road to the Press Site would be heavy.

—Norman Mailer, *Of a Fire on the Moon*

CHAPTER 7. Good-bye, *Atlantis*

STS-135: July 8, 2011

A million visitors are expected to descend on the Space Coast for the last launch of the space shuttle program on July 8, 2011, more than have visited since the launch of Apollo 11. In the weeks and days leading up to it, I see more and more news stories about the end of shuttle. Some are elegiac, focusing on layoffs and the loss to the economy in central Florida. Some strike an optimistic tone, implying that the end of shuttle will open the door for the Next Thing. In reality, the only Next Thing on the books is the Space Launch System, a stripped-down version of the canceled *Constellation* program. SLS is discussed as a replacement for shuttle with varying degrees of credulity about whether it will ever fly. But anyone who knows anything about how NASA gets funded knows that SLS has no long-term budget. To its critics, SLS is not a vehicle for getting astronauts to space so much as it is a mechanism for allowing politicians to avoid taking responsibility for canceling the future. It's a talking point, a place to put our hopes, but whether it will ever take astronauts to space remains to be seen.

When I make the trip from Knoxville to the Space Coast this time, two months after the launch of *Endeavour* and five weeks after the rollout of *Atlantis,* it's an easy drive. I've done it so many times now, I know all the landmarks by heart—the change in scenery when Tennessee becomes Georgia, which always reminds me of a line from Flannery O'Connor: "Tennessee has the mountains and Georgia has the hills." Roadside shacks, shopping malls, rest stops with peaches and boiled peanuts. The thickening traffic around Atlanta. I was curious to see whether the WHERE'S THE BIRTH CERTIFICATE? billboard would come down after the birth certificate was revealed between *Discovery*'s last launch and *Endeavour*'s; it did not. A Cracker Barrel I've become especially fond of in Valdosta, Georgia. As I pass into Florida after dark, the terrain becomes more tropical, palm trees appearing, the humidity thickening. I cut across the state on 528, a road that for some reason demands nearly seven dollars in tolls, at four different tollbooths, to travel about fifteen miles. The toll workers are invariably friendly and alert, no matter how late I pass through. This is how I know I'm almost at the Space Coast, when all the change in my ashtray has been handed out to four smiling, Hawaiian-shirted toll workers. When I was here last, I accidentally got into the lane reserved for people with those devices on their cars and missed the tollbooth altogether; weeks later I received a bill in the mail, complete with an image of my car speeding past the camera. I hung up the ticket on the corkboard in my office along with my other space souvenirs. Now I know which lane to stay in, and my change is at the ready.

After the third tollbooth, I leave the window open as I accelerate back into traffic. It's one of the small pleasures of cross-country driving: the feeling of accelerating away from a tollbooth, the perfectly legal yet still thrilling feeling of flooring the gas and letting the hot, humid night rush in past me.

I pay my last toll on 528 and approach the Space Coast a few minutes after midnight. The press badging office is scheduled to open for the day at 1:00 a.m., and even though it means I'll get even less sleep, I decide to drive out there and get badged up before checking into my motel. For this launch, I've managed to get press credentials for the first time by pitching a story to my local newspaper. Credentialing, it turned out, is a byzantine and archaic weeks-long process that involves a NASA employee speaking with my editor on the telephone to confirm that I exist, am a published writer, and am not a terrorist. It had been a harrowing wait to hear back from the media office—I still hadn't heard back the day before I needed to leave for Florida. When I'd finally called, the harassed-sounding woman on the phone promised to e-mail me, and when she did, saying that my application for credentials had been accepted, I burst into tears of relief at my computer.

The Press Site is closer to the launchpad than I've ever been: the site from which Norman Mailer watched the launch of Apollo 11, the site from which Walter Cronkite narrated the moon landings, the site from which all the space journalists have watched all the launches. Over twenty-seven hundred journalists from all over the world are expected to cover this launch (also a record unmatched since Apollo 11), and I hope not to get caught in the line for badges behind too many of them.

The press badging office turns out to be a tiny shack on State Road 3, a fluorescent-lit Apollo-era building staffed by a few slightly harried but extremely competent middle-aged women, the same women who spoke to everyone's editors on the phone. A hand-painted fifties-style sign warns us not to use the office phones, a quaint reminder of a time before each journalist carried his or her own.

A couple of other journalists are there ahead of me, chatting up the women behind the counter with the easy rhythm of coworkers. The journalists clip on their badges, both men in their fifties who have the type of physique that comes with eating bad food and sitting at press sites and on press buses for twenty-hour days. When it's my turn to check in, the woman behind the counter seems mildly irritated that I don't already know what to do—apparently most journalists who are covering this launch have been here many times before. I'm supposed to fill out a form with information about the media organization I'm representing and my emergency contacts. The media center woman looks up my name while I sign a form agreeing that I won't participate in unprofessional behavior, which includes, but is not limited to, peddling materials for profit, possessing alcoholic beverages or firearms, and autograph-seeking.

Then the woman asks for my name again, this time asks me to spell it. She looks through her files a second time.

"What organization are you with?" she asks.

"Knoxville News Sentinel," I answer. She reaches the end of her files and starts over, a doubtful look on her face.

My heart starts pounding. There's been a mistake, I didn't get press credentials at all, I'll have to find somewhere else to watch the launch from even though all the good spots have been taken for days. While I wait, a few more journalists straggle in (again, all men in their fifties), give their names, and greet the media office women like old friends.

"When did you get your confirmation you would be credentialed?" the woman asks.

"The day before yesterday," I answer. "I can show you the e-mail I got."

"Yeah, okay, that would help," she says. She comes over, takes my phone from me, and peers at the e-mail I've called up there.

"Yup, you did get accepted," she agrees. "I don't know what happened. I'm gonna make you a badge."

She types at a computer, then goes over to a laminator, which starts up with a hum. She pulls the piece of plastic off the machine, attaches a metal clip, and hands over my badge. It is still warm. I am pleased to discover that the badges have not changed since the Apollo era. Mine is much like those worn by all the journalists to have written about American spaceflight since Apollo 4.

When I finally check in to my motel—I'm at my Florida home, the Clarion in Merritt Island—it's close to 2:00 a.m. The young Indian man behind the counter, whose name tag reads PRAMOD, remembers me from the last time I was here. He types something into the computer while on the wall, a large flat-screen TV shows weather forecasts with an image of a space shuttle behind the numbers. Storms are predicted for the morning, but that can always go either way here on the Space Coast.

"Here for the space shuttle?" Pramod asks cheerily while he slips my keys into their little envelope and writes my room number inside. I always accept two keys, so no one suspects I am traveling alone.

"Yes," I admit. I would rather tell him I'm here for anything else—a cruise leaving from Port Canaveral, a vacation at the beach—anything that isn't about to happen for the very last time tomorrow. I watch him for a reaction. He knows as well as I do that tonight might be the last time this motel will be fully booked. But he seems unbothered by my answer.

"Park your car here," he says, drawing on the photocopied map with a ballpoint pen, as all motel clerks do. "Ice machine is here. Breakfast is here. Breakfast starts at 6:30. But you'll be long gone by then, won't you?"

"Yup," I agree. "I'll be long gone." I find my room, haul my things inside, and set my phone to go off in two hours.

On the morning of July 16, 1969, the morning of the launch of Apollo 11, Norman Mailer woke up in a motel room. He writes that in the predawn darkness, "the night air a wet and lightless forest in the nose, one was finally scared." He says that waking early to see a spacecraft launch reminds him of waking before dawn to invade a foreign beach, "an awakening in the dark of the sort one will always remember, for such nights live only on a few mornings of one's life."

"One was scared." An interesting turn of phrase, isn't it? Any high school English teacher will tell you this is a grammatical evasion no less than "mistakes were made" (which President Nixon would not utter until three years on). Was Norman Mailer constitutionally incapable of writing the words "I was scared"? Was Norman Mailer unwilling to tell us, without the veil of fiction, of his own terror when, as a young soldier, he woke before dawn, after only fitful sleep, in order to storm the beaches of the Philippines?

I love the smell of Florida night described as a "wet and lightless forest in the nose." There *is* a smell here, unlike that of any other place I've known. That smell has become inextricable from the feeling of waking here in the dark, knowing that, not far away, the enormous ship is steaming, creaking and groaning with fuel, coming to life for its launch.

On TV, a newscaster reports from the Kennedy Space Center. Over her shoulder, the launchpad is lit up with floodlights. *Atlantis* is stacked there, its white tiles glowing against the orange of its external tank. The newscaster talks of nothing but the weather, and she's not saying encouraging things. To use NASA terminology, the weather is only 30 percent go. Storms lurking offshore are expected to blow in later this morning, in time to interfere with the launch window. This launch attempt will likely be scrubbed, hours or minutes or seconds before liftoff. A million people will moan in unison, and we'll get up even earlier to do all this again tomorrow. All preparations are still moving forward as planned, though—NASA took a lot of criticism in the early years of the shuttle program for calling off launches based on weather predictions that never came true.

"Reporting live from the Kennedy Space Center," the young newscaster says before throwing back to the anchor, and because I have stood outside not far from where she is standing, I know she is being bitten by many vicious mosquitoes and pretending not to be. The huge countdown clock behind her continues marking time left until launch by hundredths of a second in huge orange numbers. It's now T minus seven hours.

I dress in layers, observing NASA's requirement that we wear long pants and closed-toed shoes. Last time I was here I met a writer who was turned away from his one and only chance to go inside the Orbiter Processing Facility because he was wearing shorts. I cover all exposed skin with SPF 50 and bring the bottle with me to reapply throughout the day. I bring notebooks and pens, snacks and a great deal of water. I bring my phone's charger and my computer in case I fill up my phone with pictures and recordings and need to dump data in the middle of the day. I bring rain gear, cash, and a change of clothes in case I don't have time to get back to my motel before going out to dinner with Omar and some other space friends after the launch. I make sure my press badge is securely attached to me.

I slip into my car. It is still fully night, and already sticky hot. The motel parking lot is packed to capacity with cars bearing license plates from all over the country. I feel I must be the only person awake. But out on the causeways, strings of taillights blink like fireflies, other people already heading to the Cape.

Right outside the entrance to the Kennedy Space Center squats an all-night gas station, its outdoor sodium lights pitched at such a brightness and angle it seems to be an alien starship just landed. The lights lure me in, as surely they are meant to, and I stop for coffee. Inside, the place is overrun, the coffee service area a wasteland of spilled creamer and abandoned stir sticks, devastated by the many space fans who came through even earlier than me. The people with whom I wait in line to pay are a nice mix of Launch People: first-timers overly energetic for this hour in the morning; launch veterans who play it cool, showing off their T-shirts and hats commemorating previous launches. I am wearing my press badge, and I feel a certain geeky pride when the other space fans in line notice it, then look closer at me, wondering whether I'm someone important.

As always in the hours before a launch, strangers nod and smile at each other with a shared sense of patriotism and common purpose. I hear a variety of Englishes spoken: Louisiana, New England, London. A sleepy blond mother whispers to her daughters in German. The man who rings up my coffee is wearing a name tag studded with shuttle mission pins. He smiles and tells me to have a great day, and as I thank him I wonder whether his business will suffer after the shuttle workers are laid off and few people drive past here on their way to work anymore.

I leave the gas station and find State Road 3 jammed with cars waiting to get through the checkpoint. It takes me forty-five minutes to travel about one mile, a rate reminiscent of that of the crawler transporter, by which time the sun is starting to come up. When I reach the booth, an armed guard looks over my badge with exquisite care, compares the name to the one on my driver's license letter by letter, then scrutinizes my face in comparison with the photo on my ID.

"Have a good one, Margaret," he says finally with a wink. I roll on. A few minutes later, I reach another checkpoint with another guard, and we go through the same process. This one calls me "young lady" and advises me to take it easy.

I almost miss the turnoff to the Press Site because once again I've made the mistake of using the Vehicle Assembly Building as a landmark. When I finally get there, the parking lots are already full, and another guard directs me to a nearby patch of grass to park on. As I lock up my car, I hear, then see, a black helicopter go by overhead. Then a few black SUVs. There is no mistaking it: the Astrovan is coming through. A small herd of people is running to the roadside to get a closer look.

The Astrovan convoy slows, then stops. This is unusual, the stopping. An astronaut in a blue flight suit pops out. He is along for the Astrovan ride—the astronauts going to space today are dressed in orange pressure suits. He has his picture taken with the gathered crowd. As he climbs back in, I peer at the windows of the Astrovan. I can see the astronauts' hands waving, their faces lost in shadows. I can make out the lock rings on their wrists where their gloves will connect before their suits are pressurized.

Four Americans are going to space today.

***

The Press Site at the Kennedy Space Center is just south of the Vehicle Assembly Building. Back behind the handful of buildings visible from the road lurks its largest structure, the News Center. This is where press conferences are held before and after launches, and it is also where the NASA Media Office does most of its work. The main room of the News Center has rows of Formica desks with electric outlets and data plugs, though there are not nearly as many desks as journalists today, not by a long shot, and the ones set up here have the settled look of having staked their claims many hours, maybe even days, earlier. More journalists, some in suits and ties, have camped along the walls, having plugged in their laptops and devices wherever they could find an outlet. There is something thrillingly old-school about this way of gathering news—reporters watching the monitors, getting announcements, yelling questions to the Media Office people and scrawling down the answers in those steno notebooks all the print journalists use, typing stuff up on their laptops and talking urgently into their phones.

It's pleasant for a first-time holder of press credentials to simply stroll around the Press Site. These structures of varying solidity have grown up at the Press Site over the decades, and, aside from a few losses to hurricanes, their permanence tends to correlate with age. So some of the networks and newspapers have concrete buildings that date back to Apollo 4, outlets that came later in the sixties have trailers, and the websites and foreign agencies have tents or awnings. Under each outdoor structure, a stand-up TV journalist does a standard prelaunch patter against the backdrop of the countdown clock and far-off launch stack, speaking various languages, many of them wearing shorts and flip-flops with their jackets and ties and makeup.

The overall architectural feel at the Press Site is distinctly utilitarian Apollo-era. The restroom building is a case in point, classic early-sixties sloping-roof exterior and salmon-pink tile interior. I'm surprised there were enough female journalists at the time the Press Site was built to merit the five or so stalls allocated to us. I take pictures inside the bathroom, especially of a janitor's trolley emblazoned with old mission patch stickers. It pleases me to see that even the janitors are proud of what goes on here. I have long dreamed of seeing a launch from the Press Site, and though this facility is supposed to be a means to an end, I've become fascinated with the Press Site itself, with the history of the people who have written about spaceflight, the people who have dedicated their careers to the task of telling this story. Now that it's the end, everything seems important to me, everything historic.

Now that I'm here, there is more waiting. After getting up so ungodly early, then idling in the line of creeping cars to show my badge to the guards, I had started to feel anxious that I had arrived too late, that I had underestimated the traffic, wouldn't make it to the Press Site in time. Yet now it is still not seven, and the launch is over four hours off. The other journalists, of course, had to get here so insanely early because they are putting together their coverage in real time. I am one of very few credentialed writers who is free to roam around taking in the scene, who does not have to make sense of what I'm seeing immediately. It is a great luxury.

I make my way to the center of the Press Site, a grassy field bordering on the Turn Basin, which I'm now seeing from a different angle than I did at the launch of *Endeavour*. I move downfield, close to the lip of the Turn Basin, where all the photographers are set up, nearly shoulder to shoulder now. You've seen it: the forest of enormous lenses, all pointing in the same direction across the water. The photographers got here even earlier than everyone else in order to stake their claims for prime tripod real estate, and they are the only ones who have bothered to bring lawn chairs. Oriana Fallaci, at the Press Site for a test launch of the Saturn V, commented that "journalists are always a disaster when they get together," that space journalists were even worse, women space journalists worst of all. In general, the feeling here at the Press Site is both friendly and every-man-for-himself. Leave a seat for a moment, a good vantage point, a socket where a phone can be recharged, and it will be snatched up unapologetically. This does not preclude a sense of friendliness or collegiality, however.

While I wait, I look again at what Norman Mailer wrote about his wait in this place:

> It is country beaten by the wind and water . . . unspectacular country,
> uninhabited by men in normal times and normal occupations. . . .
> To the right of the photographers was a small grove of pure jungle.
> Recollections of his platoon on a jungle trail, hacking with machetes
> entered his head. A hash of recollections.

I look over to the right of the photographers. There it is, the small grove of pure jungle. The visible line between mowed field and jungle is a border between space center and wild preserve, space and Earth, home and an alien world. The jungle is a terrain we are supposed to fear—untamed, uncivilized, teeming with poisonous plant life and vicious animal life, populated by monkeys in the trees (an astronaut is the opposite of a woman and he is also the opposite of a monkey). But, in 2011, I have no associations with jungles other than—oddly—space shuttle launches. So many writers have made much of the rockets-and-alligators contrast inherent in the landscape of the Kennedy Space Center, but that contrast, so captivating to me the first few times I visited here, has now become one of the fixtures of spaceflight itself, and at this point I can't imagine a launch of an American rocket without palm trees, humidity, and mosquitoes. I can't imagine American spacecraft being serviced by anyone but Floridians. The Cape and its remarkable geography are as much a part of the story of American spaceflight as President Kennedy's "before this decade is out," as much as the test pilot corps from which the first astronauts were selected, as much as the blue NASA meatball logo, as much as the countdown.

A text comes in from Omar: Make it to the press site ok?

Yep, I answer. Where are you?

I'm working, on north side of VAB. I'll head to the front parking lot at T-15 min.

Omar has some flexibility in his schedule, and when he wants to see a launch—which he always does—he usually requests that day off work so he can be assured the freedom to find a good vantage point. So the fact that he's chosen to be at work today means he's guessing, as I am, that today's attempt will scrub. He's gambling on it, in fact, as there's always a risk he could be engaged in some actual work at the moment of the launch.

Someone wandering by tells me that the weather is now no-go. The storm clouds must be blowing in.

"Are they continuing the countdown?" I ask him. If the answer is no, there will be an unspeakable traffic jam to get out of here, but then I'll be able to go back to my motel, take a nap, have dinner with Omar and some other spaceworkers, meet some kooky space people to get quotes from, and do all this launch business again tomorrow after a decent night's sleep. The guy looks down at his phone.

"They're continuing the countdown."

Atlantis was the fourth orbiter constructed, completed in April 1985. The name *Atlantis* comes from the oceanographic Research Vessel *Atlantis,* a sailing ship built in 1930. *Atlantis* was the primary research vessel for the Woods Hole Oceanographic Institution and is the oldest serving oceanographic research vessel in the world. The undeniably nautical feel to the name somehow blends with the legend of the sunken city, and so the space shuttle *Atlantis* has always carried with it a sense of watery mystery.

The first flight of *Atlantis* was a secret mission for the Department of Defense, as were two of its subsequent five flights. These missions, presumably to deploy spy satellites, were conducted without the usual fanfare and without the typical flood of information from NASA. In the handouts given to reporters, a column titled "primary payload," where generally one finds a long, chatty description of cargo and experiments, offers only a simple "D o D." This secrecy, along with its sleek name, made *Atlantis* seem more streamlined, slicker and sneakier, than the others.

Atlantis was the first orbiter to launch an interplanetary probe, Magellan, which traveled to Venus. On its next flight, *Atlantis* launched the Galileo probe to Jupiter. Both probes' missions were considered enormous successes, and both have greatly expanded our knowledge of the solar system. In the midnineties, *Atlantis* made seven consecutive flights to dock with the Russian space station *Mir;* when they were linked, *Atlantis* and *Mir* together formed the largest spacecraft in orbit to date.

Of all the orbiters, *Atlantis* was the one I could never quite get a handle on, the one that never really developed a personality for me, and so maybe it's fitting that it should be the last, that it should be the one I have to say good-bye to.

Within the last hour before launch, the weather has been given a go, then a no-go again, then back to go. The countdown continues. While I'm making my way back to the field in front of the countdown clock, I hear the T minus nine minute hold has been released. The weather is go again, but I don't assume it will continue to be. If I had to bet, I'd still put my money on a scrub today. It will be my first. The numbers on the huge digital countdown clock flow by, counting hundredths of a second.

People are starting to find their viewing spots. Omar is probably in place at the VAB parking lot. After the T minus nine hold is released, the photographers stop talking to each other and go into semimeditative game-face trances. They check and double-check their equipment.

T minus five minutes and counting.

T minus three minutes and counting.

Someone tall steps in front of me, covering the launchpad with his head. I tap him firmly on the shoulder. Without turning back to meet my eyes, the man steps back to where he had been. I still don't think the launch will go off, but we are getting awfully close on the countdown.

Phones and handheld radios squawk out the voice of George Diller, the public affairs officer. He sounds excited but professional. The long pauses between his comments are probably no longer than they have been all morning, but they seem troublingly long, insanely long, now that we are hanging on every word.

Verifying now that the main engines are in their start position.

Starting now the retraction of the gaseous vent arm, the vent hood.

PLT, OTC, verifying no unexpected errors.

Fuel cells going to internal, external tank camera being activated at this time.

OTC, PLT, no unexpected errors.

Flight crew, OTC, close and lock your visors and initiate O₂ flow.

T minus two minutes and counting.

T minus one minute and counting.

At T minus thirty-one seconds, the countdown pauses. There is a problem with the oxygen vent hood—it is not retracting properly. These types of small issues often crop up and get resolved without delaying the launch, but the closer we get to T minus zero the more likely it is a small problem like this one could cause a scrub. I can picture the hood, which is nicknamed the "beanie cap" (as in the transcript of crew chatter before *Challenger*'s fateful launch—Commander Dick Scobee says, "There goes the beanie cap"). But I have no idea how difficult it might be to fix one. We wait and watch and listen.

The hold is lifted and the clock starts again.

T minus ten. Nine. Eight. Seven. Six.

Go for main engine start.

Main engine start.

Five.

Four.

Three.

Two.

At one, the solid rocket boosters ignite. I see the flash on the horizon, and the unmistakable orange of that flash makes me gasp with something like horror. I clasp both hands to my chest, because it suddenly hurts. I'm aware that this is a ridiculous gesture, but I can't help myself. I'd become convinced this launch wasn't going to happen today, that I'd get the chance to do this all again tomorrow. But once the solid rocket boosters ignite, they can't be shut down. We are going to space.

Atlantis pulls itself away from the grip of gravity, slowly at first, then faster. The flames streaking from the shuttle's main engines light up the sky. Once *Atlantis* has been in the air a few long seconds, the sound reaches us, that deeply satisfying rumble, and here at the Press Site that rumble reverberates everywhere, against the VAB, against the countdown clock, against Walter Cronkite's CBS building and all the others, against the trees in Norman Mailer's jungle, against our very hearts and bodies, against the hearts and bodies of those watching with us.

"Max Q," speaks the voice of the public affairs officer one minute after launch. The shuttle has reached the peak of aerodynamic pressure. Then, at two minutes, the solid rocket boosters jettison for the last time.

Every space shuttle launch is a little different. With this launch, what I will remember most is the brightness, the intense orange flame that almost burns my eyes. Knowing that this launch is the last, and seeing it against the backdrop of such a gray and uncertain sky, I can't help but see *Atlantis*'s brightness as some sort of defiance.

"Negative return," speaks the voice of the public affairs officer, at four minutes after launch, the point past which the vehicle can no longer abort and return to Kennedy. He says it with a hint of a thrill in his voice, a satisfaction that everything has gone as planned, but to us standing with our heads tipped back, gawking at the sky, it sounds like a declaration, for the millionth time, that something we love is now over.

"Main engine cutoff," capcom says at nearly nine minutes.

"Roger MECO," the commander answers.

"ET separation," capcom says. This means the giant orange fuel tank has dropped off to burn up in the atmosphere, that now *Atlantis* is traveling by itself, the black-and-white space plane alone. Ten minutes after launch, we wouldn't be able to make out *Atlantis* even if the sky were clear. It would be too small; it's gone.

"*Atlantis* is now on orbit," the public affairs officer announces, and it's hard to believe that those hands we saw waving from their Astrovan here on Earth a few hours ago are now floating weightless, waving at black sky with stars out *Atlantis*'s windows.

Good-bye, *Atlantis*.

All around me, people are crying and hugging. The photojournalists are snapping pictures of people crying and hugging. I am still watching the now-empty sky, staring at the enormous fluffy column of steam *Atlantis* left hanging there, trying to absorb that this really happened, that the shuttle will really never launch again.

Before NASA sent men to the moon, when the Kennedy Space Center was still new, components of the Apollo spacecraft were constructed in California and brought here, romantically, by ship. They left port from the California coast and sailed south on the Pacific, made their way through the Panama Canal, then north again through the Caribbean and up the Gulf Stream to Cape Canaveral. The Gulf Stream had been discovered 453 years earlier by Juan Ponce de León who, we all agree now, was wrong to look for gold and the Fountain of Youth. These things weren't here, and he killed many people trying to find them. He took slaves instead, and the way some accounts try to make excuses for his treatment of his fellow human beings reminds me of those apologists for Wernher von Braun who try to minimize his complicity with the Nazi regime that forced slave laborers to build his rockets. We remember Juan Ponce as an explorer, a man of courage and conviction. Like Wernher von Braun, like Norman Mailer, like Captain James Cook and the other ruthless men whose stories I have learned, Ponce de León believed that the vision in his mind was more important than anything else, more important than the people standing in his way. What he saw that spring day in 1513, when he climbed out of his stinking, flea-infested galleon, is oddly similar to what I see today. Miles of marsh, a hot sky, a lot of canebrake. He climbed back into his ship and moved on. He didn't come back for eight years—the same length of time between the end of Apollo and the start of shuttle—and he came back that second time with the intention of creating a permanent colony. In between he wrote to his king, Charles V, begging for money: "That which is made or seen in those places where I shall go will be reported to Your Majesty upon my return, and I shall ask for favors. And from now on I pray they are brought to me, because I cannot imagine undertaking such a grand thing." Like Christopher Columbus, with whom Juan Ponce had made his first voyage to the New World, he faced the problem of bankrolling a second voyage when the first had been found to be culturally and geographically thrilling but financially disappointing. His tone echoes that of a NASA budget proposal, referring to lofty goals and the grand attributes of a great nation in the face of profitlessness. As historian Robert Fuson writes, "There was a need for something spectacular to come out of the voyage if support for it was to be sustained." On his second voyage to La Florida, Juan Ponce engaged in a battle with natives and died from an arrow wound to the thigh. The settlement he had dreamed of founding was a failure, and Florida would not be home to Europeans until the founding of Saint Augustine in 1561, forty years later—the same length of time since we've been to the moon.

What does it mean that we have been going to space for fifty years and have decided to stop? Maybe it's only a fantasy that the explorers of the past were met with better funding and smoother travels. Maybe they all had to beg for money; they all found themselves doing less than had been planned, less than had been hoped for. They all compromised the morals that had been the ostensible inspiration for the voyage. Maybe it was true for them as much as it is for NASA, that their discoveries are celebrated only once they have been successful. Only in retrospect does the support seem to have been inevitable. Only in retrospect does the dream seem to have fully come true.

I think of Omar, who is still on the other side of the VAB. Like me, he had guessed today's attempt would scrub, that he would be able to come back and see this tomorrow.

I text him the most direct question I have ever asked him.

Are you crying?

A minute goes by. Everyone out here is crying and hugging, texting, and describing what they saw all at once. Omar's response finally comes through.

Hahahah. Are you?

Back inside the News Center, a closed-circuit TV shows the White Room, the staging area directly outside the hatch to the crew cabin. This room is the territory of the closeout crew, whose responsibilities include strapping the crew violently into their seats one by one, making sure the right objects are inside of (and outside of) the spacecraft, closing the hatch, and pressurizing the crew cabin before taking shelter for launch.

The closed-circuit view of the White Room has shown these closeout guys all morning doing their job, which includes a lot of standing around and talking into their headsets. There were exciting moments each time one of the pumpkin-suited astronauts arrived to make last-minute preparations—donning cumbersome emergency parachutes, straightening out hoses and comm wires, then climbing through the hatch one by one to take their seats. There is always a fair amount of handshaking and shoulder-clapping, much of it ritualistic, maybe even superstitious. The closeout crew wear emergency equipment of their own—yellow safety harnesses and oxygen packs on their backs in case of disaster on the pad. They are trained, along with the astronauts, to escape clouds of toxic fuels by running down a bright yellow path painted onto the catwalk, nicknamed the Yellow Brick Road, and jumping into baskets that zip down trip wires the nineteen stories to the ground. None of this has ever been used in an actual emergency, and it's possible none of it would help anyway. But it still serves to make the closeout crew seem like badasses. They are regarded by other spaceworkers with some degree of awe, partly because of the risk and importance of their work, and partly because of their proximity to the astronauts. Every description I have ever seen of the closeout crew has mentioned that they are the last to see and shake hands with the astronauts before they leave Earth.

Now, in the aftermath of the launch, we see in the White Room one of the technicians position himself in front of the camera. He holds up a sign printed on whiteboard. At one edge is printed an image of the launch vehicle, a billowing steam cloud forming under it, against a rippling American flag. In the center of the sign are printed the words:

Thank you America!

He is, like most of them, a former-military-looking guy. His white ball cap bears the United Space Alliance logo. He stands before the camera, looking right into it, holding up his sign, and he appears to be in equal measure uncomfortable with the public nature of this act and pride-filled that he gets to carry it out. He steps away, his tool belt clanging against his legs, and is replaced by another member of the closeout crew, this one older, maybe in his fifties. His sign reads:

On behalf of all who have Designed & Built . . .

He too looks right into the camera, looking mildly embarrassed, but then he lifts his chin, almost defiantly, and holds the sign up a bit more. Both bashful and sincere, a combination I find somehow heart-rending. The idea of all these introverts collaborating in this very extroverted gesture, knowing their images would remain for all time. He is replaced by another one, this one a little more smiley and chipper. His sign reads:

Serviced & Loaded . . .
Launched & Controlled . . .

The next guy a little more laconic, straight-faced, but he too relifts his sign a few seconds into his turn, pushes it a bit more toward the camera.

Operated & Flown . . .
These Magnificent Space Vehicles

The next guy is younger, taller.

Thank you for 30 years with Our Nation's Space Shuttles!

He is replaced by yet another guy, proud to get to hold this particular sign. He is the only one to mouth the words on his sign, though he
knows we cannot hear him. Then he salutes.

Godspeed Atlantis!

Last to go is a short man with a Wilford Brimley mustache. He is the
chief of the closeout crew, Travis Thompson. He does not smile, and
of all of them he looks most solemn, most self-conscious, maybe closest to tears. He is the only one whose headset is still plugged into the
comm box behind him, a curling black cord tethering his head to the
wall. He opens his mouth as if to say the words, but then chooses not
to, or can't. His sign says:

God Bless America!

He stands there for a minute, letting his message sink in.

I watch all this on the monitor, feeling aware of the people watching around me. Some of them seem to be glued to the closeout crew's
messages and their implied import, as I am. Some of them seem to be
moved nearly to tears by it, as I am. Some glance up at the monitor,
register the signs, and keep talking to each other, messing with their
cameras and their phones, moving about as if the screen were showing nothing other than the closeout crew going about their prescribed
business.

I know I will look up this video online later, when I get back to my
motel. It's probably already on NASA TV—or if it's not yet, it will be

shortly. I know I will watch it again and again in an attempt to write about it, a document of a document. It's the best way I know of to get a moment to hold still and reveal itself.

For each of these launches I have studied videos afterward and have noticed that I always see more in the videos than I did in real time. The real experience always goes too fast, is too multisensory—a fellow space fan brushing against my elbow at *Endeavour*, struggling to keep my balance on the roof of my car at *Discovery*, the eerie storm clouds, the merciless orange numbers of the countdown clock at *Atlantis*. The lived detail of each actual launch is too much to take in. But the videos, with their finite frames and running times, those I can put words to.

In recent years much has been made of the way our ever-present cameras and connections to social media interfere with our ability to live our lives in real time through our own senses. We are too busy photographing our lunches to taste them, the argument goes, too busy Facebook messaging our friends to talk to them or listen to them. To some extent I get this—when Omar chose not to try to tilt his camera to follow *Endeavour*'s path, he was choosing the lived experience over the burden of documenting it, and in that I think he chose well. Yet the video he shot contains a permanence that the real experience doesn't, and as such it will be viewed by many people who couldn't be at the launch, including people who haven't been born yet, people for whom American spaceflight might have been only an idea, a vague claim, if not for Omar's document of that moment that lets them experience a version of it for themselves.

I know I'm supposed to value lived experiences more than I do their digital records, but for me, this video in the White Room is not a simulacrum of something else; it is precisely what its makers intended it to be. The experience of watching this video, as with videos of launches and other events I will watch over and over, *is* an experience, just as seeing the real event was, and as I watch it, through my watching, each video becomes more of what it is about.

That night, I have dinner with Omar, three photographers, and a filmmaker. It's a table only a shuttle launch could bring together—one woman and five men, all with drastically different backgrounds and interests, no two of whom live in the same state (one lives in New Zealand). But we chat happily together about what we saw today. We have chosen a local seafood restaurant popular with tourists, the kind of place with a lot of nautical bric-a-brac on the walls, restroom doors labeled BUOYS and GULLS. This place has been busy every time I've been here, but tonight it is truly overrun. Our waiter has the blank look of a person who has been harried for over four hours and has settled into his suffering, a look that tells us we won't be getting our food any time soon.

People are made patient by unusual circumstances, and the familiar postlaunch sunburn-and-patriotism atmosphere prevails even though the waitstaff can't keep drinks refilled quickly enough for anyone to really be drunk. We are all sleep-deprived and have the fuzzy giddiness that drunks and college students call "the second wind." Rather than napping this afternoon, I drank coffee and stayed up to write pages and pages of frantic notes. The photographers stayed up as well, to work on digitally processing their shots. One of them, the photographer from New Zealand, has been up for over forty-eight hours.

We talk about previous launches we've been to, how they were different from today's. As usually happens when people start comparing launch experiences, a lot of the stories are about spending hours at a viewing spot only to see the launch called off, the empty feeling of going home without having seen anything. It takes me a moment to realize that I will never see a shuttle launch scrub. For some reason this makes me feel triumphant, like I have won something.

"I'm scrubless!" I announce to the table. They applaud me politely. It's a nearly unbelievable bit of luck—the chances of seeing four launches with zero scrubs are very low. The risk of having to return to Florida for multiple attempts for each mission was great enough to make me doubt whether I should embark on this project at all. I announce my scrubless status on social media, though most of my friends will have no idea what this word means. While I'm looking in my phone, I flip through images of the launch online—shots taken by people at this table, shots by photographers from Reuters and AP, shots from random people posting on Flickr, Twitter, and Facebook. It's perhaps too obvious to bear mentioning, but the number and range of photos is astounding, the different colors and moods of the same object, the same event, the same few minutes. Each one feels different, each carries a slightly different meaning. I receive via e-mail a photo taken by a new space friend, Anna, who was standing behind me—it's a shot of the back of my head with *Atlantis* seeming to emerge from it. I show the others. This, I tell them, I will treasure forever.

One of the photographers at the table, famous for his surreally beautiful travel photographs taken around the world, mentions to us that he was referred to Omar by two different mutual acquaintances. It's an unfamiliar experience to share Omar with other people. I usually have him to myself.

"I heard about this guy named Omar who worked for NASA, and then my other friend was like, 'Look for Omar the security guard! He's really cool!'"

I flinch inwardly at the phrase "security guard," and watch Omar for his reaction. As usual he betrays none; his smile is as friendly as always. Since even before I met him in person, since I started to get an idea of what his job was, I sensed that Omar was not a security guard, but played a role more demanding and much more important. Now that I have been here as his guest on five different occasions, have seen his and his father's dedication to the project of sending people safely to space, have seen his encyclopedic knowledge of the work that has gone on here before him, the term strikes me as even more inappropriate, even offensive. I want to speak up and correct the photographer's misunderstanding, but I'm not entirely sure what I would say. Omar is an orbiter integrity clerk, a lay historian of American spaceflight, an ambassador for the Kennedy Space Center, a good friend, and a fine human being. I say nothing. No one else seems to think much of the phrase one way or the other.

Another photographer asks the table what's next, what the next step in spaceflight is supposed to be. I've been taken aback throughout the day by how tenuous a grasp of space history and space policy many of my fellow credentialed media representatives seem to have. A few of us start to answer simultaneously.

"There's a system called *Constellation*—"

"The launches to the space station will be contracted out to private companies like SpaceX—"

"A system called SLS, for Space Launch System I think, it looks like the Saturn V—"

"Wait, I thought *Constellation* was canceled—"

"But wasn't SLS part of *Constellation?* Wait, what's *Orion?*"

Even to those of us who make a point of keeping up, all this is a bit mushy. Omar tells a story about a mobile launch tower designed for *Constellation* that was being built at Kennedy, a gantry I saw on my visit for Family Day. It's now being dismantled, without ever having been used for anything, because *Constellation* was canceled. Some people were relieved when *Constellation* was canceled—I myself have referred to the decision as *Constellation* having been put out of its misery, and Buzz Aldrin called its cancellation President Obama's "JFK moment." The six of us at this table all have different reasons for being interested in spaceflight, and probably we all have different political views—but we all agree that this story about the gantry is infuriating.

Every time the shuttle takes off on the TVs, people raise their glasses and cheer.

As the six of us say our good-byes in the parking lot, Omar asks me whether I've decided to stay another day. I tell him I'm not sure.

"If you do, there's a party tomorrow you should come to," he says. "A lot of the space people on Twitter will be there. The NASATweetup people too."

"That would be fun," I say. "I'll text you tomorrow."

I'm not sure my family can spare me another day. But when I call home, Chris says they are doing fine, that I should do what I need to do so I won't have to come back again. We've agreed this will be my last trip.

Today, the day after the last launch of the space shuttle, the Visitor Complex feels different. It's busy—packed, in fact, with visitors. A lot of them wear the I WAS THERE shirts, and the festive mood persists, but these artifacts have changed somehow. I wander the displays, and all the space suits look forlorn in their display cases. I realize what it is: the last time I was here, only five weeks ago, *Atlantis* was making its way to the launchpad, and the Kennedy Space Center was a working spaceport. Now, everything has become historical. The mockup of the launch vehicle that greets us at the gates is, as of today, obsolete. Even while *Atlantis* orbits by in the sky above us, we know that never again will an orbiter be joined with an external tank and solid rocket boosters in that configuration. It's now a historical display, demonstrating something that used to happen. The surge of anger and sorrow I feel about this surprises me.

I carry this glum feeling through my afternoon at the Visitor Complex. I sit in the Rocket Garden for a few minutes, looking at the old Titan and Redstone rockets, and try to console myself with the idea that the space shuttle will take its place among them. A spacecraft that is now obsolete, but that represented an important step on the path to the next thing. But without knowing what that next thing will be, it's hard not to imagine this tourist attraction, with its boosterism and optimism for the future, becoming a depressing joke, an artifact of a more ambitious time.

On my way out, I pass through the gift shop. A table near the front always bears merchandise specific to the most recent launch, and a mob of sunburned people is now wedged there shoulder to shoulder, pawing through piles of shirts, while an employee tries to unpack a fresh box straight onto the pile. A ten-year-old girl near me picks up a shirt, looks at the tag, and starts to put it back.

"Don't put it down!" her mother shrieks. Indeed, another woman was eyeing the shirt, ready to snatch it up if the girl had dropped it.

Outside, I stop at a refreshment kiosk. The man who rings up my bottle of water is in his forties. He wears space shuttle pins on his name tag, as the gas station attendant was wearing yesterday.

"Sure is busy today," he comments while he counts out my change.

"It's crazy," I answer. "Do you think everyone's here for the last launch?"

The man doesn't hear me, or pretends not to hear me. He gives me my receipt.

"Now you have a great day," he tells me.

The whole time I'm in Florida, I keep hearing optimists say this isn't the end of American spaceflight, that this is a hiatus, a hiccup, a pause to regroup. I can't tell you how many times I've heard this week that "it's in the American DNA to explore."

Countries don't have DNA, I want to snark back. *They have policies and budgets.* I do know what these people mean—they mean they hope that maybe once we notice that we've stopped going to space, it will occur to us that we want to start going again. Maybe seeing fresh-faced astronauts like Serena Auñón in their blue flight suits will make us want to call our congressional representatives and tell them we support NASA. Maybe we will. But how long will it take us to notice? The hiatus between Apollo and shuttle was eight years—eight years when the space shuttle project was already funded, its plans already under way, as the last Apollo mission was leaving Earth. Optimists (the DNA people) predict it will be ten to fifteen years before NASA launches its next human spaceflight. Pessimists say that yesterday's launch was the last for all history.

Norman Mailer doesn't mention having visited the Visitor Complex; if he had, I'm sure his comments would have been about how fat and sweaty his fellow Americans were, how slow-moving the lines for cold drinks, how unintentionally goofy the language used in the brochures and on the signage, some of which he would quote for our amusement. Or maybe I'm being unfair to him—Norman Mailer was a snob, but like me he could also be a sucker for the broad populist appeal of space-flight, the way it can pull together Americans who have little else in common. Maybe he would have enjoyed the Rocket Garden, the simplicity of its implied phallic rhetoric: Look at these rockets. These rockets are awesome.

Norman Mailer admired the mettle of the astronauts and the technological achievement of the moon shot, yet he never gave up questioning the effort and expense—again, the contradictions. After the launch of Apollo 11, he wrote, speaking of himself in the third person, "It was the event of his lifetime, and yet it had been a dull event." I always wondered whether he still felt that way—that it had been the event of a lifetime—as his own lifetime was coming to its close. In interviews in the seventies and eighties, he didn't refer to the experience of watching Apollo 11 much, a fact I'm never sure how to interpret. Was it because his interest in spaceflight was brief, fading as soon as the book was finished? Or was it because his feelings about it were too complex? Maybe the contradictions he wrote about stayed with him, as they have with me. Maybe he both loved the spectacle of spaceflight and questioned its point. Maybe he understood the risk to be part of the heroism and simultaneously felt betrayed by the deaths, by the details of the risks that killed seventeen men and women. Maybe all this complexity kept him from making casual reference to Apollo 11, and so he soon came to sound like any other American who had never experienced a launch at all, like anyone else who wasn't sure what to believe or what to hope for.

Omar is a member of a group on Twitter called the Space Tweep Society, a thriving Venn diagram of overlapping circles of NASA insiders, outsiders, and wannabes including astronauts, spaceworkers, physicists, astronomers, engineers, technicians, journalists, writers, teachers, science fiction buffs, and nerds of all stripes. The group has over eleven thousand followers and is steadily growing. A lot of the Space Tweeps have made the trip for the last launch, and plans for this party have been under discussion for a long time. I'm not sure how the party got the name Endless BBQ (discussions of it are indicated with the hashtag #endlessbbq), but I'm relieved it's not called a Tweetup as so many Twitter-based parties are.

I've only recently joined the Space Tweep Society, at Omar's urging— I've been on Facebook forever but am still having trouble getting the hang of Twitter. For instance, if I hadn't been invited by Omar, I tell him, I never would have driven out to the home of a person I don't know to attend a party with a bunch of strangers.

"They're not *strangers*," Omar says. "We know them on Twitter."

The party is being held at the home of a local Space Tweep who used to work at the Cape with Omar but who left awhile back. Whether under the first waves of layoffs or by his own choice I don't know, but he has remained a space fan, as so many space workers are. His home is a small one-story house, like all the houses I've seen in central Florida. As we approach the front door, I notice a sign taped to it warning us that images, sound, and video from this party will be made available on social media and that by entering we are agreeing to allow this. The legal formality of the sign strikes me as odd, though upon further reflection I suppose it's more responsible than what happens at most parties, which is that people's images are shared without their knowledge or permission.

In the entryway, a table is set up where the hosts are greeting people and guests are asked to make name tags. The host whose home we're in is named Chris, but because I knew him on Twitter first, I can only ever remember his Twitter handle. Also hosting is the Space Tweep Society's founder and driving force, Jen Scheer. Jen was a shuttle technician until last year, and now she seems to be a professional social media expert and a natural leader of online enthusiasm for spaceflight. Omar introduces me to both of them, and they are both friendly even though I have not been anywhere near active enough on Twitter for them to recognize my handle—we are supposed to put our Twitter handles as well as our real names on the name tags. In fact, some people aren't bothering with real names at all.

The place is packed and loud, so Omar and I wander a bit looking for something to drink and a little more space. He knows a lot of people here, both in person and on Twitter—more than one person looks at his name tag, recognizes his handle, and hugs him. A DJ is working a console, one headphone pressed to his head (I later find out he is someone I follow on Twitter, a fellow Space Tweep). We go to the kitchen, where we are offered drinks, and I eat a pudding shot. I haven't eaten a dessert prepared as a vehicle for vodka since college, and I'm not sure why it seems like the thing to do here. I guess not since college have I been surrounded by so many people I didn't know but felt sure I had a lot in common with anyway; nor have I felt so simultaneously happy and sad that it seemed like a good idea to ingest a lot of alcohol straightaway.

As we make our way to the back of the house, I find that the host has a large screened-in pool, as so many of the little one-story houses here do, as well as a hot tub. I'm still getting my bearings, hanging out while Omar catches up with the seemingly hundreds of people he knows or who know him, when I see a woman I recognize getting out of the pool. It takes me a minute to place her because the context is so different: she is one of the space scholars I met at the conference in DC. Last I saw her, she was wearing a dark pants suit and standing on a stage at NASA Headquarters giving a PowerPoint presentation; now she is dripping wet in a red bathing suit laughing with fellow Space Tweeps. She doesn't seem as surprised to see me here as I am to see her—I guess the people who have been inside the space culture for a while are used to this kind of crossover. We talk about the conference, about the proceedings we might both be published in, about today's launch, and about our earliest space memories.

I go inside to find a quiet enough space to call home to say goodnight to my family. The kitchen is packed, as it always is at parties (on the way through I eat another pudding shot and grab a beer); the dining room is packed, entryway packed. I turn a corner to go into the living room, and for a second I'm caught up short. The room is completely darkened, blinds over the windows, with no source of light except for dozens of phones and iPads pointed up at dozens of people's glowing faces. No one here is speaking to anyone else; everyone is typing. A couple of people are speaking quietly into their devices using earbuds, and it's hard to tell whether they are shooting video of themselves narrating to their blog followers or just chatting on FaceTime.

I find an empty corner to plug in my own earbuds and call my husband.

"I'm calling you from this room," I tell Chris, "where every single person is looking at a phone rather than talking to anyone else."

"That's funny," he says.

"No, I mean, there's like thirty people in this room, and *no one* is looking at anyone."

"Sounds creepy," Chris says.

"It is," I say. "But it's also kind of cool. I've never been to a party where thirty people are *writing*."

In the coming weeks, I will read through dozens of blog posts and Twitter feeds looking for other people's accounts of today's launch, and eventually it will dawn on me that at least a few of the accounts I'm reading must have been written in that darkened room while I was there.

A bit later I'm sitting in a white plastic lawn chair talking with a computer scientist about the manicure she got for the launch: rockets on one hand and galaxies on the other. We talk about how she wanted to be an astronaut when she was a little girl. At times I feel like the only space fan here who didn't harbor that dream, and in one way I'm jealous—it's a dream that seems to have spurred each of them to accomplish things they might not otherwise have accomplished—but at the same time I'm grateful not to have gone through the painful process of letting go of that dream. Some of these people still have not entirely let it go, and this woman talks about the possibilities of civilian spaceflight—unlikely glimmers, all of them—with a goofy look of hope on her face.

A couple of pudding shots later, I find myself sitting on the concrete lip of the pool with Omar, our pants legs rolled up and feet submerged in the warm chlorinated water, drinking beer from cans and talking about his prospects for the future. He's been taking classes in computer science one or two at a time, and when he is officially unemployed he plans to finish that degree and try to get work in the space industry writing software. He is aware that he may have to move away from the Space Coast in order to make this happen. He mentions that Karen has had a couple of interviews at aerospace firms in other states.

Floating in the pool are a few space-themed inflatables, one of them a space shuttle orbiter with an absurdly wide body and tiny wings. Without the black-and-white markings and American flag, it might not be recognizable as an orbiter at all. A young woman in a bikini swims over to it, then tries to climb up onto it and straddle it as if it were a horse. This is a cumbersome process, and it may be that pudding shots are involved in her decision making. As soon as she has clambered aboard, a man who has been skulking around the pool area with a huge professional-looking camera comes to life and shoots a series of pictures of her at fashion-shoot rate, his camera's flash strobing out and blinding everyone.

"Hey," another guest shouts at him sternly, "you need to ask her before you do that." The shouter strides over to the photographer and the two have words, gesturing at the camera. I'm impressed that the sign on the door does not create carte blanche for anyone to take pictures of young women in their bikinis.

"I wonder if that's his fetish," I say quietly to Omar. "Bikini girls riding orbiters."

"He did spring into action suspiciously quickly," Omar points out.

"What would you do if Karen were offered the job at Boeing?" I ask. "Would you try to get in there too?" The alcohol has made me bold. I sneak a look at Omar—he looks thoughtful rather than offended, but then again I know him well enough to know that he wouldn't show offense no matter how inappropriate my question.

"I don't know," he says eventually. "It's hard."

I find I can't imagine Omar living in Seattle, though a job at an aerospace company might suit him. It's impossible to imagine him leaving this place, even once there are no more shuttles to care for here.

The next morning, as I pack up to leave, the parking lot at the motel is nearly empty. A chambermaid is the only person I see outside as I carry my bags to the car.

Pramod is at the front desk again when I stop in the lobby to settle my bill. He hands me my receipt with a flourish. We say good-bye and I turn to leave.

"See you for the next one," he calls to my back as I'm almost out the door. I look back at him quizzically, but he doesn't seem to be joking.

"See you for the next one," I answer.

On the drive back, I talk into the voice memo app on my phone until its memory is full. I talk about the badging office, about the light in the lobby of the Port Canaveral Clarion at 2:00 a.m., about the people in the gas station outside the south gate of the Kennedy Space Center at 4:30 a.m., about the way the sun looks coming up over the strange marshes and foliage of the wildlife refuge. About the friendly guards and the unfriendly photojournalists, the color of the tile in the women's bathroom at the Press Site, about the brightness of launch and about the people I met at the party, about what it means to be scrubless. I've been thinking of my scrublessness as a stroke of luck, of the time and money it's saved me in return trips, but then I think of Oriana Fallaci's account of a scrubbed launch attempt of an unmanned test flight in 1966.

Fallaci spent the extra two days afforded her by the scrub with the dozen or so astronauts who had made the trip. The scrub created a forty-eight-hour window during which neither she nor the astronauts had any obligations, and they spent the time sunning themselves and drinking beer by the motel pool. She got to know them, ate meals with them, got drunk with them, all because of the unscheduled days brought about by scrub conditions. I feel a sudden envy for this, for her unforgettable scene in which the astronauts in their swimming trunks take turns reciting from memory Mark Antony's funeral speech from *Julius Caesar:* "Friends, Romans, countrymen, lend me your ears."

Maybe Oriana Fallaci's moment was an even rarer one than Norman Mailer's, because of scrub conditions, because of the pre-Apollo 11 pace, and because of her gender. A moment when a writer could breeze through a motel bar with a cigarette and a martini, to be greeted with "Hi, dolly" by the chief astronaut and to respond "Hi, Deke" in return. There's a disconcerting feeling in Fallaci's book that everyone she quotes—all the astronauts, the media handlers, and even von Braun himself—wind up sounding like Oriana Fallaci, like voluble Italians, speaking in great flowing lines with little filigrees of repetition at the ends. But her physical impressions of people, especially the astronauts, are unequaled by any other space writer I have read. Is it because men are loath to describe other men? Or because Americans are loath to describe anyone? Fallaci looks at the astronauts hard, indelibly, at their skin and their gestures and their clothes and their flashing teeth. She admires them, details her attraction to them, while also noting that they are aging prematurely, that the job is making them into old men before their time, as if they live more per year than do the rest of us.

As I'm trying to remember everything that happened over the past few days, everywhere I went, everything I saw, I keep returning to the fact that the astronauts are still in space *right now,* those people I saw riding in the Astrovan, completely normal-looking middle-aged people, are currently floating in space somewhere overhead. There is simply no getting used to this—not for space fans, not for spaceworkers, not for astronauts themselves. It has never become normal, even after fifty years, not even when we know this will be the last one.

> We may remember the intense sympathy which had accompanied the travelers on their departure. If at the beginning of the enterprise they had excited such emotion both in the old and new world, with what enthusiasm would they be received on their return! The millions of spectators which had beset the peninsula of Florida, would they not rush to meet these sublime adventurers?
>
> —Jules Verne, *From the Earth to the Moon*, 1865

CHAPTER 8. The End of the Future: Wheel Stop

STS-135 Landing: July 21, 2011

The Orlando airport is one of the busiest in the country, but late at night it quiets down considerably, and after midnight, when my flight lands, it is nearly abandoned. In the rental car area, there is only one polo-shirted employee for every two or three rental company counters, and a lone janitor vacuums around the stanchions marking empty paths for customer lines. I find the glowing neon logo of the company with which I'd reserved a car shortly before getting onto my flight in Knoxville, only a few hours before. I'm fully prepared for them to have no record of my reservation and am hoping they'll have a car to give me anyway. I wait while the only other rental car patron here tonight conducts his transaction in easy, slangy Spanish. When the customer leaves, the man behind the counter finishes writing on a printout, looks up at me, and instantly switches to unaccented English.

"What can I do for you this evening?" A glance at his watch. "I mean, this morning?"

"Reservation under Dean?" I ask skeptically. He taps at his terminal.

"Dean," he says. "Got you right here. Compact?" By some miracle, my reservation has stuck. It's one in a string of lucky breaks I've had today. But as we make our way through the process of entering all my information into his computer, we hit a snag.

"Address where you'll be staying?" he asks.

"Um—I won't have one," I tell him. Only then do his eyes lift from his screen to meet mine. There's an awkward pause.

"Just need to know what *hotel* you're going to be staying at," he says, fingers twitching over his keyboard. He now wears the completely blank look of someone struggling not to betray his contempt for another person's stupidity.

"The thing is, I'm not staying in a hotel," I say. "I'm driving straight to the Kennedy Space Center, then the space shuttle will land in a few hours, then I'll drive back here in the afternoon, return the car, and get back on a plane. No hotel."

The agent blinks at me once, slowly.

"I'ma put Holiday Inn Cocoa Beach," he announces.

"Fine," I say, feeling mildly alarmed that no one else has attempted what I am trying to pull off today. Or maybe they have been smart enough to lie about it.

He does some more typing, tries unsuccessfully to upsell me on a few things, then hands me my voucher.

"Have a nice stay in Florida," he says, in a voice not entirely free of irony. I go out to the parking structure where they keep the cars, climb into a silver one, start it up, and head toward the coast.

Yesterday afternoon I got an e-mail from NASA detailing some upcoming media events, and one of them was the landing of *Atlantis*. I had known all along when the landing would be—it had at first been scheduled for July 20, then put off till July 21 at a few minutes before six in the morning, to allow the crew more time to finish up work at the International Space Station. I knew that my press badge from the launch would get me in to see the landing, and I had privately mourned a bit that I wouldn't be able to take advantage of the opportunity. Compared to launches, which are visible to anyone for many miles around, landings can only be seen by those on NASA grounds and are never open to the public. And this one will be the last landing of a space shuttle, ever; very likely the last landing of an American spacecraft within my lifetime, since none of the spacecraft proposed to replace the shuttle are reusable. But I had decided not to go—in fact, had never really considered the possibility of going—because I had promised my patient and overextended husband that I was done going to Florida. I'd said these exact words to him. As I'd packed my car for the last launch of *Atlantis,* only thirteen days earlier, he'd asked, wearily, "This is the last one, right?"

And I'd looked him in the eye and answered, "Yes. This is the last one. After this, I'll be done going to Florida." And then I'd driven away, leaving him to care for our son and our home by himself.

I've now made this trip to Cape Canaveral five times in the last calendar year—disappeared for three or four days at a time with no promise that I'll come back when I'm expected (scrubs are a part of spaceflight!) and no clear schedule as to when my next trip will be (slips are a part of spaceflight!). Each of those mornings my husband has dressed and fed our little son, driven him to preschool, and managed the grocery shopping and dishes and laundry and temper tantrums and playdates and bedtimes. Chris is fully engaged in the responsibilities of parenthood—he is not the type of man who uses the word *babysitting* to describe caring for his own child—but he's tired of doing so much by himself, and I don't blame him. For my own part, I'm tired of asking him to do it.

So I chose not to go to Houston to visit Mission Control while *Atlantis* was on orbit, though my media badge would have allowed me access, though Norman Mailer went to Mission Control while Apollo 11 was in space. This is an important difference between Norman Mailer and me—when Mailer went off to Cape Canaveral and Houston, for as long as he pleased, he left behind five children with three different mothers and does not seem to have been troubled with much guilt over who would wash their clothes or fix their meals or get up with them in the middle of the night when they wet their beds. He probably wasn't participating in these activities even when he was home. And even if by some chance he had been troubled by guilt, it would have been out of fashion to mention those feelings in his space book. Domestic life was thought to exist entirely outside the scope of his work, less relevant than his reflections on the design of the Saturn V or his reminiscences of going to war. In my world, domestic life continues to exist, even when I'm not at home to participate in it. Children need to be fed and lawns need to be mowed and cars' oil changed and dishwashers to be filled and emptied and filled again. This work gets done when I'm not there. It gets done by another writer who is giving up some of his own writing time in order to do it.

At the last launch, I'd assumed that I would see the end of the story, the symbolic counterpoint to the launch of Apollo 11, the Grand Finale. I assumed that the scene in which *Atlantis* tears into the sky as a crowd of media, space fans, and spaceworkers cry up at it from the ground would be the climactic scene of my book. But I'd found that this wasn't the end of the story, because a launch is a moment of triumph, everyone giddy from the fireworks display. Even at the postlaunch party Omar had taken me to, where everyone there was either a spaceworker or a serious space fan, a sense of celebration had drowned out the incredulous disappointment that we wouldn't be doing this again.

But that Wednesday afternoon, the e-mail I received from NASA detailing the events for the day of the landing stopped me and made me reconsider everything:

Also at about 10 a.m., Atlantis will be towed from the runway and parked outside Orbiter Processing Facility-2 (OPF-2) for several hours to give employees an opportunity to walk around and photograph the shuttle. At 11:45 a.m., [NASA administrator Charles] Bolden and [KSC director Robert] Cabana will host an employee appreciation event outside OPF-2.

Immediately after a 20 minute media question-and-answer session, the astronauts will go to the employee appreciation event to talk briefly to the work force.

I've seen OPF; I was there with Omar on Family Day and saw *Endeavour* being prepared there for its last mission. So while I was reading this e-mail I could picture the area outside OPF-2 where the employee appreciation party was to be held: empty tarmac, a wide stretch of asphalt between two hangars. The idea of holding a party out there in the brutal sun, a sad celebration for the dwindling number of still-unlaid-off shuttle workers, people who have been working nonstop for years or decades to get one shuttle after another off the ground—what sort of "party" would this be, on such a distinctly unpartylike occasion? Even with a space shuttle in attendance like the world's most expensive party decoration, even with the astronauts there, just back from space—wouldn't this be the biggest bummer of a party ever? Might some of the answers to my questions be found here? I couldn't miss it.

I sat in my office on campus and read the e-mail over and over. Some pages I'd been working on before I left rested on the top of a pile on my desk. A sentence spilling over from the previous page read, "—and now the space shuttle era is ending." I looked at it for a long time before getting a pen, scratching out the last word, and writing in, "—and now the space shuttle era is over." This is what it means to be aware of history, I suppose, but it feels oddly like living through a death, the way little reminders, little inanimate things, conspire to keep surprising you, to keep fresh the change you weren't really ready for, didn't really want.

From the moment my eyes touched this e-mail, the landing was only about fourteen hours off. Not only short notice, but maybe not physically enough time to buy a plane ticket, pack a bag, get to the airport, and make the flight that would land me in Orlando in time to drive out to the space center, through security, and out to the landing site. Probably all the flights were full or insanely expensive, but even assuming I could get a seat, if either of two flights were delayed at all, a very high likelihood so late in the day, I would miss the whole thing anyway. I opened a new browser window for a travel site, to see what it would cost. There was one seat left on a flight going through Charlotte, and it was mysteriously cheap. I had always known that

234 | CHAPTER 8

fares go up as the travel date approaches, but apparently they fall again right before the flight, the airlines finally backing down in their endless game of chicken with passengers. This flight was only a few hours away, and it was now cheaper than if I had bought it a month in advance.

The look on Chris's face when I told him about the landing, about the towback and party and the oddly cheap fare, could best be described as *be-wearied*.

"It sounds like you should try to be there," he said.

"I'd be back Thursday afternoon in time to get him from preschool," I told him. "No matter what. And I'd keep him all that day and the next, I promise."

"Do what you need to do," he said. Did Norman Mailer's wife (and ex-wives) send him off with a phrase like this? Did he even ask their permission at all, or did he simply inform them of his plans?

I clicked "buy" on the plane ticket, took my son to the pool for an hour (he'd been promised the pool, and such promises cannot be broken even for space shuttle landings), brought him home, changed out of my swimsuit, and threw a few things into a bag. Packing is much easier when you know you won't have the chance to go to bed. I kissed my husband and son, jumped into my car, and sped to the airport.

When I pass through the checkpoint at the south gate to the Kennedy Space Center, I show my badge to the armed guard a bit warily. I've confirmed more than once that the badge that got me in to the launch is still good through the end of the mission, yet I still wonder whether that can really be true. I suppose it's because of the trouble I went through to get the badge in the first place—it's hard to believe that I don't have to keep going through the same process every time I want to get past the gates. So when I hold out my badge and photo ID to the guard, there is a part of me that expects him to hand everything back, shaking his head. But he doesn't. With the combination of scrupulousness and friendliness I have come to expect from the guards at these checkpoints in the middle of the night, he greets me, examines my badge and ID letter for letter, peers in at my face to compare it to the photo on my driver's license, makes some friendly chatter about Tennessee and what a long way I have come, then sends me on my way into the humid dark. I head in toward the Press Site. It's a few minutes past three in the morning.

I've tried to describe the hugeness of the Kennedy Space Center in daylight, but now I realize it's at night that this place truly reveals its sheer square mileage, how very much empty land is separating everything. In the distance, I can see the Vehicle Assembly Building lit up like the prow of some massive ship, the row of workshops and other buildings just before it, but there are miles between here and there punctuated only with infrequent streetlights. I roll down the windows to keep myself awake on the straightaway. Outside I can hear the croaking of frogs and the strange bellowing noise alligators make. The smell of Cape Canaveral I can never quite remember when I'm not here, the night air a wet and lightless forest in the nose. Somehow, I reflect, all this feels like home now, though a home I still wonder at. A spaceport home.

I have a picture I snapped with my phone at three thirty in the morning, while I stood in line with a couple hundred other badged members of the media next to a row of idling buses. You can't see much in the photo—I'd been standing there, deafened by the idling diesels and sickened by the fumes, exhausted and annoyed that other journalists standing around had told me I needed to check in at the News Center but then after my long walk up to the News Center I was told to come back down here to the parking lot and wait in line for a bus, a process that drained some of my precious remaining energy and put me a few dozen people behind in line. I'd been stewing about this injustice, but then I suddenly remember where I am. I am at the Kennedy Space Center, well past the security checkpoint, in the middle of the night. I am on hallowed ground, a place other space fans would give their eyeteeth to be, even once. In a couple of hours, the last space shuttle is going to make its last landing. And after today, I might never get the chance to come here again.

The picture I snap of the VAB at that moment does not come out well—it was shot in the kind of light that the human eye can see but that a camera can't capture much at all, at least not the camera in my phone. I've saved the image, though, because when I look through my photos and see that blurry square that I know to be the Vehicle Assembly Building and the blurry shapes I know to be my fellow journalists, I remember what it was like to stand out there that night, the odd combination of heat and chill, of annoyance and privilege, of exhaustion and eagerness.

The bus is heading to the Shuttle Landing Facility, one of the few parts of the Kennedy Space Center where I haven't spent much time. I've seen the runway, but I've never had a clear idea of where people actually stand to watch landings. In spite of my better judgment, I keep picturing us onlookers—the astronauts' families, NASA officials, a pack of photojournalists, and me—all standing on the scrubby grass and bushes to one side of a normal airport runway, shielding our faces from the wind.

As I discover, the term "Shuttle Landing Facility" refers to a 500-acre area on the north side of the Kennedy Space Center, an area that includes the runway, an aircraft parking apron, a tow-way, a recovery convoy staging area, the mate-demate device, and the building everyone (confusingly) also calls SLF. The runway is nearly three miles long, one of the longest in the world, and with good reason. When the space shuttle comes in for a landing, it has only one chance. It has no engines to pull up, circle around, and try again, as airplanes do. It's a fact that shuttle pilots take a nontrivial amount of pride in: the winged object that's hardest to land (in early days it was nicknamed "the flying brickyard" because of its poor glide ratio) is also one with absolutely no margin for error.

Our bus parks in a field already lined with vehicles, mostly satellite uplink trucks. We pile out of our buses and start hiking up toward the SLF building. Knee-high weeds whip at everyone's ankles, barely keeping the dirt from turning to mud in the unaccustomed churning. The moon is waning gibbous. I find it hard to keep my footing in the dark, despite the floodlights. We reach the building, a sort of mashup of small-town control tower and racetrack observation deck; there are two stories of seating (all already filled with photojournalists setting up their tripods) and a concrete pad upon which many others stand about and where still more photojournalists are setting up still more tripods and stepladders. Everyone looks out toward the runway, which is, at this hour, still swallowed in darkness and whose existence we must take on faith. A digital countdown clock, much smaller than the one at the Press Site, marks the time in red LED numbers. I feel an instant prejudice against this countdown clock, solely because it is not the other countdown clock, the big one I know and love from the Press Site. The smallness, redness, and newness of this one all offend me nonsensically.

All in all, this place does not feel big enough to contain our numbers, though of course it must be noted that most landings over the past thirty years have drawn but a fraction of this crowd. Though I've never been here before, I've seen images and videos of landings on the NASA site and on people's Flickr and YouTube accounts: in them, there is always plenty of space for everyone in and around the SLF building, unlike today. And, maddeningly, the landings in the pictures are usually *daytime* landings. As of right now, I bitterly envy all the people who have ever come out here to see a landing during daylight hours. They got to see the orbiter streaking in from miles away, framed against the blue sky. We can't see a thing out there, and we know the sun will not yet have risen when *Atlantis* comes screaming toward this runway. I know I won't be able to see it until it's practically on top of us, if at all. We have come out here to witness something we might not actually be able to *see*.

I stake out a spot on the concrete to slump to the ground, my back against the wall of the building. It's T minus ninety minutes, and I discover it feels amazing to sit down. I've been up for twenty-two hours. A few feet to my left, a young journalist is similarly slumped, asleep or willing himself to sleep, his steno notebook and phone clutched in one hand, his mission badge firmly clipped to his lapel. Every thirty seconds, he swats at a mosquito without opening his eyes.

The NASA public affairs people are out here, identifiable by their blue polo shirts with the NASA meatball logo on them and by their general appearance of wakefulness and helpfulness. I don't know when these people sleep. I eavesdrop on a conversation between one of their number, a chipper middle-aged man with the physical fitness and intelligent look of an astronaut, and a journalist from Reuters (if the neckband bearing her badge is to be trusted).

Reuters woman: I thought of you the other day. On *NBC Nightly News,* the reporter was saying it was "the end of American spaceflight" and I knew you wouldn't like that.

Public Affairs guy: Well, you're right, we don't like hearing it put that way. But you know I think I watched the same broadcast and he did say "as we know it," so I think that clears up a lot of the confusion.

Reuters woman: "The end of American spaceflight as we know it"—that's better than "the end of American spaceflight"?

Public Affairs guy: Oh yes.

Then their conversation turns to other things, but I'm left wondering: do normal TV-watchers know the difference between "the end of American spaceflight as we know it" and "the end of American spaceflight"? Does the former conjure up images of the SpaceX Dragon or the Space Launch System? Having spoken to many people on these topics, I have to say I doubt it. Either way, I disagree with the public affairs man's assumption, one that seems to be embedded in most of NASA's communications of late, that the best message to send to the public is that NASA is focusing on the future, accentuating the positive, that everything is fine. Everything is not fine. We have no space vehicle anymore. Like my students, the public needs to know that American spaceflight stopped, and to feel sad about that, before they will clamor to rebuild it.

A few paces to the right of where this concrete slab ends, a waist-high chicken-wire fence separates us from other observers, dark figures who mill around in the grass and take seats on a small set of outdoor bleachers. The VIP area. This is where astronauts' families sit, NASA higher-ups, politicians, other invited guests. In their boredom, some of the journalists go over to the fence and try to lure over VIPs for interviews. The people on the VIP side are bored too, and so they drift over gamely, and from where I'm slumped I can overhear several leisurely conversations getting started at once, the opening questions, the VIPs spelling their names into the outstretched digital voice recorders of the journalists.

"Oh, it's very exciting," I hear someone say carefully. "It's the end of an era."

People around me start to complain about the wait, which is odd considering that landings involve a lot less waiting than launches, which presumably most of us have attended before. In fact, I overhear a woman, wandering by, tell another journalist that she just saw two simultaneous references to Beckett on Twitter. *En Attendant* Atlantis. *Waiting for the Shuttle.* This strikes me as a little overdramatic. Why would the wait for landing be worse than the wait for launch? Maybe we are subconsciously aware that a delay in landing means something inherently much worse. The people who stood or slumped where we are standing or slumping for the landing of *Columbia* were witnesses to the horror of *Columbia*'s absence. They waited and waited that morning, and if they hadn't given up and gone home they would still be waiting, because *Columbia* was destroyed and the crew was dead while those spectators still waited. If a launch is delayed it's a nuisance; if a landing is delayed it's a disaster.

"T minus ten minutes and counting," I hear someone say. I feel I've lost some time and wonder whether I have actually fallen asleep; all around me, people are dusting themselves off, stretching. The photojournalists are taking the lens caps off their cameras; the print journalists are finding good viewing spots. It's still full dark outside, and I'm still unclear on where we're supposed to be looking, which part of the sky *Atlantis* will appear in.

I know that the sonic boom will be coming soon, and I remember hearing *Endeavour*'s return when I was here for the *Atlantis* rollout. For that landing I was fifteen miles away, but I remember the way the sound was more momentous than what we usually call "sound"—the way it wasn't so much a sound I heard with my ears as something that *happened*. T minus five minutes on the clock. I still don't really know where to look; people aren't all looking in the same direction. When I'd first arrived here I'd had the idea that the runway is parallel to the front of the building, but now I'm not sure. How long *Atlantis* will be visible in the air before it touches down, whether it will touch down up that way or down that way or right in front of us—of none of this am I confident. And all of this seems terribly important, because I have come a long way, and gone to a great deal of trouble, to be able to see this. I'm determined not to be looking in the wrong direction when it happens.

As I am dithering over which direction I should be looking, the sonic boom tears through the sky twice in quick succession. *Boom-boom.* The sound is heart-stoppingly loud. It startles me to the core, startles everyone here. We all knew it was coming, but it doesn't matter. We jump anyway. Some of us even cry out with surprise. A few people burst into applause, as if the noise of the sonic boom were like the noise of the launch, a noise that contains an accomplishment in and of itself. Some people look around to meet another human's gaze, to share what they've just experienced, and some of those people have tears glistening in their eyes. The spectators here are all journalists, professionally unimpressed by things. Some of them have been out here for many landings and have been startled many times before. It doesn't matter. This is a phenomenon you would never get used to.

The sound rolls over the land, the way thunder does—I can hear the sound traveling away from us and bouncing off buildings and hills and gantries and then rolling on and disappearing out into the ocean. The sound will wake people, rattle windows, and set off dogs barking, including the Izquierdos' dog, for forty miles around.

"Where is it?" a few people call to each other. But most of us know that after the sonic boom it will still be another few minutes before *Atlantis* is actually visible.

Minutes go by. We stand around and wait, not sure where to look.

"There it is! There it is!" I hear people yell, and I try to follow their fingers, and I'm looking in slightly the wrong direction at first. Then I do see it, and for a second, the sight is oddly incongruous, fake. *Look, it's a space shuttle,* I want to tell people standing near me. The familiar old space shuttle as I've seen it in a million pictures and a million videos and in *The Dream Is Alive* as a child, as I've seen it up close and in person, the actual enormous space shuttle. But this time it is suspended in the air, which seems to make no sense. It's much too big to do such a thing. It hangs before me in the dark, gliding in straight toward us. Ghostly trails come off the tips of its wings and its tail fin. Of course, it's not producing noise—if we were watching a plane of comparable size, a 747, say, we'd all be deafened by the shrieking engines, but on the shuttle there are no landing engines at all. The event is not silent; there is a profound noise that comes with the air moving under the wings of *Atlantis,* but it's still eerily quiet given the sheer size of the thing we are watching barreling down toward us.

The speakers near me crackle.

"Having fired the imagination of a generation . . ." It's a man's voice—I don't know whether it's the commander, Chris Ferguson, or the public affairs officer, or someone from Mission Control. I lean in to hear better.

"Having fired the imagination of a generation, a ship like no other, its place in history secured, the space shuttle pulls into port for the last time, its voyage at an end," says the voice. Later, when I look up the audio recording of the landing online, I learn the voice is that of Mission Control commentator Rob Navias.

I lose *Atlantis* for a second in the dark, and when I find it again, it's by the screeching of rubber hitting concrete. It touches down, its tile-covered flank flashing by me like a shark flashing by the window of an aquarium. *Atlantis* has released its drogue chute and is slowing—still moving fast, but slowing, slowing.

Slowing, slowing.

Stops.

"Mission complete, Houston." This is the voice of the commander, Chris Ferguson. He speaks carefully, a little self-consciously, like he's reading off index cards prepared in advance. His language is slightly off here; usually the commander says "Wheel stop," not "Mission complete."

"After serving the world for over thirty years, the space shuttle has earned its place in history. It's come to a final stop."

"We copy your wheels stopped, and we'll take this opportunity to congratulate you, *Atlantis,* as well as the thousands of passionate individuals across this great, space-faring nation who truly empower this incredible spacecraft, which for three decades has inspired millions around the globe," replies another voice (capcom Butch Wilmore). "Job well done, America."

It's kind of sweet, I suppose, the way these speeches have clearly been scripted in advance. Somehow their formality and stiff delivery combine to make the whole exchange feel more sincere, rather than less so, like a nervous couple exchanging their scripted wedding vows.

"Hey thanks, Butch, great words, great words," Ferguson says, in what sounds like an awkward attempt to make their dialogue sound spontaneous. "You know, the space shuttle has changed the way we view the world and it's changed the way we view our universe. There are a lot of emotions today, but one thing is indisputable—America's not going to stop exploring.

"Thank you, *Columbia, Challenger, Discovery, Endeavour,* and our ship, *Atlantis.* Thank you for protecting us and bringing this program to such a fitting end. God bless all of you, God bless the United States of America."

In spite of the stiffness and prewritten tone, the names of the lost orbiters still bring tears to my eyes. Of the people around me, some seem equally moved, while others aren't really paying attention. Instead they text and tweet, tell each other their impressions of what we've just seen, pointing up at the same empty sky, which is still dark, tinged now with light gray at the horizon.

That phrase sticks in my mind: "America's not going to stop exploring." I keep hearing this kind of vaguely patriotic talk that implies another space program is inevitable simply because the American spirit demands it. But we've been proud of what space exploration says about our country all along. We have to decide it's also worth paying for.

After the landing, I stand for a long time and look out at *Atlantis,* motionless now, as the photojournalists pack up their tripods and cameras, ready to move out to the next photo op. *Atlantis* stands steaming, the heat of reentry still radiating off its skin, while specially trained crews rush in to "safe" the vehicle—to remove any residue of toxic fuel from the exterior before extracting the astronauts. A few minutes ago that object was screaming toward the runway at four hundred miles per hour; for the previous two weeks it was traveling at seventeen thousand miles per hour as it orbited Earth, faster than a bullet shot from a rifle. Now it is dead still, and it will never move under its own power again. Later today it will be towed back to the Orbiter Processing Facility, then subsequently stored in the Vehicle Assembly Building until the new museum at the Visitor Complex is ready to receive it, at which time a flatbed truck will carry it slowly down NASA Parkway to its final resting place. But for now, it is motionless, the astronauts still strapped inside, running through their postflight checklist. I still can't take my eyes off it.

Everyone piles back into the buses and rides back to the News Center at the Press Site. Most of the journalists race to grab desks, plug in

244 | CHAPTER 8

their laptops and devices. Just as at the launch, they shout facts and figures to each other, and generally cause a lot of commotion grabbing handouts, asking questions of the Media Office employees, and eventually, it seems, writing things. I assume they are throwing together breaking-news pieces and blog posts for their publications. We all watch the monitors showing replays of the landing. Some of the journalists read information loudly into their phones, as in old movies—exact times, the spelling of names. I elect not to try for a desk since I don't really need one; I didn't even bring a laptop. Not for the first time, I reflect on the luxury I have in not having to write about all this *today*. I can take in these events more fully, precisely because I don't have the burden of writing as I'm experiencing them. I'm free to wander around eavesdropping on journalists' conversations, chat with the Media Office people, page through a book of laminated bios of journalists whose names are up on the wall in metal letters under the heading THE CHRONICLERS. I can go for a walk and take pictures of things around the Press Site, think about what I'm seeing and what I've seen and what it all means to me. I can watch events replay on NASA TV. I can slump against a wall and take a nap. I do all of these things in the time it takes the journalists to pull together their first stories about the landing. When I go to write my own chapter about the landing, I will be able to use their news stories to get the details right. I will watch their videos and study their still photos and listen to their audio recordings, and that hardly seems fair. At the same time, their work of documenting what happens today, as challenging and important is it is, will be done by the time they leave the Press Site today, while my self-appointed job of reflection will just be beginning.

The monitors show the live feed on NASA TV, where the astronauts are being helped out of *Atlantis*'s hatch. They wear the same expressions that astronauts always wear upon returning to Earth—tired, elated, a little confused by the unaccustomed pull of gravity, an expression of a child shaken from a happy dream.

Nearby, I hear two journalists greet each other.

"Boom-boom."

"Hey, and a *boom-boom* to you as well."

A sign posted on the wall in the News Center reminds us that we aren't to go anywhere other than the Press Site or the Launch Control cafeteria without an escort. After passing this sign a few times, it occurs to me that the implication is that we *are* allowed to go to the Launch Control cafeteria without an escort. I ask a journalist wearing a Mars rover T-shirt whether we can really cross the street to go to the cafeteria, and he answers "of course," with a look as though I am crazy for asking.

"The food's not great, though," he warns me, as if I came here for the cuisine.

Walking to the cafeteria, I stop at a crosswalk on VAB Road to let a tour bus go by. The visitors riding the bus look out at me with great curiosity, their faces shadowed by the smoked glass. It occurs to me that they probably think that I work for NASA, that I'm an engineer or a physicist or even an astronaut. I wave at them experimentally; several wave back. One mother points out the window at me, and her children lean in to wave as the bus disappears around the bend.

The Launch Control cafeteria seats a couple hundred people, and judging from the colors and materials, I'd guess it hasn't been updated since the mideighties. It's relatively empty at this hour, 9:30 a.m. or so, but by some miracle they are still serving breakfast. I order eggs, hashbrowns, an enormous biscuit (another notch in the "central Florida is part of the South" column), and coffee. As I eat, I scribble notes, and though I sneak looks at my fellow diners, none of the few badged employees eating nearby seems to recognize me as an interloper. They pitch their voices low, either because they are discussing something classified or because they don't want to disturb me. I wish they wouldn't—I'd love to hear what they're talking about. Even when I can make out what people are saying, I keep losing the threads of their conversations in my exhaustion. The space workers all eat quickly and get back to work, but I linger over a second cup of coffee, killing time before the next scheduled photo op: the towback.

The area where we wait to board the buses to take us to the towback is unsheltered, and though no one has passed out completely, we are all starting to wilt a bit in the unrelenting sun. It's over 90 degrees and nearing 100 percent humidity. I tried to plan ahead for a range of temperatures—I've already peeled off several layers—but I still have a serious problem: I have no sunscreen with me. If I'd packed any, security restrictions would have forced me to check a bag on my flight, and a wait at luggage claim might very well have made me miss the landing. Some people knew to cover their heads, but a lot of journalists still insist upon dressing in some version of professional attire, which precludes shade-giving hats. A few enterprising journalists have made makeshift hats out of handkerchiefs by tying knots in the four corners. I am wearing a white cotton scarf I had the good sense to throw around my neck before heading to the airport—it helped keep me warm this morning before the sun came up, but now that the sun is beating down, I've draped it over my head like Lawrence of Arabia.

Not nearly as many of us have elected to watch the towback, I realize when I climb onto the bus. It's a smaller bus than the one we rode out to the Shuttle Landing Facility this morning, and not nearly as luxurious. I also soon realize that I am the only person on the bus without cameras, tripods, and bags of other equipment. This is, apparently, a photo op, but not an event print journalists feel the need to view in person. It makes sense, I suppose—there will probably be a live feed of the towback on closed-circuit TV that one can watch from the air-conditioned comfort of the News Center, and seeing with one's own eyes the sight of *Atlantis* being towed back to the hangar from the runway would not in any way add to the veracity or detail of the stories most of the journalists are writing. I feel self-conscious finding a seat on the bus carrying only my notebook. I am also the only woman here.

As the bus grinds through its gears, I realize that it is something like the converted school bus that Norman Mailer rode for Apollo 11. Rather than being completely un-air-conditioned, as Mailer complained his was, this bus does have air-conditioning—at least it boasts air-conditioning *vents*—but the system seems to lack the wherewithal to stand up to fifty sweating journalists, many of them oversized. The temperature inside is probably similar to that outside, only more stagnant and fragrant. After about ten minutes, the bus pulls over right where a tow road leading from the landing strip connects with Kennedy Parkway. We pile out of the bus. The photographers' shirts are stained with enormous sweat spots. And the mosquitoes have come out as well, tiny vicious mosquitoes. It occurs to me that in addition to having no sunscreen, I also have no bug spray.

"This *sucks!* I'm never coming to one of these *again!*" cries out a huge sweating journalist. Everyone laughs.

The roadside at the intersection is uneven, moist without quite being swampy, the ubiquitous canebrake brushing against everyone's pants legs. Running parallel to both roads are ditches filled with brackish water. One of the more experienced photographers points out to us an alligator lurking in the ditch on our side of the road. It is a safe distance away, but I've been told alligators can move surprisingly fast. We all keep one eye on it as we move around finding our vantage points. The photographers busy themselves setting up their tripods and stepladders; a few intrepid stand-up journalists attempt to smooth themselves out enough to appear on camera. Judging by the logos on their microphones, none of them are from networks or news agencies I have ever heard of, and I wonder whether they now regret the idea of attempting to speak briskly into the camera as *Atlantis* rolls by behind them, whether it has now become clear to them that this was not a good plan.

We see the caravan coming a long way off.

First a black SUV.

Then the convoy command vehicle, a converted motor home that's used as a sort of mobile mission control during safing procedures after landings.

Then a stair car. It had never occurred to me that NASA must own stair cars, but of course the astronauts have to get out of the orbiter somehow. This pleases me unreasonably.

These lead vehicles are moving exquisitely slowly, barely a slow walking pace. Behind them, soon, we can see the silhouette of *Atlantis,* its enormous tail fin and the curved shape of the orbital maneuvering system pods against the sky. In the minutes it takes the orbiter to come fully into view, the photographers scurry around, revising their guesses as to where the best vantage points will be. The few stand-up TV journalists run through their patter, all of them speaking earnestly into their cameras, all of them turning now and then to gesture toward *Atlantis.*

As *Atlantis* comes near enough that we can make out more details, we see that there are people walking alongside it, men and women, wearing work clothes and jeans. They walk slowly and reverentially, pall-bearers, and though I know from my reading that this towback is always done slowly, today it seems intentional that they move as slowly as a funeral procession.

I hear a single pair of hands clapping behind me, and when I turn to look it's a photographer's assistant who has tucked his camera pole under his arm to applaud. He holds his chin up a bit self-consciously, knowing everyone is looking at him, but he has decided to go through with this gesture. Maybe he knew for weeks he wanted to do this, or maybe he's only decided right this moment, when those people came into view, the workers walking beside *Atlantis,* hugging close to its side. Even from here we can see that the spaceworkers are not chatting, are not smiling or drifting off thinking about what they are going to do after work or what to make for dinner. They face straight ahead, their expressions solemn. They can see the clump of us journalists on the roadside; they know they are having their pictures taken, and this is the face they want to wear in these pictures. A lot of them are going to get their layoff notices tomorrow, Omar has told me, but for right now it is their privilege to walk alongside their spacecraft. This is what makes me tear up, finally, as more and more people around me pick up the applause, *photojournalists actually let go of their cameras,* let their cameras dangle from their neck straps, to clap as loudly as they can, holding their arms up so our applause can be seen by those we are applauding. Unencumbered by equipment, I tuck my phone into my back pocket and clap until my palms sting. I'm moved by the sight of the great ship, now forever flightless, crawling along with its keepers at its sides.

We stand on that roadside forever, watching *Atlantis* go by, still keeping one eye on that alligator. We are in no hurry to leave. We watch patiently as *Atlantis* slowly passes us in its own sweet time. And then we watch it navigate the soft turn onto Kennedy Parkway, and we watch it make its way up toward the area outside the Orbiter Processing Facility, where the employee appreciation party is under way. We watch until we can see only the outlines of the tail fin again, and as *Atlantis* navigates into its place of honor at the head of the area where the party is to be held, we hear a cheer rising from the crowd gathered there.

Once we've all piled back into the stagnant, fragrant bus, we sit motionless for a long time. Our driver, who bears an uncanny resemblance to Nelson Mandela, keeps the bus idling in a vain effort to get us some air.

Waiting long periods of time in close quarters makes people chatty. The photojournalists strike up conversations. They gossip about others among their number who couldn't make it to this event. They gossip about layoffs, journalism being another one of the occupations, like space work, in which even the best among them are being laid off in large numbers. The photojournalist who made the joke about not coming back has decided to give nicknames to those sitting closest to him. A tiny videographer carrying a giant camera is dubbed Gator Bait; soon everyone is calling him that. The journalists swap stories of previous space events, and the discussions spread out to more rows of seats as they call out mission numbers and the names of orbiters. I was here for the last launch of *Columbia.* I was here for the last *landing* of *Columbia.* I was here for return to flight after *Columbia.*

I WAS HERE. All of us, it seems, were here for the last launch of *Atlantis*, only thirteen days ago. That feels like another lifetime.

"Get any good shots?" my seatmate asks me, casting a curious eye over my small bag and empty hands.

"I'm not a photographer," I answer, and then because he seems to be waiting for something more, "I'm a writer."

"A writer. What do you write?"

"I'm trying to write about the end of the shuttle era. Trying to make sense of what all this means." I gesture vaguely toward *Atlantis*. As I speak, I'm aware of how very iffy this all sounds.

"Huh." He is quiet for a minute. "And what *does* it mean?"

I look out the window at a Japanese film crew packing up their elaborate setup, huge sheets of plywood they have laid out on the grass to enable them to get a smooth dolly shot, and I can't imagine they got any images anywhere near worth the effort, but we watch while they haul all their equipment back into the van piece by piece against the totally unacceptable heat and humidity. The futility of their task seems to signify something.

"I have no idea what it means," I tell him truthfully. "I've been out here for everything, and I have even less of a clue than when I started."

He seems unsure of what to say to this, as if I've told him I'm dying of cancer. I'm struck with an idea. I turn in my seat to face him.

"What do *you* think it means?" I ask him. "You've been out here taking pictures, right? What do you think it means that we're not going anymore?"

He takes a deep breath, leans his head back against the bus seat. I'm not sure whether he's thinking or taking a brief nap.

Finally he speaks. "I don't think it means *any*thing, it means we've decided to stop," he says. "It means a lot of people on this bus are about to lose their jobs."

When we finally start moving, the bus circles around and delivers us to the opposite end of the Orbiter Processing Facility from where

Atlantis is now displayed. We get out and look around. A small crowd presses toward a low barrier set up to keep us from touching the orbiter. People take turns snapping each other's photos with it. Bins of ice cream and bottled water are on offer, and I immediately help myself to both. A number of awnings are set up—under one, people are invited to sign a banner commemorating this mission that will be hung in the Vehicle Assembly Building. I find a blank spot and write my son's name and the date. Under another awning, a live band is playing R&B covers. They are with the Air Force Reserve, and they remind me of a high-end wedding band; they even have a horn section. Nearby, a woman in a union T-shirt is handing out cardboard fans with the NASA logo, and not far from her a man is handing out little American flags. People wandering by are taking one of each; I accept a fan and after a moment's thought I decline the flag, thinking the stick is probably too long and pointy to carry on board my flight. The man handing out the flags scowls at me.

As I slink away, I see Omar emerge from OPF. I shout and wave, but he only raises a single hand to waist height to acknowledge me, looking totally unsurprised to find me here. I've texted him I was coming, and we've managed to find each other at other launches and events, but this one feels different. It's an event for NASA employees only, and my sense that I'm not really supposed to be here, that I somehow got in on a technicality, makes me feel giddy about catching sight of my one friend who is also an employee.

Omar grabs two ice cream bars out of the nearest container and tosses me one. I don't mention that I ate one two minutes ago and eat this one too.

"Want your picture with *Atlantis?*" Omar offers, and we make our way up to the barricade. We trade phones and take each other's pictures with the orbiter peeking over our shoulders. It's funny that so many of the people here, including Omar, have worked with these machines every day for years, yet they still clamor to take pictures with them like first-time tourists. Being close to this orbiter today is still a privilege.

A dais is set up with a microphone toward the center of the barricade, not far from where we have worked our way to the front of the crowd, and soon Charles Bolden, the NASA administrator, takes the stage to welcome us. He speaks for five minutes, somehow not repeating anything I heard him say at the history conference but not really saying anything new either. Then we hear from the crew of *Atlantis*. They have changed out of their orange reentry pressure suits and into blue flight suits (and, presumably, have showered). One by one they speak, thanking the people here for keeping them safe, for taking such good care of their ship. As Chris Ferguson steps aside to let Rex Walheim come to the microphone, I notice he stumbles over his feet a bit, a misstep then overcorrection, as if he is walking on the deck of a boat encountering swelling waves. I realize that what I am seeing is his readjustment to gravity.

"Isn't it weird," I say to Omar, "that these people just got back from space?" Even as I say this, I know the observation is idiotic. Of course they're just back from space; that's why we're all here.

But Omar nods. "It really is," he says.

After the speeches are over, the Air Force Reserve band tries to get the crowd dancing, but with limited success. A lot of partygoers are standing around watching amiably, maybe clapping along, but no one is dancing. If these bottles we're holding contained beer instead of water, maybe. But at work in the middle of a weekday with no alcohol—not a chance.

But then one dude steps forward. Tall and rangy, probably not any older than me but with a weathered face that reflects years spent in the Florida sun. He dances by himself, to "Celebrate Good Times," and his footwork is reminiscent of Chris Ferguson's stumble at the microphone. This man appears to have somehow gotten some alcohol on base, and he is dancing accordingly. Everyone still stands around, but now we are all watching him.

Where he went wrong was in taking the word *party* literally, when the event is not in fact a party but a wake. Best to stand around somberly. A wake with speeches from astronauts and NASA officials, a wake with *Atlantis,* fresh from its reentry into the atmosphere, in attendance. A wake with ice cream, in hundred-degree heat, a party where most of the partygoers know they are about to be laid off. We watch him dance a few minutes more, then avert our eyes and move on.

Omar and I walk around. The crowd thins out more the farther we get from *Atlantis,* and past the entrance to OPF-1 there is almost no one. We step over a set of train tracks, built to deliver the solid rocket boosters directly to the Vehicle Assembly Building from the contractor in Utah. Past that, the cliff wall of the VAB. One of the high bay doors is open, and I shield my eyes, straining to see inside.

"Trying to see *Discovery?*" Omar asks, following my eyes. *Discovery* has been in the VAB, having its engines and other working parts removed, in preparation for transport to the Air and Space Museum. Omar has been tweeting and posting on Facebook about this dismantling process, and though he doesn't go on and on about it, it's clear he finds it disturbing, the lifelong mandate to keep the orbiter safe from harm suddenly reversed into overseeing its dismemberment.

"She's in there," Omar tells me. "But I don't think you'll be able to see anything from here." As we move toward the fence, Omar wonders aloud whether he might be able to get me past the gate.

"I'm not supposed to take you in there," Omar explains, then thinks something over. "It might depend on who's working security, though."

As we get closer, we see an idling black SUV with a single guard in it. He steps one foot out onto the tarmac and juts his chin at Omar.

"She wanted to try to see inside the VAB a bit," Omar says in a chummy, what-do-you-say-bro tone of voice. I can tell he doesn't know this guy at all.

"Badge?" the guard asks. Omar hands over his work badge. I unclip my media badge and hand that to him as well.

The guard looks me over thoroughly.

"Sorry, dog," the guard tells Omar, handing us both back our badges. "I can really only let in folks specifically badged for VAB." It occurs to me only then that he might have thought Omar was trying to impress a date, and that maybe we'd have had better luck if I kept my media badge to myself. I feel a little disappointed, partly because

I want to see *Discovery*, wanted to walk into the cool, dark VAB with Omar and no one else. But also because the guard seemed to be basing his decision on something other than our badges, and I can't help but think if I had been younger or cuter he would have let us in.

As we walk away, Omar is apologetic about not getting me into the VAB, and I tell him he has nothing to be sorry for, after everything he *has* gotten me into. I wonder privately what Omar would have done in that guard's place—it's impossible to imagine him bending the rules, but also hard to picture him failing to come through for a coworker asking a favor.

After some more wandering around, Omar tells me he has to go back to OPF—he's working today, and people are taking turns coming out to the party. For a while after he's gone I linger, watching the band, eavesdropping, eating more ice cream, watching *Atlantis*, and watching people watch it. A call goes out for media people to get back on the bus, but I ignore it. Even though I've signed a form saying I will stay with media escorts and won't wander around unaccompanied, I feel pretty confident that I won't get in any trouble today. If I'm caught, I will say I missed the last bus, which will more or less be true.

Eventually, when the crowd starts to thin out, I set out to head back to the Press Site by circling around the VAB on foot, a project that, I only now start to realize, is going to take me a while. For the millionth time, the building has fooled me with its hugeness. The sun is fully blazing now in the early afternoon, I realize it's been hours since I applied some sunscreen I begged off a Scottish journalist, and I put my Lawrence of Arabia scarf back on my head. I haven't slept for thirty-two hours. I walk and walk and walk and the huge building next to me hardly seems to change as I walk. It is city blocks long.

Then something strikes me: I am walking, by myself, next to the Vehicle Assembly Building in the middle of the day. I'm loose on the grounds of the Kennedy Space Center. I'm walking through a strange landscape I have come to know so well in my mind it feels like another home to me, yet it still feels like a setting for science fiction.

This is where the spaceships are assembled, and I will never get used to that—the people who assemble the spaceships themselves say they never get used to that—even as the spaceships are retired and will be assembled no longer.

For the many minutes it takes me to circumnavigate the enormous beige edifice, I look up at it. I think of the way architecture, over time, can become transmuted into pure emotion. I haven't really been seeing the VAB, I just feel an overwhelming wonder and admiration and loss. But now I look closely. Turkey vultures circle endlessly overhead, as they always do. Seeing it this close up, I finally notice the many imperfections on the facade, places where the beige-gray paint has been touched up after hurricanes and doesn't quite match, the way the corrugated surface, seen from directly below, distorts the huge NASA logo. When I pass the high bay doors, I squint inside again to try to catch a glimpse of *Discovery*. It's too far away.

I get back to the Press Site, where my rental car waits in the parking lot, baking in the heat. It took me longer to walk back here than I thought it would, and I really need to be getting on my way to the airport. But before I get in the car, I decide to visit the grassy field with the countdown clock at the edge of the Turn Basin. I don't know whether I'll be able to visit the Press Site again, whether there will be another event that will allow me to get badged, whether I will ever have an excuse to come to the Kennedy Space Center again at all.

The press parking lot is still half full, and I imagine things are still bustling inside the News Center. But no one is out here near the countdown clock; nothing is launching. I compare in my mind what this grassy field looked like on the day of the launch, thirteen days ago—the tents and awnings and cameras and tripods and mic booms and thousands of journalists in clumps and pairs and singly, speaking a dozen different languages. All heady with excitement. The land shows no trace of this, except for some tire tracks cutting through the long grass. I look out at the Turn Basin, its calm water. I look at the countdown clock, now powered down, counting nothing. With my phone, I snap a picture of the clump of tropical foliage at the edge of the grassy field. All along I've been thinking that Norman Mailer had an experience similar to mine, that he and I saw similar events from the same vantage point. But now that a certain sense of history is catching up with those at my end of the rope, it seems more and more clear to me that what Norman Mailer and I saw could not have been more different. What he saw was a moment that felt like it was going to be the start of an era. I have never really tried to imagine what it would feel like to be inside that moment, the sixties optimism that my parents' generation is always trying to make people younger than themselves understand, not yet ground down into a cliché but a real palpable hope, an actual optimism that here, *now*, people could make things different. That things could start to be better than they had been from that moment on. For as long as I've been alive that idea has been demonstrably false. But on the morning of the launch of Apollo 11, even the gruffest, most cynical of Americans, even Norman Mailer himself, could inhabit that optimism for a moment. For that moment, he thought it might be true that the achievement of going to the moon would permanently change the human condition. I've always envied him the simple experience of watching that launch, but now that I've come to understand what he saw, my envy is an entirely different kind. Because what must *that* have been like? To think everything was about to get better, that people, all of them, were going to change for the better, once and for all?

It's true what I scribbled in my notebook when I first arrived here to meet Omar, back in the fall of 2010, for Family Day: Norman Mailer's generation got to see the beginning of things and mine has gotten the ends. But though Norman Mailer thought he was seeing the start of something, he was wrong. In fact, he was seeing its pinnacle. I have the sad advantage of traveling to Florida knowing I'm seeing the end. I'm glad, I suppose, to know exactly what I'm seeing.

It is one of the ironies of history that what is not discovered is often better remembered than what is discovered. This is certainly the case with Juan Ponce's first journey to the land he called La Florida, for when one hears the name Ponce de León, the first thing that comes to mind is the Fountain of Youth.

—Robert H. Fuson, *Juan Ponce de León and the Spanish Discovery of Puerto Rico and Florida*

CHAPTER 9. The Future

Discovery Day, Air and Space Museum, Washington, DC, April 19, 2012

SpaceX Dragon launch attempt, May 19, 2012

When I flip through all the notebooks I've been carrying back and forth to Florida over the past year and a half, I see the same sentence scrawled over and over again, in different pens under different dates: *The story of American spaceflight is a story with many endings.* This always seems meaningful to me as I'm writing it, as if it will be the key to something, but I've never been sure what. The first time I wrote it, I was thinking of the many times in the past when it had seemed spaceflight might end—the early rocket failures before the successes of 1961, then the Apollo 1 fire, then the premature cancellation of Apollo, then the compromises and threats to the developing shuttle project. Then *Challenger,* then *Columbia.* Each of these events put its mark on the fate of the program, but only the last did in fact cause American spaceflight to end.

After the landing of *Atlantis* in July of 2011, I returned home again to try to make sense of the whole mess. I organized my receipts and labeled my photos and videos and uploaded all the texts in my phone. I save all of it, even the blurry photos, even the texts that are nonsensical out of context, because I never know what might help me piece together some detail, the detail that turns out to be that surprising spark that can illuminate it all.

I'd filled another notebook, which I added to the knee-high pile in my study. Coffee-stained, sunscreen-stained, margarita-stained, sun-bleached, and humidity-warped, some of their bindings breaking down from being left in my oven-hot car for long Florida afternoons. Some of them have grains of sand caught in their bindings, tiny smashed bugs, little bits of vegetation from those times I sat on the ground while I was waiting for something to happen. Stuck between the pages are brochures from Florida attractions, business cards from people I've met, a McDonald's straw wrapper, ticket stubs from the Visitor Complex, a NASA meatball sticker, and a temporary tattoo of Yuri Gagarin's helmeted head that one of the Space Tweeps gave me. Omar's home address is scrawled on the back pages of at least three of them, and the cell numbers and Twitter handles of my new space friends. There are descriptions and half-descriptions and single-word triggers to remind me of the moments I've witnessed on all my trips to Florida, all the bizarre and beautiful and mundane things I have seen, all my research and all my childhood memories and my interviews and notes from the books I've read. The notebooks are as messy as the inside of my head, and I'm convinced that somewhere within them is the story I've been trying to write, the answers to the Question: What does it mean that we went to space for fifty years and now we are stopping?

And the books themselves: they've long since overfilled the shelves allocated to them, shelves that were already full after I finished my *Challenger* novel, and they've piled up in great vertical drifts that don't seem like they should be able to balance. From time to time I'm inspired to try to organize the piles into categories: a JFK and Mercury stack, a Gemini and Apollo stack, a special stack for Apollo 11. A Kennedy Space Center stack including histories of Florida, the Cape, the voyages of Ponce de León. A shuttle development stack, an eighties-

and-nineties shuttle stack, a *Challenger* disaster stack, a *Columbia* disaster stack. A Norman Mailer stack, his self-referential meditations on topics that always just eluded his understanding, like feminism or the Vietnam War or Hitler or Marilyn Monroe. But some books defy piling. What to do with, for instance, the science fiction novel Buzz Aldrin cowrote in the nineties? It includes scenes that take place on a fictional space shuttle, but it hardly goes with the factual shuttle books, nor does it seem to go with the Apollo 11 books, where I keep other titles by and about Buzz. The mass-market paperback floats from pile to pile, nagging at me every time it catches my eye. And what do I do with the books I've read about the voyages of Captain James Cook in the eighteenth century, a subject that has nothing to do with anything except that two of the space shuttle orbiters were named for his ships, a connection that has led me to read about Captain Cook's voyages late at night after my family is asleep, after I've written all I can for the day but still want to press forward on this project somehow, want somehow to be rocked to sleep on the creaking wooden sailing ships *Discovery* and *Endeavour,* their names and adventures evoking the odd image of galleons sailing straight up into the night sky with the aid of external tanks and solid rocket boosters?

I keep thinking at some point I will step back and the larger pattern will pop into focus. Sometimes I think I can almost see it out of the corner of my eye, almost sense a passing glimmer of an answer. When I pull out my notebook to try to catch it, I hesitate, not knowing how to start. I get a pen and write: *The story of American spaceflight is a story with many endings.* Then I don't know what to write next.

Even before the last launches, NASA had announced the final destinations for each of the orbiters—*Endeavour* to the California Science Center in Los Angeles, *Atlantis* to the Visitor Complex at Kennedy Space Center, and *Discovery* to the Smithsonian National Air and Space Museum, where I spent so much of my childhood. Each of the orbiters will be displayed in a different configuration: *Endeavour* will be stacked vertically as if for launch with a mock external tank and mock solid rocket boosters; *Discovery* will be standing on its wheels horizontally as if having just landed; and *Atlantis* will be hung from the ceiling, tilted at a forty-five-degree angle with its payload bay doors open and robotic arm outstretched, as if working in space. Omar approves of the multiconfiguration plan—he likes the idea that a visitor to all three exhibits would get to see what the shuttle looked like throughout its workflow—but he admits that he doesn't care for the idea of *Atlantis* being displayed at an angle. "It's like taxidermy," he told me, with a look of distaste.

Omar and I have said many times that we both plan to be at the *Discovery* welcoming ceremony at Air and Space in DC, and I hope he is serious—partly because I'd like to see him, but also for the murkier motivation that I think it will be poignant to see him say his goodbyes with *Discovery,* and I want that scene for my book.

In October, a few months after we saw each other at the landing of *Atlantis,* I send Omar a chunk of what I have been writing, about fifty pages that tell my experiences with the final launches of *Discovery, Endeavour,* and *Atlantis.* Family Day is left out entirely, as is the landing, as is a lot of other stuff he helped me get access to, and I feel self-conscious about how my shaping of the story will come across to Omar, who will know, better than anyone, what I am leaving out.

Omar texts me back within hours, God bless him.

> A very good read!

He corrects a technical error (diplomatically, of course)—I've misunderstood the meaning of the abort mode known as negative return. I'd written that negative return marks the point after which the shuttle could no longer safely return to Earth, when, in fact, Omar explains, negative return means only that the shuttle can't return to the runway at the Kennedy Space Center. It can still land at one of the emergency landing sites elsewhere around the globe. Somehow, my error feels symbolic, maybe because the term itself is so poetic. It seems significant that I'd thought things were a little worse than they actually are.

Nearly six months later, I'm standing around with Omar in a roped-off VIP area in a large grassy field outside the Air and Space Museum's Udvar-Hazy Center near Dulles Airport. This is a second site the Air and Space Museum added in 2003, a pair of hangars large enough to display more of the museum's many airplanes, spacecraft, and other artifacts than can the smaller marble building on the National Mall that I still think of as being Air and Space.

The ceremony isn't due to begin for over an hour, and while we talk, Omar and I watch the final stages of the setup. Folding chairs in the first two rows are marked with signs that read RESERVED FOR ASTRONAUTS, each one with a small American flag resting on it. The sound system is put through its final preparations; the opera singer who will perform the national anthem does a brief sound check, singing the song's first line and then its highest notes, "and the rockets' red glare . . ."

Omar is wearing a neon orange wristband that a few minutes ago I pried off my own wrist and slipped to him surreptitiously through a fence separating media and VIPs from the general public. I wasn't even supposed to have press credentials myself, hadn't thought to register for them, but last night at my hotel I ran into my space friends Anna and Doug, whom I met at the launch of *Atlantis,* and they let me tag along with them to the media registration table and allow myself to be mistaken for a journalist with the same publication. Once I had the orange wristband, it became clear to me what its value would be, that the spacious area directly in front of the dais was open only to accredited media and to VIPs designated by NASA—mostly astronauts, administrators, and museum officials. Omar and I had been texting each other all morning, and I was pleased with myself when I hit upon the plan to sneak him in, pleased that I could get him in somewhere he wouldn't have been able to get into otherwise, as he has done for me so many times.

Discovery had left the Kennedy Space Center for the last time two days earlier. Omar was there working that day, watching and taking pictures as *Discovery* rolled out of the Vehicle Assembly Building on its way to the mate-demate device that would lift it atop the back of the shuttle carrier aircraft—I got to see his, and other space fans', pictures of it all day on Twitter, Facebook, and Flickr. Yesterday I drove from Knoxville to Washington, and it felt odd to head north instead of south, to drive eight hours rather than twelve. I'd thought the drive would be easier, but I didn't find it to be so—I didn't know any of the landmarks, never knew where would be a safe place to stop, how much farther I had to go. It was oddly disorienting.

Enterprise has already been pulled out of its old spot in the museum and parked on a paved area behind the dais. It's already wearing the tail cone that will help stabilize it on its trip to New York. *Discovery* is going to be pulled up in the other direction, and the two orbiters will be posed nose to nose for a few hours, a rare sight.

Enterprise was the first orbiter to be constructed, assembled without engines or tiles for early flight dynamics tests. It was flown atop the shuttle carrier aircraft repeatedly to test the safety of the mated configuration, then was dropped from a plane and landed manually by astronauts to test its gliding abilities. All this happened in 1977, when I was in kindergarten. The original plan had been for *Enterprise* to be fitted with engines and to become the second working orbiter, after *Columbia,* but a number of design changes were made as *Columbia* was being assembled, making it more practical to refit an existing test frame as a new orbiter and to retire *Enterprise.* The test frame became *Challenger,* and *Enterprise* went on a goodwill tour of the world before being sent to Air and Space. It was in storage from 1985 until 2003, when the Udvar-Hazy Center opened and there was finally enough room to display it. The one thing people seem to remember about *Enterprise* is that it was going to be named *Constitution* until a letter-writing campaign convinced President Gerald Ford to ask NASA to change the name to that of the spaceship from *Star Trek.* When *Enterprise* rolled out of the plant where it had been assembled in Palmdale, California, it was feted in a ceremony including some of the original show's cast. It's a distinct moment of midseventies culture: in the pictures from that day, Leonard Nimoy, George Takei, and NASA managers are all wearing leisure suits. I've never seen *Enterprise* in person, and I find it strange to look at. In size and proportion it's identical to the other orbiters, as is its black nose. But the fuselage and payload bay doors are wrong, solid white without the familiar tiles that protect working space shuttles. And the whole thing is too clean, without the wear and tear that *Discovery* and the others have earned over dozens of space flights.

As we wait, Omar and I catch up on what's been going on since we saw each other last. It doesn't feel at all unusual to be standing with him in a grassy field with a lot of other people milling around waiting for something to begin, but it feels wrong not to be doing so in Florida. Omar always acts as a host, subtly, when we are together at the Cape, answering my questions, introducing me to people, making sure I get a clear view of whatever we are looking at. Here in DC he doesn't know any more than I do, and I find that disorienting too.

"Thanks again for getting me in here," Omar says, flashing his wristband.

"It's the least I could do," I answer. "It would be wrong if you couldn't see the ceremony, after you've dedicated so much of your life to *Discovery*."

"Still," Omar points out, "if they let in everyone who's ever worked with *Discovery*, there wouldn't be any room for anyone else."

The ceremony gets started. Michael Curie from the NASA Communications Office directs our attention to a countdown being displayed on video screens. He tries to lead the crowd in counting down from ten, but it's a little awkward, and most people don't join in. I fold my arms and remain silent. There is something sacred about the poetry of countdown, and I feel it's not to be evoked inappropriately. At *six*, the video creates the sound of main engine start, and when the countdown reaches *zero* the screens display footage of *Discovery* launching, that fire under the launchpad and the steam billowing up, the bright light as the spacecraft starts its climb against gravity. People applaud, but I scowl at the video screen. There is something awful about showing video of launch today when everyone here would rather be at a launch than at a museum dedication. I sneak a look at Omar, who looks skeptical but is clapping.

Then Michael Curie explains to us that as *Discovery* returned home from space, the twin sonic booms always announced its arrival, and that now we should listen for that telltale sound. The sound system then produces a recording of the sonic booms, such a faint facsimile of the real thing I feel a flare of anger. Most people here have never heard the shuttle's sonic boom and never will, and to play them this weak recording and tell them it's what the shuttle sounded like, I feel, is a disservice to all. I wonder whether Omar feels the same way, but he is watching the far end of the tarmac, the direction from which *Discovery* will approach us.

"Here she comes," Omar says. As *Discovery* creeps closer, we can see that it is accompanied by astronauts wearing their bright blue flight suits. I recognize a few, including Eileen Collins, the first woman to serve as a space shuttle commander. As they walk, one of the astronauts pats the landing gear door affectionately, the way you'd pat a horse. I feel Omar flinch almost imperceptibly next to me. The imperative to keep people from touching *Discovery*'s tiles will never leave him.

As promised, *Discovery* is pulled nose to nose with *Enterprise,* and the crowd applauds this sight.

Speeches ensue: One from the director of the Air and Space Museum, who gets choked up and has to take a moment to compose himself. Then the NASA administrator, Charlie Bolden, who starts out by recognizing the spaceworkers who have made the trip today, the people who worked on *Discovery* with their own hands. This earns a huge round of applause.

The rest of Bolden's speech emphasizes that the next steps are under way: NASA is partnering with private companies to get astronauts and cargo back and forth from the International Space Station, and NASA will now focus on long-range spaceflight. The same story we've been hearing all along, yet the Space Launch System is still underfunded and unpopular with many spaceflight advocates. In a best-case scenario, SLS won't get astronauts back into space before 2021, and won't get us any farther than we've already been until 2025 or later. This is tough to get excited about, especially when so many in Congress are eager to make a name for themselves by killing this relatively unambitious plan altogether.

John Glenn is introduced by the secretary of the Smithsonian Institution, Wayne Clough, who uses the same F. Scott Fitzgerald quote to introduce him that I used to introduce Buzz Aldrin two years ago: "There are no second acts in American lives." I am seized with horror that this quote I thought was so clever is actually incredibly obvious, that maybe Buzz listened to me reading it so confidently in my introduction of him and rolled his eyes, having heard it a million times before. "Now *Discovery* begins its own second act as an engine of imagination, education, and inspiration," Clough finishes.

John Glenn takes the podium. He is ninety years old. Like all of us, he has been sitting out here for over an hour in the beating sun. Some people a fraction of his age are looking worse for wear, but he stands straight as a stick and looks out at us with bright eyes. I think of Oriana Fallaci's fantastic description of him when he was in his forties: he reminded her of the GIs who showed up to liberate Italy and gave her chocolate when she was a child. "[A] whirlwind of freckles and strong white teeth . . . a pair of sparkling green eyes, whether shrewd or innocent I couldn't tell." The description is still oddly fitting despite the passage of forty-five years. Same freckles, same sparkling green eyes. John Glenn begins.

"Perhaps it started with the pioneers who first lived in this new land, but Americans have always had a curious, questing nature that has served us well." He is a born public speaker; we are in the palm of his hand.

John Glenn points out that the wagon trains that took settlers west in the nineteenth century considered ten miles to be a good day's trip. *Discovery,* the spacecraft upon which he became the oldest astronaut in history at age seventy-seven, could cover the same distance in less than two seconds. He reminds us that only twenty-three years after railroads replaced the wagon trains, the Wright brothers flew their first plane at Kitty Hawk. Only fifty-nine years after that, John Glenn became the first American to orbit Earth. Seven years later, Neil and Buzz walked on the moon. Some of us do math in our heads, dismayed. How long will it be until we can add another leap?

John Glenn gives a rundown of the accomplishments of *Discovery*. Then he hits a part of the speech that gets everyone's attention.

> The unfortunate decision made eight-and-a-half years ago to terminate the shuttle fleet, in my view, prematurely grounded *Discovery* and delayed our research. But those decisions have been made, and we recovered and now we move on with new programs and possibilities unlimited.

It's one sentence of criticism, immediately followed by a hedge. The line gets applause, but it's not entirely clear whether the crowd is clapping for the criticism, for the "new programs and possibilities" line, or because he has paused. Omar raises his eyebrows in surprise and we exchange a look. No one at any of these events has ever said anything even vaguely negative about the decision to retire the space shuttle—the closest you'll hear is the word *bittersweet*. But here John Glenn himself has criticized the retirement directly. I feel oddly elated.

He closes with this:

> We recently celebrated a 50th anniversary of our first orbital flight. In a speech to Congress following that flight, I closed with a statement that I would repeat today. "As our knowledge of the universe in which we live increases, may God grant us the wisdom and guidance to use it wisely." Thank you.

A document officially transferring ownership of *Discovery* from NASA to the Smithsonian is produced. It's signed with great flourishes, John Glenn serving as witness.

For nearly as long as I've been reading about spaceflight, I have had strong and conflicting emotions about John Glenn. He is, on the one hand, the most charismatic Mercury astronaut, the appealingly boy-ish bow-tied moralist who earned the ire of the others by suggesting that they not cheat on their wives. At the same time, he is the man who testified at the 1962 hearing on the possibility of letting women into the astronaut corps that it is "a fact of our social order" that women don't belong in space, who found it so hard to grasp the simple fact that the women in the same room with him harbored the same dream he did. I don't know whether John Glenn regrets saying what he did in 1962, or whether he no longer believes it to be true. But I do know that in 1998 he chose to climb into space shuttle *Discovery* with a woman, Chiaki Mukai, among his crewmates, thereby trust-ing his life to her competence. There are no reports of his having had any qualms about doing so.

The director of the Smithsonian formally introduces *Discovery* as the newest holding in the museum's collection, and though every-one claps, I'm surprised by how awful that sounds to me. I knew I was coming here to see *Discovery* put into a museum, yet it still catches me off guard, the finality of the sentence. *Discovery,* which has flown into space thirty-nine times, which I personally watched tear into the sky on two different occasions ten years apart, which Omar has dedicated his adult life to keeping safe, is now officially a museum piece.

For most of the afternoon, the two orbiters stand nose to nose while people converge and disperse, taking each other's pictures. Omar stands out on the field for a few minutes, shading his eyes, looking at *Discovery* and *Enterprise.* I watch him, trying to put myself in his place. Omar has been around space shuttles since before he can re-member. *Discovery* specifically he has spent many hundreds of hours with—he has seen it standing on the launchpad readied for flight and parked in the Orbitor Processing Facility for repairs and rolling hori-zontally to the Vehicle Assembly Building and rolling vertically on the crawler out to the launchpad. He has seen *Discovery* slung up on its harness dangling from a crane affixed to the ceiling of the VAB, being joined to its external tank and solid rocket boosters. He has seen it steaming on the runway fresh from its return to space. Omar has crawled inside the crew compartment, sat in the commander's seat, and felt how his weight settled in that position from which astronauts have waited so many hours to launch. He has traveled to California, twice, to help out when *Discovery* was forced to land at Edwards Air Force Base and overseen it being mated to the shuttle carrier aircraft. He has seen *Discovery* on rainy days and on sunny ones, when there have been threats of hurricanes and while its engines were removed after its last flight, when it was being prepared for the end of its life. The engineers who created *Discovery* and kept it working have not spent nearly as many hours in the personal company of *Discovery* as Omar has. Certainly not the astronauts themselves, who live in Houston and train in simulators, visiting the actual orbiters only briefly before flying in them.

I try not to show that I am watching him surreptitiously, watching for a profound moment.

Omar Izquierdo stood in the bright sun, a wistful look of affection on his face for "his bird," Discovery.

Omar Izquierdo stood watching as Discovery *shone in the sunlight for the last time before being forever interred in the dark museum.*

Omar Izquierdo stood vigil with his orbiter for the last time, his jaw grinding in anger as he struggled to accept that his bird would never fly again—

"Hey, you want to know something I've never really noticed before?" Omar breaks into my thoughts. "You can see the old worm logo on *Discovery*. You see, right there? You can see where they removed it but it's still sort of showing through."

Omar is right—I can see where the letters of the worm logo have been removed, their traces still visible only from this distance and in bright sun. For all the time he's spent with *Discovery*, for all the sacrifices he's made in order to be part of preparing it for flight, there are still things Omar doesn't know, still new things to learn about it even as it's being put away for the last time.

"Do you like the worm?" I ask, just to have something to ask. The things I really want to ask him are unaskable.

"Yeah, I guess," he answers. "It's pretty seventies. I like the meatball better."

"Me too."

We stand for a long time feeling—what? The mandatoriness of emotion, I guess. All the people waving little American flags and the little kids wearing their astronaut suits and the grown-ups wearing their red I WAS THERE shirts and the press shouldering past one another steadying their enormous cameras, all of us trying to tell ourselves that this is the last time we are ever going to be able to see a thing like this, that nothing like this will ever happen again.

Later, when we are standing inside the hangar where *Discovery* has been parked, the brand-new rope to keep visitors at a safe distance being installed all around it, Omar and I glance at a map of the room, a schematic with labeled outlines corresponding to the artifacts. In the center of the rectangle representing the room is an outline of a space shuttle orbiter, the word *Enterprise* printed next to it. Omar points to it.

"Wrong," I say, and we laugh.

A couple of hours later, I hug Omar good-bye and wish him safe travels. He's headed to the airport to catch his flight back to Florida. I'm not sure when I'll see him again, and it's the first time since we met that this is true.

In the car on my way home from DC, I hear a new pop song, "Starships." It's a generic dance hit, an attempt to build on the popularity of the "baby, you're a firework" song, which is still getting radio play. I hear "Starships" enough times that I start to learn the words:

"Starships were meant to fly. / Hands up and touch the sky. / Let's do this one last time."

As with "Firework," this song is not about the space shuttle, only a pop confection urging us to dance and to think much of ourselves, like all the other pop songs. Still, it's hard not to hear in it a reference to what I've just seen, an odd confluence of disparate emotions, a celebration of something sad.

When I get home, my family has already gone to sleep. I stay up for a while to organize my notes and upload data from my phone. As I noticed at the *Atlantis* landing, it seems to be NASA policy to consistently thumbs-up the decision to retire the shuttle program, to always emphasize the importance of looking ahead. And I still can't fault them for this—it's really their only choice. Criticizing the decisions of lawmakers who determine its future budgets is not judicious for any government agency. Yet I can't help but feel there has to be a way of conveying a more complex reaction to these retirements than this false celebration. NASA will always do as much as they can with what they are given. We saw this to be the case at the end of Apollo, when the grand visions of an orbiting shipyard and transports to Mars were compromised down to the space shuttle. Surely Charles Bolden believes, as I do, that when we are sending American astronauts to space again in American spacecraft launched from Florida, that will be better than what we are doing now, which is putting our only working spacecraft in museums and paying the Russians to ferry our astronauts to the International Space Station. This is why it meant so much to me to hear John Glenn say what he said. Just to hear the words *unfortunate* and *prematurely* at one of these events, in front of God and Charlie Bolden and *Discovery* herself.

I realize now how much I was hoping to see Omar betray some emotion, but as always, Omar chooses to see the best side of things. Certainly he doesn't seem as angry as I am.

As I scribble notes, the pictures and videos and voice memos in my phone are uploading into my computer, each of them showing itself briefly before being replaced by the next. I become distracted watching my own photographic experience go by: A picture of *Enterprise* alone wearing its tail cone. A picture of a row of folding chairs, each of them marked by a sign reading RESERVED FOR ASTRONAUTS and a little American flag. A picture of the two orbiters nose to nose; from this angle, they seem to be kissing. A picture of John Glenn I snapped surreptitiously, standing close enough to reach out and touch his arm, though I didn't. Pictures of children wearing miniature orange astronaut suits posing in front of the two orbiters nose to nose. I have no pictures of Omar with *Discovery*—I offered repeatedly throughout the day, but each time he refused.

The last video is taken from within the dark interior space of the Udvar-Hazy Center and shows *Discovery* moving, bit by bit, into the museum. It's broad daylight outside, so the first seconds of my video are too bright, crushed out to white. But as *Discovery* slowly creeps inside, its nose and wings become visible in sharp detail. As I shoot this video I'm as close as I've ever been to a space shuttle orbiter. *Discovery* gets bigger and bigger in my frame, then the massive hangar door slides closed behind it. Once the door is shut, the light changes, the camera adjusts, *Discovery* is suddenly sharply detailed in the newly balanced light. I take in the spaceship before me. It will never move again.

Good-bye, *Discovery*.

When he came back from covering the moon landing and finished writing his space book, Norman Mailer embarked on an experiment. He rented a house in Maine and spent part of the summer there with five of his six children to demonstrate that he could care for them and run a household himself. He had something to prove, because his fourth wife, Beverly Bentley, had just left him, claiming that her career as an actress had been buried under the domestic work necessary to let Norman Mailer go out into the world and be Norman Mailer.

Though the original challenge was to show he could do everything himself, Mailer almost immediately hired a local woman to do cleaning

272 | CHAPTER 9

and laundry. He also depended on the oldest three children, all girls, who "did their chores and helped the boys to dress and go to bed, aided with the cooking and the dishes and the pots and with the wire perambulators in the shopping marts." Then he called in his sister for two weeks and, after she'd left, a "mistress" who at first came for a brief stay, but soon returned for the rest of the summer. It's hard not to imagine that the sister and the "mistress" took over much or all of the work of running the household, the very work Mailer had meant to demonstrate he could do. Some scorekeepers might say he cheated at his own game—my husband certainly would. But when I imagine which aspects of Mailer's account of this challenge would most frustrate Beverly, it's that the experiment had an end date, that it required him to do this work for only a finite and predetermined period of time. Even on the worst rainy afternoons, he knew that at the end of the summer he could give the children back to their mothers and go back to being Norman Mailer. None of his children's mothers had that luxury, had any end point in sight. They wouldn't be able to set down this burden for the years or decades until their children were grown. This distinction Mailer seemed to have missed altogether, or chose to miss. Yet he did claim to have taken one lesson from the experience: "Yes, he could be a housewife for six weeks, even for six years if it came to it, even work without help if it came to it, but he did not question what he would have to give up forever."

What he would have to give up forever: his writing. His life's work, his ego, his fame. His travels, his affairs, his one-night stands, his television appearances, his campus lectures, his outrageous interviews. His freedom to accept when *Life* asks him to go to Cape Canaveral to cover the launch of Apollo 11. All the powerful and ruthless men I've been reading about—Juan Ponce, James Cook, von Braun, the Mercury astronauts—had this freedom; they also had wives and children who carried on without them with varying degrees of success. This admission of Norman Mailer's does not carry the power of transformation, or even of any type of insight, because he attributes his freedom to the biological fact that he's a man: "[H]e could not know whether he would have found it endurable to be born a woman." He guessed that being a woman might have driven him insane.

An interesting thing happened at the end of the summer of 1969: more than the usual number of marriages in Norman Mailer's social circle broke up, including his own. There is a weird moment toward the end of *Of a Fire on the Moon* when, just home from Cape Canaveral, Mailer catches sight of Beverly at a party.

> Aquarius watched his wife at the other end of the lawn and knew again as he had known each day of this summer that their marriage was over. Something had touched the moon and she would never be the same.

Something had touched the moon. Mailer reminds us throughout his book of the possibility that some spiritual balance would be altered by the violation of man's boot touching a celestial body, the feminine moon. Something magical, mystical, astrological. He does, after all, refer to himself as Aquarius throughout and gives a great deal of attention to the astrological signs of the astronauts. Why not blame on the boots of Armstrong and Aldrin the tectonic shifts in a woman's heart, rather than his own failure to take seriously his wife's work?

Immediately after the launch of Apollo 11, the press corps was taken around to visit the wives of the three astronauts then on their way to the moon. Norman Mailer found Jan Armstrong appealing in a plain and hardworking way; Pat Collins he found unremarkable. But Joan Aldrin he found quite captivating. He didn't fail to notice that, like his own wife, she was an actress who had given up her craft for a husband with an overwhelmingly public career. He saw in the theatricality of her answers to reporters' banal questions a hint of the frustration he saw in his own wife. Mailer couldn't have known that Buzz and Joan Aldrin were to divorce, just like Beverly and himself, shortly after.

What would Norman Mailer think of me, a mother and wife, following in his footsteps at Kennedy? If time could fold back upon itself, if he and I could both be standing on that field of grass by the countdown clock at the Press Site on the same hot Florida day rather than days separated by forty-two years, what would we see in each other? I doubt very much that our encounter would be anything like those I've had with other space people in my own time—I doubt we'd swap stories of slips and delays, of lonely nights in Space Coast motels, of bad food and sunburns, of the finer points of liquid fuels and hypergolic thrusters. Would he walk right by me, assuming me to be somebody's secretary, somebody's wife, a nonwriter, nonartist, nonego with nothing to contribute to the world but to care for and feed a male ego and his babies? He'd said not long before that "the prime responsibility of a woman probably is to be on earth long enough to find the best mate possible for herself, and conceive children who will improve the species."

Or would he, out of boredom and isolation and the lowered standards that come with launch conditions, attempt to bed me? Would he corner me at a space party, ask me to dinner, ply me with wine? Does it make me shallow that of these scenarios, the latter seems least depressing, because in trying to seduce me he'd at least have to pay attention to me, look me in the eye, talk to me and pretend to listen?

It's important to remember that, as destructive as attitudes like Mailer's were to women (both the individual women he knew and women as a group in society), it was also a loss to men of his time that they were denied the pleasures of taking care of children, the pleasures of home life to which they contributed more than a paycheck and a last name. And they were denied the honest uncomplicated friendship of women: professional collaboration and respect, intellectual rapport, gossip, comfort, advice, simple favors one friend does for another, games of online Scrabble. As much as I envy Norman Mailer the events he got to take part in, I can't really envy him his era. He and I never could have been friends in it. I would not have been allowed to be a writer in it. Or if I had, if I'd managed to make a place for myself as Joan Didion and Susan Sontag did, readers would have hastened to assure each other that, smart as I may have been, I was a bad mother, a bad wife, not pretty or nice enough. This is familiar from the narratives about women astronauts—you can go, but we'll say you abandoned your children. You can go, but we'll say you are unnatural for choosing not to have children. It's a dream still, the dream of being allowed full participation. The dream is alive, I suppose. The dream is still in the process of coming true.

Just as it did the last time I was driving toward the south gate of the Kennedy Space Center in the middle of the night, the gas station on State Road 3 beckons to me with its alien landing lights, its promise of coffee. I haven't stopped here since the launch of *Atlantis,* ten months ago, and as I park to go inside I remember how overrun this place was that day, space fans from all over the world sloshing coffee on the counters and waiting in line to pay for their snacks before heading out to see something historical. There are only a couple of cars parked here now, and I know it will be different today, but I'm still not prepared for how different the scene is when I walk in. A young woman is mopping the floor while a bored-looking man stares into space behind the counter. I am the only customer, and every surface is clean. Neither employee wears any space pins or patches.

As I push back out into the humid night, I hear a sound coming from the other side of the gas station. Instead of getting back into my car, I wander around the corner of the building to try to hear it better. Back there it's surprisingly undeveloped, the type of wetland that covers the Merritt Island National Wildlife Refuge. It still takes me a second to place the sound: it's alligators bellowing to each other in the dark.

I'm once again back on the Space Coast, once more adding another visit after the one I had thought would be my last. On the drive here, which I now know so well, I felt happy. Part of me had been missing Florida, had been trying to think of an excuse to come here again.

I think of Oriana Fallaci heading back to the Space Coast—the first time she came here, she'd described it as being "so ugly that if you saw it you'd agree to go to the Moon, which might not be better but certainly couldn't be worse." But after several visits, after making the acquaintance of astronauts and engineers and managers and seeing a launch, Fallaci started to feel the same way about the Space Coast that I do.

> I was on my way back to Cape Kennedy: happy to see my friends, to see the launching of the Saturn rocket, to be going home. Now I liked Florida that I'd described so cruelly. . . . Suddenly it was my home.

I'm here to see the first launch from Cape Canaveral operated by a private company, SpaceX. Today SpaceX will attempt to launch its own spacecraft, the Dragon, to dock with the International Space Station and deliver supplies. This would be a first, and it would make SpaceX the front-runner to become the contractor NASA hires to get people and cargo up and down to the International Space Station. Even if today's launch is successful, Dragon will have to fly many more re-supply missions, over a period of years, before it can be considered safe for astronauts.

I've never been a believer in privatized spaceflight—getting to space as cheaply as possible with an emphasis on catering to paying customers only serves to rob spaceflight of the things I love most about it. But I started to notice how many of my space friends—people I would have thought would be NASA-only snobs like me—were getting excited about the SpaceX launch, were posting updates about it online and making plans to come out for the launch. The NASASocial (the new, more inclusive name for NASATweetup) organized around this launch seemed to engender more chatter than many of them in the past. SpaceX has established a significant launch operation here in Florida but isn't hiring many ex-NASA people. The rumor is that the company doesn't want workers who have been steeped in NASA culture, especially NASA's extreme concern for safety (and, I can't help but cynically suspect, the relatively high wages, solid job security, and generous benefits of government contractors). If Omar were somehow to get hired at SpaceX in spite of this bias, it would likely be with a cut in pay and certainly a cut in benefits.

I found myself wondering what this launch was going to be like, how it would be different from shuttle launches both in terms of the rocket itself and in terms of the social experience of seeing it. A lot of the space fans I know are laid-off, or soon-to-be-laid-off, shuttle workers. What would this launch experience be like for them?

So I started making plans to go. Thankfully, this launch fell after the end of my semester and before my son's preschool ends, a quieter time than usual at my house and less disruptive for me to be gone. Still, the number of trips beyond the "definitely last one" is now three and growing, which is lost on neither my husband nor me.

Today's launch is scheduled for 4:55 a.m. Unlike the shuttle, the SpaceX Dragon has an "instantaneous launch window," a phrase whose implications I don't care for. Whereas the shuttle had a ten-minute window in which to get off the ground (even longer back in the days when they weren't trying to rendezvous with the International Space Station), Dragon has much less capacity to maneuver in space and so must arrive on a pinpoint trajectory from Earth. If it doesn't launch at exactly 4:55, they will have to scrub and try again another day.

It's only a few minutes from the gas station to the south gate of the Kennedy Space Center, but when I reach the gate it's closed and barricaded.

"What the hell?" I ask out loud in my car, of no one.

I sit for a minute, trying to think of what to do next. The north gate, the only other gate I've ever used, is up by Titusville, a half-hour drive away. That can't be what I'm supposed to do. So after a moment's contemplation, I text Omar:

South gate is closed ??

Omar's answer comes through right away. Gotta go to gate by VC.

VC means Visitor Complex, I know that much. But I'm still not sure what he's talking about, because this isn't the way I usually go to the Visitor Complex, and because the iPhone map offers no details within a restricted government installation, and because it's three in the morning.

Another text from Omar comes through: Where are you? I'm on my way

I text: Badge office

He answers: Hang on, be there in 30 secs

Twenty-nine seconds later, I recognize Omar's silver Mustang pulling into the lot. He rolls down his window just long enough to flash a smile and gesture for to me to follow him. Once he takes the turnoff toward the Visitor Complex, I realize where we are and what he was talking about—this little side road offers a second way in.

After we both get past the checkpoint, Omar gives a wave and drives off heading north. He is going to try to watch from the Vehicle Assembly Building roof. He still works here; his layoff has been rescinded one more time. I head toward the Press Site. We've made plans to have breakfast after the launch and the postlaunch press conference.

It's a new experience to be at the Press Site for a non-NASA launch. I would have thought the NASA Media Office people would hold themselves at arm's length from this one, but they seem to be doing their traditional fine job of getting us the information we need and answering our questions. They are handing out packets of material with the SpaceX logo on them in exactly the same way they used to hand out packets bearing the mission patch corresponding to each space shuttle launch. On the closed-circuit TVs, the SpaceX Falcon (the rocket that carries Dragon, the spacecraft) is steaming nicely on the launchpad.

So much of the answer to the question of what the end of the shuttle means depends upon what comes next. The existence of a next step already in development, the space shuttle, gave space fans living through the end of Apollo a sense that we were still moving forward, gave them an event to look forward to, even if it was still years off. For me, commercial spaceflight doesn't adequately fill this gap, for several reasons. One: the type of big, grand, daring spaceflight projects I'm interested in are, by definition, not good investments. They are exploratory, scientific, ennobling, and expensive, with no clear end point and certainly no chance of making a profit. *What will we find when we get to the moon?* people wondered in the sixties. They didn't know, but they were pretty sure they wouldn't find anything that could come close to compensating them financially for the cost of getting there, and they were right.

Two: as long as spaceflight is run by a government agency, any American child can reasonably dream of flying in space one day. For many of them, that dream will shape their early lives in important and beneficial ways. If spaceflight belongs to private companies, space travel will be a privilege of the incredibly wealthy, and space-obsessed children will have no particular motivation to do their algebra homework or serve in the military, knowing that their only hope of earning a seat lies in getting rich.

Three: since the beginning, it has been part of NASA's mandate to make its projects available to the American public. This means that everything—images, films, discoveries, transcripts of crew chatter—belongs to all of us. Not so with SpaceX. As a private company, SpaceX can keep private whatever they want, and they do. Some of my online space friends have been indignant to learn that they can't download specs and diagrams for Dragon and Falcon, as we have always been able to do for shuttle and other NASA spacecraft—the SpaceX designs are industry secrets. NASA makes moon rocks available to scientists all over the world for the asking, and they have let scientists send experiments to space on their spacecraft for very negotiable fees, often negotiated down to nothing. SpaceX is under no obligation to do anything of the kind, and I don't expect they will.

But maybe the privatization proponents are right that NASA has actually been holding us back. Maybe the end of shuttle will be like the meteor that killed the dinosaurs. Only with the behemoths gone could the little mammals that became our ancestors start to make a place for themselves.

At about four thirty in the morning, people start heading outside to the grassy field at the Press Site. Before I even get close I see a familiar orange glow on the horizon, and I can't believe it: it's the countdown clock. I look at the people on my left and right, looking to see whether they are incensed as well, but no one else seems to notice.

The light from the countdown clock is so bright, it's a little eerie. Since it's still full dark, without even any moon, the light of the countdown clock in my face makes it hard to see where I'm stepping, and I trip and stumble on the uneven ground. Rather than looking down into the useless dark surrounding my feet, I look out into the field and follow the swarm of glowing rectangles, one for each phone of the spectators. Bleachers have been set up, as they were for *Atlantis,* and many of the glowing phones are clustered there. Many of these are the NASASocial people, I can tell, because they are excitedly narrating into their phones or, in some cases, tiny video cameras. In fact, maybe it's all NASASocial people out here—maybe all the print journalists are watching on NASA TV from the safety of the News Center rather than stumbling around out here getting bitten by mosquitoes.

I walk all the way down to the lip of the Turn Basin. The SpaceX launchpad is not dead center ahead of us, as the Apollo and shuttle launchpads were, but off to the right, almost hidden behind the foliage making up Norman Mailer's jungle. I learn I've been looking in the wrong direction only when I hear some NASASocial people point out the launchpad to each other. I follow their fingers and see a bright haze rising from the horizon, the rocket lit up by floodlights.

I stand by the Turn Basin for a minute before I realize I'm hearing a splashing sound coming from the water. The sound is intermittent and quiet but distinct. Then I hear a faint *ribbit*. It's nocturnal frogs that live in the Turn Basin, going about their froggy business. Just as at the gas station, the sounds of wildlife are coming through now that everything is quiet.

At T minus nine, I move toward the bleachers to try to get a good spot to watch from. The chatter coming over the speakers is a little different for this launch, as one would expect—it's different people in a different launch control room using different procedures to prepare a different spacecraft. I feel hostility toward this countdown, a strong conviction that they are using the wrong language, are doing everything wrong. When the flight director (or whatever SpaceX calls her) polls the room (or whatever SpaceX calls it), one of the managers in the sequence doesn't answer when called on for a "go" or "no go." A few seconds of silence go by. I look around at some of the NASASocial people and we share an eye-roll-y look. NASA flight directors would never fall asleep at the wheel like that, we agree silently.

Someone shouts and points straight up.

"There goes the ISS!"

Everyone looks up. The sky is a bit overcast, so I think the shouting man might be overoptimistic, but when I look up in the direction he's pointing, I see it. It's unmistakable. The International Space Station. Brighter than any star, it moves surprisingly fast. I know the ISS is as long as a football field, has the volume of a three-bedroom house, that it's two hundred miles away and moving at seventeen thousand miles per hour.

"We're sending you up some stuff!" one of the NASASocial people shouts. Some of them try to take video of it, uselessly.

As always, I get caught up in the countdown. *Ten. Nine. Eight. Seven.* The NASASocial people are so excited, it's hard not to share their enthusiasm. I count along.

Five. Four. Three. Two. One.

At *zero*, we see a quick flash on the horizon. *Flash* isn't even quite the word. It's more like the hazy halo over the launchpad gets more intense for a second, then goes back to normal. An uncertain cheer rises around me. I wait to see the spacecraft enter my field of vision—I know from experience how slow the first seconds of launch can appear to be—but it never does.

The announcer on the speaker tells us there has been an abort, that the spacecraft is now being safed. I stand, gawking openmouthed in the direction of the launchpad. I was fooled by the light on the horizon: in the days of the space shuttle, the solid rocket boosters couldn't be shut down, so if you saw a light, you could be sure you were going to space today. But the SpaceX Falcon is powered by liquid fuel, which means it can shut itself down. And did, at the first sign of a problem. We all look at each other, a little bewildered. I hear someone say the word *scrub* into his phone, narrating the event to his followers. Only then do I understand: this is a scrub, my first. I tweet, "No longer scrubless," and get some sympathetic responses from space friends who have woken up to watch the launch live online. It's an odd feeling to come so far and wait so long to have everything called off in a fraction of a second. This is a feeling that many space fans have had many times. It's only fair that I should experience it once.

People start making their way back up to the News Center. I look at Twitter to see what's being said about the scrub, and I see a new tweet from André Kuipers, a Dutch astronaut living on the International Space Station. He has tweeted a picture he took of Cape Canaveral just a few minutes before as he passed overhead. The image is like any satellite image taken at night, mostly black, the landmasses and causeways traced in pale yellow light. It's brightest right where we are standing.

I follow all the astronauts living on the ISS on Twitter, so I see the pictures they take of Earth passing below them every day. I always stop to look at them because they are insanely gorgeous. But I've never seen a picture taken from space that I know I am in. I was standing on that ground looking up at him while he was looking down at us, and the image is one I'll save.

I hang around the News Center for a while waiting for the press conference. It had been scheduled for 7:00 a.m. but is being moved up because of the scrub. While I wait, I curl up for a short nap on the floor with my head pressed up against the wall. When I awaken, the monitor turned to NASA TV is showing an image of the rocket on the pad, presumably having been safed. A crawl at the bottom of the screen reads "*Endeavour* launch scrubbed." I blink at it a couple of times.

Then those words disappear and are quickly replaced with "SpaceX/ Falcon 9 launch scrubbed."

I poke around the News Center a bit, and against one wall I find a floor-to-ceiling shelf offering material of all kinds for journalists to take. All of this information is presumably online as well, but I am apparently not the only writer who is still tempted by paper handouts. The shelf holds packets specific to each mission as well as other packets providing information of all kinds about the space program. There are also copies of a newsletter for space center workers called *Spaceport News*. I grab a copy at random and start reading.

Guards watch over Discovery during final rollover
By Rebecca Sprague
Spaceport News

Nearly every Hollywood celebrity has at least one bodyguard on their payroll. At any given time, NASA's three space shuttles have about 80.

Officially called access control monitors and orbiter integrity clerks, the "guards" make sure the shuttles are safe and secure in Kennedy Space Center's orbiter processing facilities, the Vehicle Assembly Building, on the launch pads and when they're on the move.

The article describes the last rollover of *Discovery* from the Orbiter Processing Facility to the Vehicle Assembly Building; only then do I realize that this issue of *Spaceport News* must be an old one. I find the date: September 17, 2010.

Dressed in jeans, sneakers and blue United Space Alliance (USA) collared shirts, Discovery's guards stood watch about 50 feet away.

"Obviously, people like to get as close as they can, so we have to maintain some sort of control," said USA's Omar Izquierdo, who specifically is designated to guard Discovery. "We have a list of who gets to be how close and then we control that."

I smile and shake my head. Of course Omar was the one the writer approached; I'm not even surprised to find him here. The article goes on to quote the vehicle manager for *Discovery,* Jennifer Nufer: "These folks perform a very critical job for America's space program."

I stash a copy of the newsletter along with some other handouts in my bag. September 17, 2010, was just eight days before I came here for Family Day. In the intervening week, *Discovery* was mated with an external tank and two solid rocket boosters in the Vehicle Assembly Building. Then it was rolled out to the launchpad for the last time. The photo on my phone is still the snapshot I took of *Discovery* on Family Day, riding by in Omar's car, and whenever I see it I remember that day, that sense of possibility even as we knew this would be *Discovery's* last flight.

The SpaceX press conference is pretty much what you would expect—a lot of reminders that this is a new rocket, that spaceflight is an untested business, a lot of cautious optimism for the next attempt, which won't be for a few days because of a scheduled Soyuz docking that takes precedence. I get my first good look at Gwynne Shotwell, the president of SpaceX. She is whip smart in that put-together way you would expect in the president of an experimental tech company. But she is also intense and sincere and kind of adorable. She smiles a lot, her eyes twinkle. Her answers to questions are thoroughly well considered—her pauses between thoughts remind me of the pauses politicians leave themselves to scan what they are about to say for possible controversy—but a real love for what she does shines through. I came here planning to dislike SpaceX, and while Gwynne Shotwell doesn't exactly defy my every expectation, I still find myself liking her in spite of myself. In part, I know that I am a sucker for women involved in spaceflight, for women in jobs traditionally closed to them, and I can't help but suspect that Elon Musk, SpaceX's founder, had this appeal in mind when he chose her to run his space company.

I'm at a postlaunch party, my second official EndlessBBQ ("It really *is* endless," I joke on Twitter, before noticing how many other people have made the same joke), standing on the deck behind the Cocoa Beach Brewing Company with a few dozen space people. The sun is setting as I drink one of the microbrews made here and talk with Omar and some of the people I've met at launches and on Twitter. A lot of them are here with the NASASocial. It's a beautiful evening, not too humid for once.

I wind up in a long conversation with Jen Scheer, a woman I met at the party after *Atlantis* but never really talked to. I know her well from Twitter because she tweets avidly about space and is the founder and organizer of the Space Tweep Society, which makes her a celebrity of the online space community. Jen worked maintaining the hypergolic systems in the orbital maneuvering system pods and was one of the few female techs to work at the space center. Tonight, while we drink beer, I'm quizzing her about safety procedures—I've been trying to get a handle on whether NASA became overly safety conscious after *Columbia,* as some insiders have told me, or not safety conscious enough—when Omar drifts over. Jen asks about how work has been, and he tells her how unnerving it's been that visitors are now allowed to touch the orbiters.

"Hey, Omar," Jen starts with a big smile, "do you know what we used to call the tiles?"

"What?" Omar asks warily.

"Wrench cushions." Jen waits, open mouthed, for his reaction. Omar flinches.

"Aaagh," he moans quietly. "Don't put your wrenches on my tiles."

Jen laughs, "Of course if any tiles got damaged the tile techs would replace them," she assures me.

"I'm going to get another beer," Omar says, "and when I come back we'll be talking about something else."

Omar has told me how upsetting it's been seeing procedures change after the last landings, watching equipment that had been maintained with exquisite care now torn apart for scrap. Seeing visitors invited to touch things he spent years of his life making sure never got touched seems to elicit something like primal panic in Omar, and if he were less good-hearted that panic might metastasize into rage and resentment. Instead, he seems a little fuzzy these days, a little confused. When he comes back from the bar, we do talk about something else. Jen has been out of the space center workforce for a while now, so she has had time to get used to the changes. Omar still goes in every day, still walks through the same motions, but with no real purpose.

Later I strike up a conversation with Andy Scheer, Jen's husband, also a spaceworker. Andy tells me he is a pad rat, which means that rather than working with a specific orbiter, he works on a specific launchpad.

"Was there a rivalry," I ask him, "between people who worked at one pad or the other?"

"Oh yeah," he says. "Just like anyplace. Pad A people made fun of Pad B people, Pad B people made fun of Pad A people. Then it came down to one pad, and the people who were left had to work together."

I've heard a rumor that Andy was at work the day James Vanover, the engineer who had tried to rescind his early retirement and was told he could not, committed suicide by jumping off the launch tower, back in March 2011. When it had first happened, I'd thought I should ask Omar about the meaning of Vanover's gesture, but when I saw Omar next, the morning of the launch of *Endeavour,* it didn't seem right to bring it up. But now I decide to ask Andy.

"Yeah, I was there," Andy tells me. He's quiet for a minute.

"We'd walk around the pad first thing when we started a shift, looking for loose debris or anything out of place, and out of the corner of my eye I thought I saw something fall. I was the closest to him when he hit. I knew right away what had happened."

"That's awful," I say. I don't know what else to add.

"Yeah. Paramedics came pretty quickly. But until they arrived, there was nothing I could do except to sit with him."

We both look down into our beers.

"I know he cared about what he did," Andy adds. "I know he loved what he did and loved that place. His whole life was out there and that was coming to an end."

Put this way, it's remarkable that there haven't been more suicides, more violence, more family tragedies. Vanover's whole life was out there, and that was coming to an end, and the same is true for tens of thousands of people.

"So what's your book about?" Andy asks. "Omar said you're writing a book."

"Oh, it's about the end of shuttle," I answer. "I'm asking what it means that we went to space for fifty years and have decided not to go anymore."

"Good question," Andy says. I used to feel silly repeating this question, but I've come to realize that no one feels confident about having a good answer to it. Everyone says it's a good question. "What do you think is the answer?"

"I don't entirely know yet," I tell him. "But I think it has to do with the beginning, with how it started. The start was an accident. Without Sputnik, and a new president, and the Cold War, and then that president getting assassinated—without the German rocket designers who fled to the United States instead of the Soviet Union—it never would have happened at all."

Andy is quiet for a long moment. I'm afraid I've offended him by calling his life's work an accident.

Omar waves us over—he wants to show us something on his phone.

"Check this out," Omar says. He's found a video on NASA TV documenting the *Discovery* Day event we were at together. Exciting electronic music plays over a montage of *Discovery* arriving at Dulles and *Enterprise* being wheeled out of the museum.

"Look, right here!" It's a swooping crane shot of *Discovery* moving toward the building—I remember seeing the crane with the movie camera on it when we were out there—but then suddenly, in the bottom of the frame, I see Omar and myself, the backs of our heads, standing shoulder to shoulder watching *Discovery* roll by. We are unmistakable, Omar in his white ball cap, me with my blond ponytail, trying to take a picture of *Discovery* with my phone.

Omar seems pleased to find himself in the video commemorating the celebration of his bird, and he should—it's a document he can show his grandchildren. *I was there.* The video already has more than thirty thousand hits. But I find it disconcerting. I'm trying to write about these things that I've experienced, and in trying to write about them I often consult pictures and video I find online to help me understand where everything was, to reconstruct what things looked like. It's an unsettlingly postmodern experience to find myself in one of these documents, like looking up a word in the dictionary and finding my own name.

As the evening goes on, people talk about whether they will come back for the next attempt or not. I will not. This will be my first time leaving Florida with the spacecraft I came to see launch still on the ground.

As I'm getting ready to leave, Omar asks if I'd like to set off a model rocket with him in the morning. He's bought a scale model of the SpaceX Falcon, and he offers it as a sort of consolation because I didn't get to see the real one go off.

I answer immediately, "Of course!" We make plans for when to meet up. I have a twelve-hour drive tomorrow and really should be hitting the road as early as possible. But I like the idea of seeing Omar one more time before I go, and besides that, I sense a metaphor.

What does it mean that we've done so much, and what does it mean that we've decided to stop? I talked to Andy about the unlikely chain of events that led to the start of NASA and Project Mercury, and though it goes against some of the patriotic pride we usually take in our space program, I've had to accept that the political will to keep spaceflight going just doesn't exist anymore, hasn't for a long time. We have been infected by the myth of public support for spaceflight for so long, it's kept us from properly understanding how we got to where we are. As historian John Logsdon writes, "Apollo was a product of a particular moment in time. . . . Its most important significance may well be simply that it happened. Humans did travel to and explore another celestial body." It happened, but we never quite understood why we were doing it. There was never enthusiastic public support for human spaceflight for its own sake. I should probably say this again: *There was never enthusiastic public support for human spaceflight for its own sake.* At best, there was support for beating the Soviets at a game that they had grabbed a head start on, a game that seemed to have to do with military, not scientific, superiority. People said they didn't want to go to bed under a Soviet moon, and they were serious. The power of that brief surge of emotion was enough to start Apollo, but the moon project had lost its relevance as a national project by the time it was actually accomplished. The power of that brief interest, combined with the immense fun and pageantry and good feeling brought about by the successes of the heroic era, and its heroes, has been enough to fuel fifty years of NASA. This is remarkable in and of itself, of course. Few projects based on such short-lived support have shown themselves to have such endurance.

But maybe this is a part of the answer to the question I've been torturing myself with all this time: *Why are we stopping this when everyone seems to like it?* The answer is that public support for spending the money, to the extent it ever existed, was long gone by the time I was born. The whole thing depended on a confluence of forces that can't be re-created. Those of us who love it should count ourselves lucky that it somehow accidentally happened at all, and, I suppose, we should accept the fact that it's finally run its course.

I discovered at this attempt that it's simply impossible to stand outside in the middle of the night watching an enormous object on the horizon try to launch itself into space and not root for it. At least, it's impossible for me. And once you've stood out there and rooted for it, you kind of hope for it to succeed even once you're not watching it in person anymore. A few days later, I will set my alarm for the middle of the night in order to wake up and watch the second attempt to launch Dragon. I will be pleased and confused when it does launch successfully. I find I have started to care about this spacecraft. Not in the same way that I care about the space shuttle or the Saturn V, or even the Redstones and Atlases—nothing would ever come close to that—but when the little white Dragon on my phone's screen slowly pulls itself up into the sky, the way spaceships do, I will feel a surge of joy for it, clap my hand over my mouth to keep from waking my husband. Then I will have to stop and think about what that means.

What does it mean that we went to space for fifty years and then decided not to anymore? This question is as difficult to grapple with as ever because, I've discovered, it's actually many questions at once. What does it mean to stop exploring? What does it mean to disappoint children? What does it mean to cancel the future? What does it mean to hobble the one government agency that people feel good about? What does it mean to hope for private companies to take over something we used to do as a nation? What does it mean to stop spending the money?

One thing I notice every time I'm at the Cape is how literal all the workers are about their work. I've kept calling the work here some kind of dream, yet what I see over and over is that, to the people who do the work, nothing is a dream, a metaphor, a fairy tale: everything is exactly what it is. If the work here results in something beautiful, it is beautiful by accident, as form follows function. It is the reflected beauty of our intentions I'm seeing, not someone's abstract idea of beauty.

Hugely wasteful, hugely grand? If we wanted to go back to the moon now, we couldn't do it. We'd have to start over. But here's the thing I keep coming back to: the goal itself was beautiful, beautiful in its imagery and in its impossibility. It was a dream that even the literal-minded could share—even Neil Armstrong, as a boy, had dreamed a recurring dream that he could hover above the earth by holding his breath. The dream came true, even if it was only a fluke. Even if it was only for a while.

In the morning, I find Omar at the park, a perfect location with four full-sized soccer fields, all of them unused today. We walk into the center of the four fields, leaving as much empty space as we can around us. Omar carefully unpacks the model's pieces and starts setting it up, telling me about how it works as he assembles it. But a piece is missing; it must have fallen out in his car. He heads back to the parking lot to find it, a five-minute round trip. To pass the time, I snap a few pictures of the rocket and tweet one along with the words:

w/ @izqomar: Failure is not an option.

Ten seconds later, I look up to see Omar heading back toward me with the missing piece held aloft triumphantly. He's still far away, but I see him startle, then make an expression exactly as if his phone has just vibrated in his pants. He fishes the phone out of a pocket, looks at it, and smiles. He's seen what I put on Twitter.

"That's pretty funny," he calls out as soon as he's within earshot. A second later, my phone buzzes. Omar has retweeted me, and now a few of his followers are weighing in—he has over five hundred. Now with all the pieces in hand, Omar kneels down to finish assembling the rocket.

"Now, I've made a few mods," Omar explains from his position on the ground. He shows me where a tube meant to guide the rocket along a metal rod had fallen off the fuselage earlier—Omar had replaced it by supergluing a fast-food straw in its place. This adaptation held together through one previous launch, but today it looks to be coming apart. Soon the straw comes off in Omar's hand. He grunts in exasperation.

"That's definitely a scrub," he announces, disappointed.

"But I've already tweeted that failure is not an option," I point out. I'm only kind of joking.

"Do you have any duct tape in your car, or anything like that?" Omar asks. I don't, but I start thinking about other ways to attach the straw to the body of the rocket. I come up with the idea of using my hair elastics, and that seems to work. Our jury-rigged rocket is set up on its stand, its white body striped with my brown hair elastics, poised for launch. Omar and I step away as far as the detonator cord will let us. Omar is extremely careful working with the wires and the deto-nator, and he describes what he's doing as he does it, probably a safety thing he learned at work. Once everything is set up to his satisfaction, Omar takes a deep breath and says, "Okay. You ready?"

"Ready."

"You want to push the button?" he asks.

I'm surprised at first that he doesn't have a more technical term than "push the button." But I suppose none of the terms used in space-flight quite apply here. "Go for main engine start" isn't quite accurate. "Ignition" would technically be correct, I suppose, but isn't easily made into a verb in this context ("You want to ignite?"). "Liftoff" seems overly grand when we're talking about pushing a small plastic button. Or maybe Omar doesn't want to make a joke of this moment—maybe he wants to enjoy this model rocket for what it is rather than pretend it's something it's not.

"No, you do it," I say.

"You sure?" Omar sounds genuinely disbelieving that I am refus-ing the pleasure of firing the rocket. To me, his skepticism only under-scores that he considers it a privilege to push the button, and that only makes me want all the more to let him be the one to do it.

"I'm sure," I say, and get out my phone to record a video of our tri-umph. "Light this candle."

I have in my phone a thirty-second video of the model rocket launch. The video starts at the moment the rocket begins to lift itself off the stand, and I wish I had thought to start recording a few seconds ear-lier because I would like to know whether Omar and I counted down before launching. I don't think we did.

In the video, Omar is holding the detonator button in his left hand, his white polo shirt and light khaki shorts blinding white in the Florida sun, his skin a glowing brown. As his thumb comes down on the button, I swing over to look at the rocket, and the camera finds it already lifting off, already a few inches off the ground, by the time I get there. Within a couple of seconds it's flying so fast and so high I have trouble finding it again. A thin smoke trail streaks out behind it, adorably, a tiny echo of the enormous steam trail of the shuttle, and my camera follows that white stripe on the sky up, up, up, far higher than I had ever expected this little model rocket could go, and when I almost can't see it anymore it stops traveling up and levels off, the curve it makes against the bright blue sky exactly like the curve made by *Challenger* in my childhood. A few seconds later, the smoke trail waning, the rocket slows way down. Its recovery chute has detonated, and soon it's possible to make out the white smudge that is the parachute against the sky. Now it will drift down toward us, at a leisurely pace, quite a way downrange of us—it's a good thing we left as much space as we did. The rocket swings crazily back and forth under its parachute.

As the exhausted rocket drifts down and down, I can make out the dark stripes of my hair bands along its fuselage. The horizon heaves itself up into the frame—a row of perfect white clouds, a soccer goal, a faraway stand of perfect green palm trees, some stucco houses. Florida. Watching the video today, on a cool gray day in Tennessee, the sight of those palm trees stirs in me something like homesickness, though Florida has never been my home, though I still don't understand it. What was the metaphor I thought would present itself in this rocket launch? When I watch the video, I can't quite remember. Something about a success after yesterday's scrub, a joke about SpaceX or about my scrubless record, but when I watch the little video in my phone I feel only the weird spaceport homesickness, that Florida nostalgia, and then the surprise and pleasure of how high and fast the actual model rocket flies. After it finishes drifting back to earth and plops itself unceremoniously onto the grass, the camera swings around again to find my friend Omar walking toward me, a huge smile on his face.

"That was a success," my voice says, and Omar laughs happily, and then the video ends.

Планета есть колыбель разума, но нельзя вечно жить в колыбели.
(This planet is the cradle of human reason, but one cannot live in a cradle forever.)   —Konstantin Tsiolkovsky, 1911

There can be no thought of finishing [work on rockets], for "aiming at the stars," both literally and figuratively, is a problem to occupy generations, so that no matter how much progress one makes, there is always the thrill of just beginning.   —Robert Goddard, 1932

EPILOGUE

On August 6, 2012, the Mars rover Curiosity approached the surface of Mars after a nine-month journey through interplanetary space. At NASA's Jet Propulsion Laboratory in Pasadena, California, a room full of flight controllers and engineers bit their nails and paced the floor while Curiosity went through its complicated and daring entry sequence, nicknamed the "seven minutes of terror." Flight control erupted in emotion when the signal indicated that Curiosity was safe on Mars. A record number of people (3.2 million) watched the landing live online, so many that the server became overloaded and temporarily shut down. A crowd gathered in Times Square to watch the landing on the big screen together, and after the successful touchdown chanted "NASA! NASA! NASA!" Millions more watched subsequently on YouTube. The flight director, a young man with a Mohawk named Bobak Ferdowsi, became an instant Internet celebrity and gained twenty thousand Twitter followers in twelve hours.

The enormous level of enthusiasm for Curiosity was encouraging for space fans like me still mourning shuttle. NASA's deft handling of social media seemed to come to the attention of more people than ever. Curiosity has 1.4 million Twitter followers who watch its progress each day on the surface of Mars. The extent to which so many people seem to feel a personal connection to a robot, the sort of mission that used to be dismissed as too boring to keep the public interest, gives me hope. And the enthusiasm only serves to underscore the frustrating notion that Twitter might have been able to save the shuttle, if only it had come along a few years earlier.

In the middle of drafting my last chapter, I text Omar:
> What does the 'days to launch' sign say now?

His reply:
> It doesn't. It's covered with a bag that says 'Safety is no accident.'

When I show him an early draft of this book, Omar is surprised to see my account of James Vanover, the engineer who jumped from the launch tower, whose death I was too shy to ask Omar about. It turns out Omar was there too, on the pad with *Endeavour*, the day Vanover jumped. Omar was on the launch tower, two levels above Vanover, he tells me when I ask three years later. He'd been watching the external tank to make sure birds didn't damage it when he heard someone yelling. If he'd happened to be looking down through the open grate floor, he tells me, he would have seen Vanover silently slip over the railing to his death.

A few days later, Omar writes to tell me that the McDonald's in Merritt Island has removed the giant plastic space shuttle from its play area. "So it's really over," he adds. I've come to know him well enough to know that this is both a joke and also a sincere observation, a moment that makes him truly sad.

I come across a photograph of Wernher von Braun taken in the last year of his life, standing in the main lobby of the National Air and Space Museum, the hushed interior of my childhood. It's a portrait filled with quiet emotion, though it's possible the emotion is all mine, imported from my sensory memory of Air and Space, from my knowledge that von Braun won't live much longer. Under his polished dress shoes lies the red carpet; behind him loom the marble walls. His face is strangely tragic, his posture noble. It's as though he knows his greatest achievement is already on its way to being forgotten, and that he won't live long enough to see the next thing. As much as he has done, he will never get to go to space himself.

In the summer of 2012, I took my husband and son to the Space Coast for the first time. I got to lead them through the Rocket Garden, introduce them to Omar, and play with them in the surf at Cape Canaveral. I showed them the Visitor Complex, and we rode the air-conditioned tour buses with the regular enthralled visitors through the roads I now know so well, through the place that has taken me away from them so many times. We went on the public tour of the Vehicle Assembly Building, which had just a few weeks before opened to limited numbers of visitors for the first time since the seventies. I held my son's hand while he walked into the VAB, looked up, then caught sight of *Atlantis* in one of the high bays. His little face lit up with wonder, and he looked at me to confirm that he was seeing what he thought he was seeing.

"Wow," he said.

The economy in Brevard County saw a sharp downturn, as everyone predicted, at the end of shuttle. The combination of the ongoing recession and the precipitous layoffs had a serious effect on the area. About eight thousand people lost their jobs at the Kennedy Space

Center as a result of the end of shuttle, half of the workforce there. A ripple effect resulted in an estimated twenty-five thousand more lost jobs, further depressing an area that had already suffered from higher unemployment than the rest of the state and the country. Underemployment—highly skilled workers hired at lower salaries and with stripped-down benefits—is widespread. Housing prices fell and foreclosures increased.

There have been signs of hope, however. More aerospace companies have established sites in central Florida than had been anticipated, including SpaceX, Boeing, Embraer, and XCOR, taking advantage of a skilled workforce and tax incentives. The unemployment rate in Brevard County remains higher than state and national averages, but the foreclosure rate is slowing. Whether these new jobs will fully replace the role the Kennedy Space Center has played in the local economy remains to be seen.

Omar received his fourth and final layoff notice in January of 2013. Perhaps fittingly, the day Omar worked at the Kennedy Space Center for the last time and turned in his badge, March 1, 2013, was also the day a SpaceX Dragon successfully docked with the International Space Station for the first time. My Twitter feed was filled with descriptions of, and celebrations of, the SpaceX launch and, simultaneously, a long stream of condolences for Omar.

In May 2013, Omar accepted a job at the badging office at the Orlando airport.

Andy Scheer, the pad technician I met after the SpaceX attempt, left NASA and started work at SpaceX in a similar position in March 2013. Andy and his wife, Jen, the former orbital maneuvering system technician, welcomed their first baby, a girl named Fara, on April 26, 2013. Andy and Jen's many combined followers kept apprised of Jen's progress the day she gave birth via the hashtag #spacebaby. Fara was born with a shock of dark hair in a fauxhawk that earned the instant Twitter approval of Bobak Ferdowsi, the Jet Propulsion Laboratory's Mohawk guy. The congratulations included a lot of jokes about Fara being a future astronaut, Fara being the first American to set foot on Mars. So many of the people I have met at launches are people who took the dream of flying in space seriously as children and young adults and let that dream shape their lives; what will it mean for Fara to grow up on the Space Coast in the coming decades, both her parents still immersed in spaceflight? This too gives me some hope.

After ten months at SpaceX, Andy left in frustration. He had enjoyed being back at work on a launchpad, he says, but despite his years of experience, he had been hired on contract rather than as a salaried worker. He grew tired of the long hours away from his family, and he is now back at Kennedy working at the Space Station Processing Facility.

Frank Izquierdo, who retired from NASA after the last launch, now fills his time with travel, fixing up an old Camaro, and home improvement projects. He says he feels grateful that his thirty-year career at NASA fit so perfectly the thirty-year life span of the space shuttle.

Plans for the Space Launch System continue to move forward. The Orion capsule is being tested for its ability to safely return astronauts to Earth using a design similar to that of Apollo. NASA still gives 2021 as the date for the first crewed missions, though budget wrangling and political debate show no signs of stopping. NASA continues to plan for and educate the public about SLS and Orion, but their fate is far from certain.

SpaceX continues to develop its Dragon V2 spacecraft for transporting crews to the International Space Station. The company continues to promise crewed flights on a short time frame, but no specific dates have been set.

I am often asked what I think will happen with American spaceflight in the future. How many years will it be before astronauts can get to space again on an American spacecraft? Will a human flight to Mars take place in my lifetime, and if it does, will its voyagers be NASA astronauts or will they be wealthy pleasure seekers? As much as I like to talk about space and to hold forth on what I know, I tend to evade answering these questions. I know that NASA has plans, fantastic plans, that it would like to put into practice, but the conditions it would take for those dreams to be funded are as uncertain as they have ever been since before NASA started. The progress made by private companies like SpaceX has been impressive. But the space programs I love most are the ones that are so ambitiously expensive only the federal budget of a superpower could support them. Altogether, Apollo cost about $110 billion in today's dollars. The entire shuttle program cost about $200 billion. A trip to Mars might cost twice what shuttle did; the war in Iraq has cost five times that as of this writing.

What would it take to get us back on the path it seemed we were on more than forty years ago? In 2012 the Chinese space agency announced a robotic mission to the moon, to be followed by human moonwalkers. When I read about this I felt a surge of hope unlike any I've felt in a long time. If Americans thought Chinese taikonauts were headed to the Sea of Tranquility with the intention of pulling up Buzz's American flag and in its place staking a Chinese flag, we might have the conditions necessary for another trip to the moon—namely, an enemy threatening to get there before we get back.

Once in a while when I climb into my car at night in hot weather, the smell of the baked upholstery and dashboard wafts up and brings with it a memory of my trips to the Space Coast, the hot asphalt, sunscreen, canebrake, Coca-Cola and the taste of ice melting in a wax fast-food cup, bugs big and small, pop music that was in Top 40 rotation in 2011, the crackly voice of the NASA announcer saying *PLT, OTC, no unexpected errors* and *go at throttle up,* the slickness of the brown bedspreads at the Clarion Merritt Island, a swell of enthusiasm and patriotism, the bright light of the space shuttle's main engines burning liquid oxygen and liquid hydrogen, the sound of helicopter blades choppering through a steam trail, the taste of the von Braun ale at the Cocoa Beach Brewing Company. In these moments I am suddenly conscious of a feeling that I know is with me always, a feeling that I need to get back to the Space Coast, an unsatisfiable desire to get back there in order to finally understand it, or to be accepted by it, though I never will understand it, never will belong there. The moments I've come closest have been those hot sunburned evenings I've spent with space fans and spaceworkers, with people who have touched the space shuttle with their own hands and whose work has made the space shuttle fly, and that those people have become my friends, because of this strange thing we have in common, pleases me.

In my dreams, sometimes, I still return to the Vehicle Assembly Building. The other night, I dreamed I found myself sitting in its vast interior on a beige metal folding chair, in a field of folding chairs, the rain clouds swirling 525 feet above our heads, just under the vanishingly far-off ceiling windows. The folding chairs are flimsy and they keep trying to close themselves under us, their rubber feet skittering on the hard concrete of the Vehicle Assembly Building floor. I know without being told that these chairs have been set up for all the writers who have written about the American space program, though most of the chairs appear to be empty. Norman Mailer is sitting next to me, which makes me faintly nervous. I can also make out Tom Wolfe, Jay Barbree, J. G. Ballard, Lynn Sherr, Oriana Fallaci, Walter Cronkite, and fields of others, some long dead. Nearly all are men, nearly all are white. It occurs to me that we space writers are all asked the same question all the time: *Would you go?* Mostly we say yes, but we know we are lying. We'll never be given the chance anyway. We all feel Norman's masculine envy at being left behind, but our envy is beside the point. We know that someone needs to stay behind and write about what it feels like to watch it from the ground.

We wait on our folding chairs. We are waiting for something to happen, but we wait and wait and it never gets started.

MILESTONES OF AMERICAN SPACEFLIGHT

Precursors

March 1926: First successful liquid-fueled rocket launched by American physicist Robert Goddard

October 1942: Successful German test launch of the first ballistic missile, the V-2, later used on Allied cities near the end of World War II combat in Europe

October 1947: Sound barrier broken by American test pilot Chuck Yeager

October 1957: Soviet Union launch of Sputnik, the first artificial satellite; beginning of the space race

February 1958: Launch of the first American satellite, Explorer 1

July 1958: Establishment of the US National Aeronautics and Space Administration (NASA)

April 1961: First human spaceflight: Soviet cosmonaut Yuri Gagarin

The Heroic Era: Mercury, Gemini, Apollo (1959–1972)

Project Mercury: Putting the First Americans in Space (1959–1963)

Six single-astronaut missions

May 1961: First American to travel into space: Alan Shepard

May 1961: President John F. Kennedy's charge to Congress to put a man on the moon by the end of the decade

February 1962: First American to orbit Earth: John Glenn

Project Gemini: Moving toward the Moon (1962–1966)

Ten missions to develop hardware and techniques for travel to the moon

March 1965: First flight to carry two astronauts

June 1965: First American spacewalk: Ed White

December 1965: First rendezvous of two American spacecraft

March 1966: First docking of two American spacecraft

Project Apollo: Walking on the Moon (1963–1972)

Eleven crewed missions, including six successful trips to the lunar surface

January 1967: All three Apollo 1 astronauts—Roger Chaffee, Gus Grissom, and Ed White—killed in a cabin fire during a launchpad test

December 1968: First trip to lunar orbit on Apollo 8

July 1969: Apollo 11 crew makes first moon landing; Neil Armstrong and Buzz Aldrin walk on moon

April 1970: Apollo 13 crew prevented from landing on the moon by oxygen tank explosion

July 1971: First use of lunar rover on Apollo 15

December 1972: Final moon landing Apollo 17

The Shuttle Era: Ongoing Access to Low-Earth Orbit (1981–2011)

135 total flights of the orbiters *Columbia, Challenger, Discovery, Atlantis, Endeavour*—133 successful missions and two disasters resulting in loss of spacecraft and crew. Deployment and repairs to satellites, including the Hubble Space Telescope; assembly of the International Space Station over 37 missions.

April 1981: First test flight of space shuttle *Columbia*

June 1982: Last test flight of *Columbia;* shuttle program officially operational

April 1983: First flight of *Challenger;* first shuttle spacewalk

June 1983: First American woman in space: Sally Ride

August 1983: First African American in space: Guy Bluford

August 1984: First flight for *Discovery*

October 1985: First flight for *Atlantis*

January 1986: Explosion of *Challenger* 73 seconds after launch, destroying the spacecraft and killing all seven crew members, including teacher Christa McAuliffe

May 1989: Venus probe Magellan deployed

October 1989: Jupiter probe Galileo deployed

April 1990: Hubble Space Telescope deployed

May 1992: First flight for *Endeavour*

June 1995: First shuttle docking with Russian space station *Mir*

December 1998: First International Space Station assembly mission

February 2003: Breakup of *Columbia* upon reentry of Earth's atmosphere, destroying the spacecraft and killing all seven crew members

February 2011: Final flight for *Discovery*

May 2011: Final flight for *Endeavour*

July 2011: Final flight of the space shuttle program *(Atlantis)*

The remaining shuttles become museum displays: Discovery *at National Air and Space Museum, Washington, DC;* Atlantis *at Kennedy Space Center Visitor Complex, Florida;* Endeavour *at California Science Center, Los Angeles.*

SELECTED BIBLIOGRAPHY

Aldrin, Buzz, with Ken Abraham. *Magnificent Desolation: The Long Journey Home from the Moon.* New York: Harmony/Random House, 2009.

Burrows, William E. *This New Ocean: The Story of the First Space Age.* New York: Random House, 1998.

Cabbage, Michael, and William Harwood. *Comm Check . . . : The Final Flight of Shuttle Columbia.* New York: Free Press/Simon & Schuster, 2004.

Cernan, Eugene, with Don Davis. *The Last Man on the Moon: Astronaut Eugene Cernan and America's Race in Space.* New York: St. Martin's, 1999.

Chaikin, Andrew. *A Man on the Moon: The Voyages of the Apollo Astronauts.* New York: Viking, 1994.

Collins, Michael. *Carrying the Fire: An Astronaut's Journeys. 40th anniversary ed.* New York: Farrar, Straus and Giroux, 2009.

Fallaci, Oriana. *If the Sun Dies.* Translated by Pamela Swinglehurst. New York: Atheneum, 1966.

Feynman, Richard P. *"What Do You Care What Other People Think?":* *Further Adventures of a Curious Character.* New York: Bantam, 1989.

Fuson, Robert H. *Juan Ponce de León and the Spanish Discovery of Puerto Rico and Florida.* Blacksburg: McDonald and Woodward, 2000.

Government Printing Office. *Columbia Accident Investigation Board Report.* Washington, DC: US Government Printing Office, 2003.

Hansen, James R. *First Man: The Life of Neil Armstrong.* New York: Simon & Schuster, 2005.

Hickam, Homer H. Jr. *Rocket Boys.* New York: Delta/Random House, 2000.

Hough, Richard. *Captain James Cook: A Biography.* London: Coronet/ Hodder and Stoughton, 1995.

Lathers, Marie. *Space Oddities: Women and Outer Space in Popular Film and Culture, 1960–2000.* New York: Continuum, 2010.

Launius, Roger D., and Howard E. McCurdy, eds. *Spaceflight and the Myth of Presidential Leadership.* Champaign: University of Illinois Press, 1997.

Lennon, J. Michael. *Norman Mailer: A Double Life.* New York: Simon & Schuster, 2013.

Lipartito, Kenneth, and Orville R. Butler. *A History of the Kennedy Space Center.* Gainesville: University Press of Florida, 2007.

Logsdon, John M. *John F. Kennedy and the Race to the Moon.* New York: Palgrave Macmillan, 2010.

Mailer, Norman. *Of a Fire on the Moon.* Boston: Little, Brown, 1970.

McCurdy, Howard E. *Space and the American Imagination.* Baltimore: Johns Hopkins University Press, 2011.

Murray, Charles, and Catherine Bly Cox. *Apollo: The Race to the Moon.* New York: Simon & Schuster, 1989.

Neufeld, Michael J., ed. *Spacefarers: Images of Astronauts and Cosmonauts in the Heroic Era of Spaceflight.* Washington, DC: Smithsonian Institution, 2013.

Neufeld, Michael J. *Von Braun: Dreamer of Space, Engineer of War.* New York: Vintage/Random House, 2008.

Office of the President. *Report of the Presidential Commission on the Space Shuttle* Challenger *Accident.* Washington, DC: Office of the President, 1986.

Schmitt, Harrison H. *Return to the Moon: Exploration, Enterprise, and Energy in the Human Settlement of Space.* New York: Copernicus, 2006.

Shepard, Alan, and Deke Slayton. *Moon Shot: The Inside Story of America's Race to the Moon.* Atlanta: Turner, 1994.

Sherr, Lynn. *Sally Ride: America's First Woman in Space.* New York: Simon & Schuster, 2014.

Vaughan, Diane. *The* Challenger *Launch Decision: Risky Technology, Culture, and Deviance at NASA.* Chicago: University of Chicago Press, 1997.

Verne, Jules. *From the Earth to the Moon* and *Around the Moon.* Translated by Harold Salemson. New York: Heritage, 1970.

Weitekamp, Margaret A. *Right Stuff, Wrong Sex: America's First Women in Space Program.* Baltimore: Johns Hopkins University Press, 2004.

Winters, Dan. *Last Launch:* Discovery, Endeavour, Atlantis. Austin: University of Texas Press, 2012.

Wolfe, Tom. *The Right Stuff.* New York: Farrar, Straus and Giroux, 1979.

ACKNOWLEDGMENTS

It was a privilege to be able to tell this story, and I would like to extend thanks to the many people who helped me to do so:

To Omar Izquierdo and the Izquierdo family for inviting me into their world and letting me write about it. To Chris and Elliot for their support and enthusiasm (and for wearing the T-shirts). To my launch friends, especially Anna Leahy, Doug Dechow, Jen Scheer, Andy Scheer, Stu Maschwitz, Kara Tonolli, Trey Ratcliff, Gordon Laing, Scott Kublin, Christopher Shaffer, Megan Prelinger, Matthew Cimone, and Ryan Kobrick. To Laurel Litzenberger and Stephanie Schierholz at NASA, and to Nancy Glasgow and Andrea Farmer at the Kennedy Space Center Visitor Complex. To the space journalists and the space historians, especially Michael Neufeld and Margaret Weitekamp. To my colleagues in the Department of English at the University of Tennessee, especially Michael Knight, Marilyn Kallet, Chuck Maland, and Stan Garner; most especially to my core committee Katy Chiles, Amy Elias, Heather Hirschfeld, Lisi Schoenbach, and Urmila Seshagiri. To Michael Shum for research assistance. To my colleague Stephen Blackwell for the translation of Tsiolkovsky. To the Tennessee Arts Commission and to the National Endowment for the Arts. To my former professors and classmates at the University of Michigan, especially to Thomas Lynch for encouraging my first efforts in creative nonfiction. To my generous early readers Emily Carney, Christopher Hebert, Omar Izquierdo, Mitchell Lazarus, Jen Scheer, and D'Anne Witkowski. To J. L. Pickering at Retro Space Images. To the staff and my fellow regulars at store #8536. To my students, especially the students who took the time to help me understand what the young people know: Stephanie Ammons, Olivia Cooper, Taylor Goff, Stephen Graves, Benjamin Heller, Anthony Karnowski, Ian Parker, and Stephanie Riggs.

Special thanks to Julie Barer and everyone at Barer Literary. Special thanks to Steve Woodward, Katie Dublinski, Fiona McCrae, Robert Polito, Erin Kottke, Marisa Atkinson, Jeff Shotts, and everyone at Graywolf Press.

Lastly, I want to thank the men and women of the Kennedy Space Center, past and present. Your work made something beautiful come true. May it never be forgotten.

JUDGE'S AFTERWORD

Of a Fire on the Moon, Norman Mailer's 1970 account of the Apollo 11 moon landing, was the first book I "covered" as a freshman arts reporter for my student newspaper, the *Heights,* after negotiating Boston's subway maze from Boston College to Harvard Square one sharp April night to hear him read. Originally a serial in *Life, Of a Fire on the Moon* would not be published for months, and Mailer read from typescript—a gorgeous sequence about the engineering and metaphysics of the launch, followed by an analysis of the mysterious reverberations of the event for himself, his family, his friends, the nation. There were numerous characters inside the psychic playhouse of Norman Mailer, but at the podium of Sanders Theatre his stance was magisterial—a dazzle of science, history, art, politics, and Manichaeism—his command subtly disconcerting to an audience who mostly was there in anticipation of the legendary bad behavior.

When I was able finally to pore over *Of a Fire on the Moon* the following fall, I was at home with the worst flu of my life—and my spiking temperature prompted a delirious effect I've never experienced again. I found that merely by looking at them I had memorized pages of Mailer's prose, and at night as I struggled to sleep the

314 | JUDGE'S AFTERWORD

sentences wouldn't stop racing through my head. That his sentences already were speedy, febrile, and unforgettable only intensified my twilight nightmares:

> Presumably, the moon was not listening, but if, in fact, she were the receiving and transmitting station of all lunacy, then she had not been ignoring the nation since. Four assassinations later; a war in Vietnam later; a burning of Black ghettos later; hippies, drugs, and many student uprisings later; one Democratic Convention in Chicago seven years later; one New York school strike later; one sexual revolution later; yes, eight years of a dramatic, near-catastrophic, outright spooky decade later, we were ready to make the moon.

My first—literal—fever dreams.

In my *Heights* piece I strained over otherwise pointless flourishes, such as boxing metaphors, which at that moment must have sounded Mailerish to me. Fortunately for us, Margaret Lazarus Dean in *Leaving Orbit: Notes from the Last Days of American Spaceflight* shuns such ready-made stylistic traps. Yet as divergent as Dean in 2015 should be from Mailer, *Leaving Orbit* is haunted by *Of a Fire on the Moon,* along a resonant personal and historical continuum that ultimately proposes comparisons with such notable contemporary nonfiction classics as Geoff Dyer's *Out of Sheer Rage* (Dyer in conversation with D. H. Lawrence) or Nicholson Baker's *U and I: A True Story* (Baker in conversation with John Updike). As early on Dean focuses what she tags the "heroic" versus the "shuttle" eras of spaceflight, she confesses her "jealousy" of Mailer:

> With Norman Mailer, especially . . . I feel as though he and I are tugging on opposite ends of the same thread, a thread forty years long. I am often struck with jealousy for the era he lived in. Sometimes it seems as though Norman Mailer's generation got to see the beginning of things and mine has gotten the ends.

From the outset she frames her own project via his: "What would it mean to go to the last launch and write about it the way Mailer wrote about the launch of Apollo 11?" Dean actually rereads *Of a Fire on the Moon* while she waits among the Florida throngs for *Discovery* to take off, and, whenever possible, correlates notes. "In his book about Apollo 11, Norman Mailer wrote that the Vehicle Assembly Building may be the ugliest building in the world from the outside," she recalls, "but that from the inside it was a candidate for the most beautiful. I can finally see what he means." Dean recognizes that she and Mailer share an "envy" of the astronauts:

> The masculine envy of which he speaks is not masculine at all. It's integral to the experience of watching people soaring into the heavens while we, with pen and paper, are stuck on the ground. I feel it too, and that envy is at the heart of a kinship between Norman Mailer and me that transcends forty-two years, a change in space vehicle, and even gender—a difference not insignificant to Norman Mailer, who once remarked to Orson Welles in a television interview that all women should be kept in cages. But I understand him, I feel him, just the same. I've read accounts of the launch of Apollo 11 by each of the three men on board, by the flight director and dozens of other people closely tied to the mission, and I've clung to every word; yet it's Norman Mailer's wrestling with his own detachment, his own desire to feel something for that gray stick, that stays with me, that makes me feel I've been let in on what it was like to be there.

Despite this unanticipated "kinship," Dean (as here) refuses to flinch from their contrasts—generational, circumstantial, and tonal, or of gender and class. The gifted writer of *Leaving Orbit* also steadily positions herself as a mother, wife, and teacher. "This is an important difference between Norman Mailer and me," she says, "when Mailer went off to Cape Canaveral and Houston, for as long as he pleased, he left behind five children with three different mothers and does not seem to have been troubled with much guilt over who would wash their clothes or fix their meals or get up with them in the middle of the night when they wet their beds. He probably wasn't participating in these activities even when he was home. And even if by some chance he had been troubled by guilt, it would have been out of fashion to mention those feelings in his space book." Shading the visionary into the everyday, Dean shows us, for instance, her students reading Mailer and Tom Wolfe on the astronauts, or herself attending a conference on space history in Washington, DC. She also shows us what she must miss due to other duties and roles—"mornings my husband has dressed and fed our little son, driven him to preschool, and managed the grocery shopping and dishes and laundry and temper tantrums and playdates and bedtimes. . . . So I chose not to go to Houston to visit Mission Control while *Atlantis* was on orbit, though my media badge would have allowed me access, though Norman Mailer went to Mission Control while Apollo 11 was in space."

As Dean advances, though, "Norman Mailer" isn't just the author of a space book she admires, or a ghostly oversized personality who spurs and vexes her, but her surprising metonymy for tracking a transformed America over the half century from JFK's audacious 1961 challenge to land a man on the moon "before this decade is out" to the anticlimactic final shuttle flight, in 2011, of *Atlantis*. "I'm asking," she writes, "what it means that we went to space for fifty years and what it means that we've decided not to go anymore." Mailer, she reluctantly realizes, wasn't so much witnessing "the start of something. . . . In fact, he was seeing its pinnacle. I have the sad advantage of traveling to Florida knowing I'm seeing the end."

Whether because of this alertness to national diminishment, or her own microcosmic artistic temperament, the most startling wonders of *Leaving Orbit* tend to rise from minute, spectral looks—her canny notice of an astronaut who "knows she will never get to fly on a space shuttle, that they will all be sealed up in museums by the time her training is complete"; her empathetic and comic dramatization of her fellow "Space Tweeps" in a darkened room where all are punching tweets and posts into their phones; her exchanges with her hero Buzz

Aldrin, and with crackpots, such as "moon hoax True Believers"; her moving portrait of Omar, a Facebook friend who works at the Cape as an Orbiter Integrity Clerk and emerges as her handy, loyal Virgil; her skeptical invocation of the first privatized spacecraft; and her internal dialogues with Mailer, Wolfe, and Oriana Fallaci about space then and now.

Come Dean's finish, though, her yearning for the 1960s folds inside out, and during a recurrent dream, anyway, the dynamics of the initial jealousy of Mailer and Co. shift. "I know without being told that these chairs have been set up for all the writers who have written about the American space program," she recounts, "though most of the chairs appear to be empty. Norman Mailer is sitting next to me, which makes me faintly nervous. I can also make out Tom Wolfe, Jay Barbree, J. G. Ballard, Lynn Sherr, Oriana Fallaci, Walter Cronkite, and fields of others, some long dead. . . . We space writers are all asked the same question all the time: Would you go? Mostly we say yes, but we know we are lying. We'll never be given the chance anyway. We all feel Norman's masculine envy at being left behind, but our envy is beside the point. We know that someone needs to stay behind and write about what it feels like to watch it from the ground."

Her dream is what NASA dubs a "scrub," a postponed, or maybe an aborted mission. "We wait on our folding chairs. We are waiting for something to happen, but we wait and wait and it never gets started."

Robert Polito
Chicago

THE GRAYWOLF PRESS NONFICTION PRIZE

Leaving Orbit: Notes from the Last Days of American Spaceflight by Margaret Lazarus Dean is the 2012 winner of the Graywolf Press Nonfiction Prize. Graywolf awards this prize every twelve to eighteen months to a previously unpublished, full-length work of outstanding literary nonfiction by a writer who is not yet established in the genre. Previous winners include *The Empathy Exams: Essays* by Leslie Jamison, *The Grey Album: On the Blackness of Blackness* by Kevin Young, *Notes from No Man's Land: American Essays* by Eula Biss, *Black Glasses Like Clark Kent: A GI's Secret from Postwar Japan* by Terese Svoboda, *Neck Deep and Other Predicaments* by Ander Monson, and *Frantic Transmissions to and from Los Angeles: An Accidental Memoir* by Kate Braverman.

The Graywolf Press Nonfiction Prize seeks to acknowledge—and honor—the great traditions of literary nonfiction, extending from Robert Burton and Thomas Browne in the seventeenth century through Daniel Defoe and Lytton Strachey and on to James Baldwin, Joan Didion, and Jamaica Kincaid in our own time. Whether it is grounded in observation, autobiography, or research, much of the most beautiful, daring, and original writing over the past few decades can be categorized as nonfiction. Graywolf is excited to increase its commitment to the evolving and dynamic genre.

The prize is judged by Robert Polito, author of *Hollywood & God, Savage Art: A Biography of Jim Thompson, Doubles,* and *A Reader's Guide to James Merrill's* The Changing Light at Sandover, and formerly director of the Graduate Writing Program at the New School in New York City. He is currently president of the Poetry Foundation in Chicago.

The Graywolf Press Nonfiction Prize is funded in part by endowed gifts from the Arsham Ohanessian Charitable Remainder Unitrust and the Ruth Easton Fund of the Edelstein Family Foundation.

Arsham Ohanessian, an Armenian born in Iraq who came to the United States in 1952, was an avid reader and a tireless advocate for human rights and peace. He strongly believed in the power of literature and education to make a positive impact on humanity.

Ruth Easton, born in North Branch, Minnesota, was a Broadway actress in the 1920s and 1930s. The Ruth Easton Fund of the Edelstein Family Foundation is pleased to support the work of emerging artists and writers in her honor.

Graywolf Press is grateful to Arsham Ohanessian and Ruth Easton for their generous support.

MARGARET LAZARUS DEAN holds a BA from Wellesley College and an MFA from the University of Michigan. She is the author of *The Time It Takes to Fall* (Simon & Schuster, 2007), a novel about the space shuttle *Challenger* disaster. Her work has appeared in *StoryQuarterly, FiveChapters,* and *Michigan Quarterly Review.* She is a recipient of a National Endowment for the Arts fellowship, a Hopwood Award for the novel, and a Tennessee Arts Commission fellowship. An associate professor of English at the University of Tennessee, she lives in Knoxville.

Book design by Rachel Holscher. Composition by Bookmobile Design & Digital Publisher Services, Minneapolis, Minnesota. Manufactured by Versa Press on acid-free, 30 percent postconsumer wastepaper.